day trips® from
st. louis

help us keep this guide up to date

We would love to hear from you concerning your experiences with this guide and how you feel it could be improved and kept up to date. Please send your comments and suggestions to:

editorial@GlobePequot.com

Thanks for your input, and happy travels!

day trips® series

day trips® from st. louis

first edition

 getaway ideas for the local traveler

dawne massey

gpp®

travel

Guilford, Connecticut

All the information in this guidebook is subject to change. We recommend that you call ahead to obtain current information before traveling.

To buy books in quantity for corporate use or incentives, call **(800) 962-0973** or e-mail **premiums@GlobePequot.com**.

Editor: Kevin Sirois
Project Editor: Lynn Zelem
Layout: Joanna Beyer
Text Design: Linda R. Loiewski
Maps: Design Maps Inc. © Morris Book Publishing, LLC.
Spot photography throughout licensed by Shutterstock.com

ISBN 978-0-7627-7936-9

Printed in the United States of America
10 9 8 7 6 5 4 3 2 1

contents

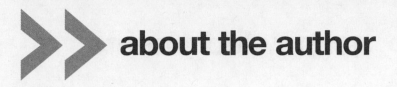

about the author

Dawne Massey has lived and worked in St. Louis for more than 15 years, writing about the city for a variety of publications including the *St. Louis Post-Dispatch*, *St. Petersburg Times*, *AAA Magazine*, the *Official St. Louis Visitors Guide*, and *Guest Informant*. She is the author of *Insiders' Guide to St. Louis* (Globe Pequot Press).

acknowledgments

Many thanks to all of the convention and visitors bureaus, chambers of commerce, and tourism industry professionals who provided suggestions and information about places to go, things to do, and stuff to eat in their particular part of the world. Thanks also to all of the friends, foodies, and outdoor enthusiasts who provided insight and additional recommendations to help round out the book's offerings. I couldn't have done it without you!

And thank you to the editors and copy editors who took all of this information and made it into a coherent guide book. I appreciate your patience and your expertise.

introduction

As if there wasn't already enough to do in St. Louis! But, if you've got a bit of road warrior in you, your need to hit the open road is understandable. Luckily, St. Louis is situated in the middle of some pretty interesting country, so you're only a couple of hours from a diverse collection of entertaining things to see and do.

From exploring rock formations and the prehistoric past to wandering through the heart of America's diverse history, there's something around here for just about everyone. History buffs can trace the path of explorers Lewis and Clark from St. Charles, MO, or walk in the footsteps of honest Abe Lincoln in Springfield, IL. Wine aficionados can sample their way through Missouri's wine country west of St. Louis, and hikers and bikers can get some serious trail time along the beautiful Katy Trail. Actually, there are a number of wine countries in the bistate area, including in and around Ste. Genevieve, MO, and Shawnee National Forest in Illinois. Those who just can't get enough time behind the wheel will enjoy the natural beauty along the Great River Road as well as the nostalgic photo opportunities along historic Route 66. Shop in unique boutiques and specialty stores or prowl for brand-name bargains at area outlet malls—after all, the thrill is in the hunt.

From the most quaint bed-and-breakfast inns to the kitschiest greasy-spoon diners, chances are you can find whatever it is you're looking for somewhere within a two- to three-hour drive of the Gateway City. All of the suggested destinations are close enough that you can make it back to St. Louis for the evening, and just far enough away to feel like you "got away from it all." Happy trails!

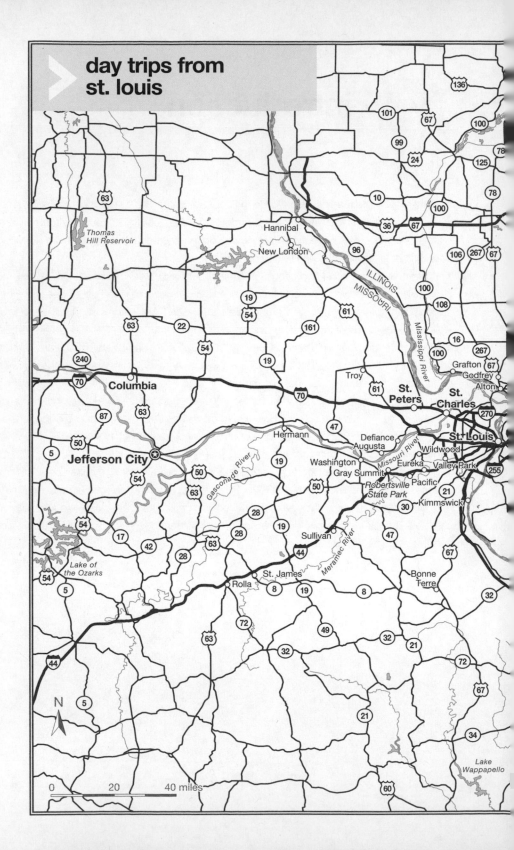

day trips from st. louis

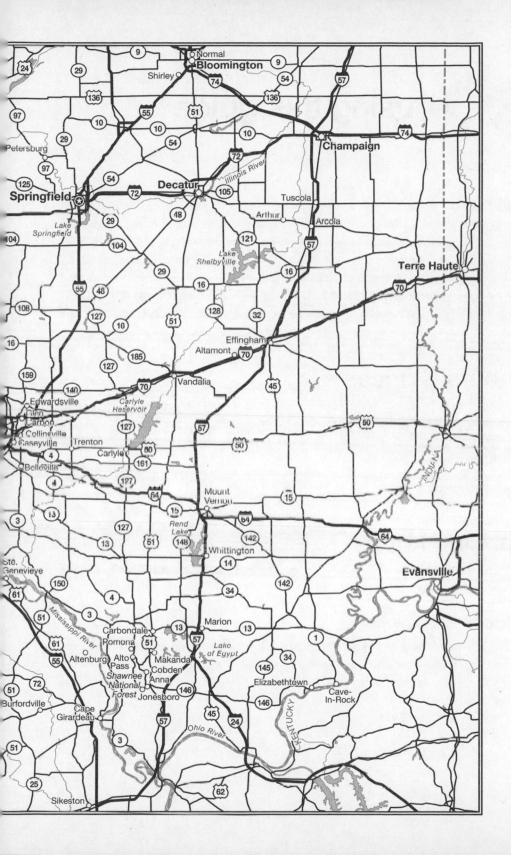

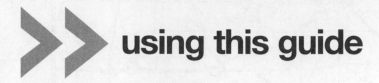

using this guide

Day Trips from St. Louis is organized by standard compass points, starting with points north and going clockwise: north, northeast, east, southeast, south, southwest, west, and northwest. The day trip destinations start with the ones closest to St. Louis and go from there. They don't include everything there is to see, but they represent a cross section of treks designed to appeal to adventurous types looking for additional slices of life in the heartland of the country. Depending on how strongly you adhere to the posted speed limits, most of the destinations can be reached from St. Louis via major interstates and highways in 2.5 hours or less—although "off-roading" and spontaneous exits are always encouraged.

hours & prices

Because hours of operation and prices are subject to change without notice, the information included here is given in general terms. Please call ahead to get the most up-to-date information, as websites are not always reliable. If you have questions, contact the establishments directly for specifics.

You can assume all establishments listed accept major credit cards unless otherwise noted. For details, contact the locations directly.

pricing key

The price codes for accommodations and restaurants are represented as a scale of one to three dollar signs ($).

accommodations

The price code reflects the average cost of a double-occupancy room during the peak price period (not including tax or extras). Please also note that during peak season in some areas, a two-night stay (or more) is required. Always check online or call to find out if any special discounts are available.

$	less than $100
$$	$100 to $175
$$$	more than $175

restaurants

The price code reflects the average price of dinner entrees for two, not including cocktails, wine, appetizers, desserts, tax, and tip (and please don't forget to tip!). Usually, lunch and/or breakfast pricing will be lower.

$ less than $20

$$ $20 to $40

$$$ more than $40

driving tips

- St. Louis is located at the intersection of four interstate highways—I-55, I-64, I-70, and I-44—so it's accessible from every direction. All four highways converge in downtown St. Louis, just south of the Gateway Arch.

- Locals refer to I-64 by its previous moniker, Highway 40.

- The Poplar Street Bridge, or "PSB" as it's called on local traffic reports, links St. Louis to Illinois via three interstate highways: I-64, I-55, and I-70.

- Plan your route before you hit the highway. The GPS is a great tool/toy, but it's not always accurate.

- In Missouri the speed limit on rural stretches of interstate highways is 70 mph and slows to 60 mph in urban areas.

- You'll need to take it a little slower in Illinois, with interstate speed limits set at 65 mph in rural areas and 55 mph in urban stretches.

- Both Missouri and Illinois take advantage of warmer-weather months to handle road construction projects, so slow down in those construction zones and check www.MOdot.org and www.Idot.org to see where the guys in the orange vests will be working during your trip.

highway designations

Major highways are typically listed in terms of their numbered designations, such as I-70, US 67, etc., but be aware that residents of St. Louis will almost always refer to I-64 as Highway 40. Some road abbreviations to be aware of include "IL," for Illinois state highways/routes like IL 100; MO for Missouri state highways; US for US highways; and CR for county roads.

travel tips

hours

Hours for restaurants, shops, and attractions are given in general terms. Because some may close on particular holidays and hours can change seasonally or at the whim of the owner, it's always a good idea to call ahead.

seasonal issues

During cold-weather months many of the area hotels and B&Bs offer great deals and discounts, although prices may spike to in-season rates for New Year's Eve and Valentine's Day. Speaking of winter, from December through February the weather in the region can be anything from treacherous and bleak to mild and uneventful—you never really know what you'll get. Interstates will be plowed and passable, but there's no guarantee the side roads in suburbs or smaller towns will be safe for travel. Call the folks at your destination for insight on how accessible the roads are—chances are if they don't answer, they stayed home too.

As is the case in most Midwestern cities, Memorial Day is typically when in-season pricing kicks in for hotels and B&Bs, so if you want to sneak in a stay before then, you'll often get a cheaper rate. Remember that summer in the Midwest does not always mean hot and sunny—although it usually means warm and humid—so you should plan a few rainy-day options just in case. For fall foliage trips, October usually offers the best viewing, and some destinations offer fall foliage maps or suggested routes to make the most of your leaf-peeping experience. Check online or call the area's visitor center to find out what they recommend.

sales tax

Sales tax in Missouri and Illinois varies, so if you're concerned about how much it will affect the cost of your trip, it's a good idea to call ahead and find out the specifics. Some attractions will quote prices that include sales tax, but it's always wise to ask. Be prepared to pay a state sales tax on top of most published prices as well. Hotels rarely include sales or occupancy taxes or gratuities in their published rates, and depending on the county and/or municipality, it could raise your hotel rate by 15 percent or more.

selected lodging & restaurants

Most destinations have chain hotels and restaurants, which are generally not included in the listings in each chapter, as they operate on similar standards across the country. The lodgings and restaurants highlighted are typically locally owned and are designed to offer a unique lodging or dining experience.

where to get more information

The day trips attempt to cover a variety of interests and include activities for adults and children of all ages, but if you're looking for additional info, there are plenty of places to find it. Most states and cities, and even some smaller towns, have their own tourism bureaus, so for most trips they are listed first as a "Where to Go" location. They are a good place to start, offering comprehensive websites and insider tips, and they welcome visitors' calls, e-mails, or requests for printed visitor guides, brochures, and maps.

In addition to the resources in this book, some additional sources of information include:

illinois

Illinois Office of Tourism
500 E. Monroe
Springfield, IL 62701
(217) 785-6278
www.enjoyillinois.com

Alton Regional Convention & Visitors Bureau
200 Piasa St.
Alton, IL 62002
(618) 465 6676 or (800) ALTON-IL
www.visitalton.com

Illinois Amish Interpretive Center
125 N. CR 425E
Arcola, IL 61910
(888) 45-AMISH
www.amishcenter.com

Illinois Route 66 Scenic Byway
700 E. Adams St.
Springfield, IL 62701
(217) 525-9308
www.illinoisroute66.org

Mississippi Bluffs Ranger District
521 N. Main St.
Jonesboro, IL 62952
(618) 833-8576
www.fs.usda.gov/shawnee

Rend Lake Information Center
80N I-57 North
Whittington, IL 62897
(618) 435-4155
www.rendlake.com/pages/lake/visitorcenter
.htm

Shawnee National Forest
Hidden Springs Ranger District
602 N. 1st St./Route 45 North
Vienna, IL 62995
(618) 658-2111

Springfield Convention & Visitors Bureau
109 N. 7th St.
Springfield, IL 62701
(217) 789-2360 or (800) 545-7300
www.visit-springfieldillinois.com

The Tourism Bureau Southwestern Illinois
10950 Lincoln Trail
Fairview Heights, IL 62208
(618) 397-1488 or (800) 442-1488
www.thetourismbureau.org

missouri

Missouri Division of Tourism
PO Box 1055
Jefferson City, MO 65102
www.visitmo.com

Cape Girardeau Convention & Visitors Bureau
400 Broadway, Ste. 100
Cape Girardeau, MO 63701
(573) 335-1631
www.visitcape.com

City of Columbia, MO, Convention & Visitors Bureau
300 South Providence Rd.
Columbia, MO 65201
www.visitcolumbiamo.com

City of Ste. Genevieve Department of Tourism
66 South Main St.
Ste. Genevieve, MO 63670
(573) 883-7097
www.visitstegen.com

Eastern Missouri Parks District
2901 US 61
Festus, MO 63028
(636) 931-5200
www.mostateparks.com

Greater Saint Charles CVB
230 S. Main St.
Saint Charles, MO 63301
(800) 366-2427
www.historicstcharles.com

Hannibal Convention & Visitors Bureau
505 N. 3rd St.
Hannibal, MO 63401
(573) 221-2477
www.visithannibal.com

Jefferson City Convention & Visitors Bureau
100 E. High St., PO Box 2227
Jefferson City, MO 65101
(573) 632-2820
www.visitjeffersoncity.com

Missouri Wine Country
www.missouriwinecountry.com

north

>>>

day trip 01

north

>>> **great river road:**
alton, il; grafton, il

The Great River Road from Alton to Kampsville, IL, is one of America's National Scenic Byways, a stretch of road recognized for its archeological, cultural, historic, natural, recreational, or scenic qualities by the US Department of Transportation. If you get tired of the beautiful views of the mighty Mississippi River, you can take a break and enjoy the soaring limestone bluffs on the other side. These bluffs were first noted by 17th-century explorers Marquette and Joliet. On the bluffs just north of town you'll see an image of a piasa bird painted on the bluffs. The fierce, serpent-like bird of Native American legend gives the area its name, Piasa Country.

alton, il

After the settlement was created in 1818, Alton became a thriving steamboat landing and one of the largest communities in the state. Civil War history is woven throughout the town's past, thanks to Illinois's status as a free state, while its neighbor across the Mississippi River—Missouri—was a slave state. Alton resident Reverend Elijah Lovejoy became a vocal opponent of slavery and published the *Alton Observer,* an abolitionist newspaper. The Underground Railroad, a secret route used by slaves to escape into free territory, went directly through Alton. In 1858 the final Lincoln-Douglas debate was held in the city, and it set the stage for Abraham Lincoln's future presidency.

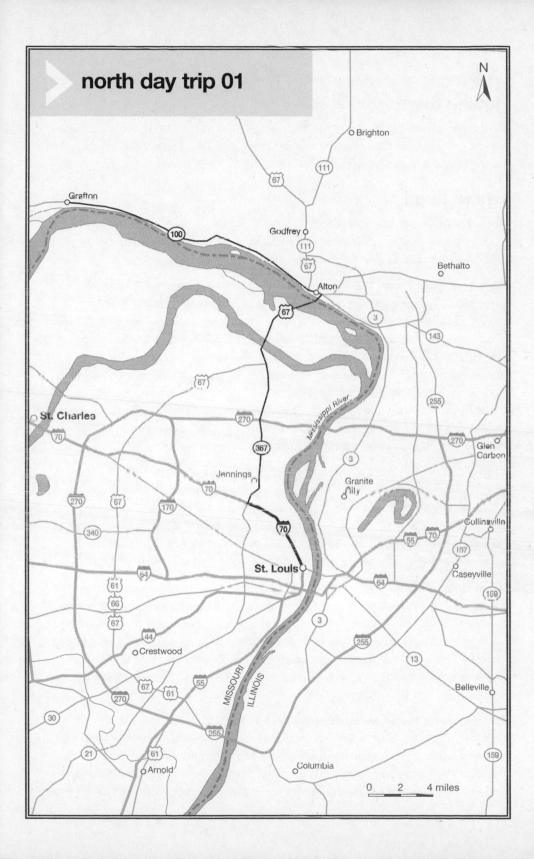

N

Brighton

111

67

Grafton

100

Godfrey

111

Bethalto

67

Alton

67

3

143

67

255

St. Charles

270

70

367

Mississippi River

270

Glen Carbon

3

Jennings

270

67

70

Granite City

Collinsville

170

340

70

55

70

157

Caseyville

64

St. Louis

64

159

61

66

67

3

255

44

13

Crestwood

MISSOURI

ILLINOIS

Belleville

55

270

67

61

30

255

21

61

159

Arnold

Columbia

0   2   4 miles

getting there

From downtown St. Louis, take I-70 West to exit 246A to merge onto N. Broadway. Make a slight left onto Halls Ferry Road. At the traffic circle, take the second exit onto MO 367 North/Lewis and Clark Boulevard. Continue onto US 67 North into Alton.

where to go

Alton Visitor Center. 200 Piasa St.; (618) 465-6676; www.visitalton.com. Pick up a visitor guide, maps, or brochures for many of Alton's most popular attractions and get information on local accommodations and restaurants.

Alton Hauntings Tours. Tours depart from the Alton Visitor Center, 200 Piasa St.; (888) 446-7859; www.altonhauntings.com. Alton has been called one of the most haunted towns in the country, and local legend places the blame on the abundance of limestone in the area. A local "ghost hunter" claims the stone is able to hold psychic energy and emotional history, and many of the area's buildings are made from limestone or are built on foundations of reused limestone blocks. Whatever the reason, Alton's Hauntings Tours are an entertaining way to explore the region's colorful history, and they include tales from such haunted hot spots as the Mineral Springs Hotel, Cracker Factory, First Unitarian Church, old Alton Penitentiary, and the Enos Sanitarium. Tours also highlight scary stuff from the Underground Railroad and the town's infamous McPike Mansion. Available Apr through the end of fall.

Argosy Casino. #1 Piasa St.; (800) 711-GAME; www.argosyalton.com. Get your game on at the riverfront casino that offers the usual lineup of slot machines and table games like blackjack, craps, and roulette. Argosy's Music Hall hosts live performances by luminaries such as Chuck Berry, the Turtles, Ozark Mountain Daredevils, and the Shirelles, as well as comedians like Craig Ferguson and Vicky Lawrence of *Mama's Family* fame and the occasional "ladies' night" with the world-famous Chippendales.

Great Godfrey Maze. 1401 Stamper Ln., Godfrey; (618) 463-1183; www.godfreyil.org. Every September the nearby village of Godfrey embraces its agricultural heritage with a giant corn maze. Located in Robert E. Glazebrook Park, 0.5 mile west of US 67/Godfrey Road, the 7-acre maze is the centerpiece of a fall festival that includes hay rides, a cow train, a corn crib, and a corn cannon for target practice. In mid-October the maze turns "haunted" and spooky treks through the labyrinth are offered via flashlight. Open weekends through the fall.

National Great Rivers Museum at the Melvin Price Locks & Dam. #2 Locks and Dam Way; (888) 899-2602; www.mvs.usace.army.mil/rivers/museum.html. River buffs can explore the history and cultural significance of the Mississippi River in the museum and get a firsthand look at the technology used to control Old Man River on the dam. A 25-minute film, *Power of the River,* offers an overview of the watery transportation corridor from its source to the mouth and provides insight into some of the culture and river cities along its banks. The 20-plus interactive and educational exhibits include a large river model and the chance to "steer" a barge or explore the plant and animal life in and around the river. Tours are available of the Melvin Price Locks and Dam, a structure that consists of a 1,160-foot-long dam with 9 tainter gates.

Segway Tours. Tours depart from National Great Rivers Research and Education Center, One Confluence Way, East Alton; (314) 289-4439; www.slsc.org/AdultProgrammings/SegwayPrograms.aspx. Produced in conjunction with the Saint Louis Science Center, there are 2 Alton-based Segway tours available, and both offer a quick training course to make sure you are comfortable on your machine. The 3-hour Glided Tour of Alton includes background on the Melvin Price Locks and Dam, the Lincoln-Douglas debate, the first-of-its-kind Clark Bridge, and historic sites in downtown Alton. The Taste of Alton tour includes all of the aforementioned locations as well as lunch at the popular downtown Alton eatery My Just Desserts.

where to shop

Alton Antiques & Decor. 301 E. Broadway; (010) 433-2778. Located in the Mineral Springs Mall, the store is a mix of antique furniture, glassware, knickknacks, and one-of-a-kind items. The shop is actually located in the Crystal Room, which was once part of the historic Mineral Springs Hotel.

Alton Stained Glass Works. 412 E. Broadway; (618) 462-4145; www.altonartglass.com. This working art-glass studio offers a number of handcrafted lamps, windowpanes, ornaments, sun catchers, and glass beads. In addition to the decorative items, they can help you design a custom piece or teach you to make one yourself. Some of the classes offered are Introduction to Stained Glass, Glass Bead Making, and Glass Kiln Work, and they are available as part of an overnight accommodations package at the Tiffany Inn located upstairs.

Mississippi Mud Pottery. 310 E. Broadway, (010) 462-7573; www.mississippimudpottery.biz. The in-house "Mud Team" is in the studio daily making everything from dinnerware and casserole dishes to lamps and planters. They specialize in raku pottery and custom-designed pieces made from Midwest-mined natural clay materials and use lead-free glazes on their pieces, so everything's safe for the microwave, oven, and dishwasher.

Prairie Peddler Antiques. 413 E. Broadway; (618) 465-6114; www.theprairiepeddlerantiques.com. The shop features 2 floors full of 18th- and 19th-century American antiques and specializes in formal and early American/primitive furniture and accessories. The buyers make frequent trips "back East" to collect many of their additional treasures, which range from folk art and portraiture to textiles, ceramics, and antique clocks.

where to eat

Bossanova Restaurant & Lounge. 112 W. 3rd St.; (618) 462-1175; www.bossanova martinilounge.com. After dinner the Bossanova becomes a hipster lounge, but foodies will love the globally inspired fusion menu of options like pork tenderloin wonton tacos and white clam or buffalo chicken pizettes, and entrees like salmon beurre blanc or a Southwestern strip steak. The chef sources locally grown and produced foodstuffs, which complement the nice wine list and assortment of specialty beers and martinis. Open for dinner only; no reservations accepted. $$.

Gentelin's on Broadway. 122 E. Broadway; (618) 465-6080; www.gentelinsonbroadway .com. Owners Sara and Ryan Gentelin created a menu of seafood, steaks, pastas, and comfort foods that's upscale but still casual enough to be a relaxing dining experience. Specialties include sesame-encrusted tofu, toasted wild mushroom ravioli, lobster mac and cheese, peppercorn seared ahi tuna, and the dessert Chocolate Two Ways (a milk chocolate cup filled with a dark chocolate and Chambord mousse, garnished with fresh raspberries and Chantilly cream, and served with a chocolate Grenache brownie topped with vanilla bean ice cream and a cashew Dutch crumb). Located in historic downtown Alton, the restaurant offers a very good wine list and an assortment of scotch and spirits, as well as a great view of Alton's famous Clark Bridge. $$.

My Just Desserts. 31 E. Broadway; (618) 462-5881; www.myjustdesserts.org. If you have a sweet tooth, you won't need your GPS to find your way here. My Just Desserts is "downright famous" for their homemade pies and Toll House brownies. Made fresh every morning, the 10 or so pie varieties are joined on the menu by such mouthwatering delicacies as rhubarb cobbler and the restaurant's equally famous half-pound chicken salad sandwich, soups, and salads. Open daily for lunch until 4 p.m. $.

Tony's Restaurant. 312 Piasa St.; (618) 462-8384; www.tonysrestaurant.com. Offering upscale dining for more than 50 years, Tony's is one of Alton's best restaurants. Its signature dish is the Tony's Pepperloin, which is hand-trimmed whole tenderloin that's marinated in a house-recipe marinade, rolled in half-cracked black peppercorns, and grilled to order. The menu also includes various seafood and pasta options, along with a respectable wine list. The eatery's more casual 3rd Street Cafe offers Tony's bar menu with specialty entrees like chicken Kiev, veal parmigiana, and lobster tail, along with pizzas, paninis, and a Bambini menu for the small fry. $$–$$$.

where to stay

Beall Mansion. 407 E. 12th St.; (618) 474-9100; www.beallmansion.com. The Beall is one of the region's most popular B&Bs—in fact, it was the state's best in the *Illinois Magazine* readers' poll. Located on Alton's "Millionaire's Row" and designed by Lucas Pfeiffenberger, the 3-story, 10,000-square-foot home was built in 1903 and is listed on the National

Register of Historic Places. The elegant mansion features 2 king-size and 2 queen-size rooms, all with whirlpool tubs, and a 300-square-foot third-floor guest suite. All have private baths, feather beds, and access to the 24-hour "all you can eat" chocolate buffet. $$–$$$.

Jackson House. 1821 Seminary St.; (618) 462-1426; www.jacksonbb.com. Located in the Upper Alton Historic District, Jackson House offers a trio of very different B&B experiences. The Main House is an oversize Victorian with a relaxing wraparound porch that's surrounded by trees; guests can opt for the king-size bed in the Master Bedroom or the cozier queen-size bed in the Fireplace Room. Two more-secluded options are also available on the property: The Barn offers quiet, rustic luxury complete with a whirlpool tub, enclosed porch, and open deck. The Cave features a tranquil yet luxurious atmosphere inside a cozy earth house under the trees. You won't be roughing it here—there's a king-size bed, fireplace, secluded patio, and whirlpool built for two. $$.

grafton, il

Founded in 1832 by James Mason, Grafton is located at the confluence of the Illinois and Mississippi Rivers. During the heyday of the steamboats, the town was a busy stop for paddlewheel riverboats. Today's river traffic includes regular runs of the Brussels ferry, which takes cars and trucks across the Illinois River, and Grafton's Main Street is home to restaurants, shops, and spectacular houses.

getting there

From Alton, head north on N. Alby Street and take the first left onto E. 3rd Street. Continue to Market Street and make a left turn, then take the first right onto W. Broadway. Continue onto IL 100 North/Great River Road/McAdams Parkway for a little more than 14 miles, then make a right onto Oak Street.

where to go

Eckert's Grafton Farm. 20995 Orchard Ln.; (618) 786-3445; www.eckerts.com. Eckert's offers city-folk a chance to experience life on the farm and an opportunity to "pick your own" seasonal produce—it doesn't get much fresher than this. Hit the fields and bring back anything from strawberries, peaches, and blackberries to apples and pumpkins, depending on what's ripe at the time. The year-round entertainment area offers something for kids of all sizes—and the people who drive them there—including feeding the farm animals, swinging on an old-fashioned tire swing, or hitting the links for a round of miniature golf.

Historic Museum of Torture Devices. 301 E. Broadway; (866) 465-3205; www.mineral springshauntedtours.com. Yep, you read that right. Located inside the friendly confines of the Mineral Springs Mall is the Historic Museum of Torture Devices, which offers self-guided tours of a collection of torture devices from around the world. In addition to pictures and written explanations about how and when the items were used, the museum includes such torture devices from the Middle Ages as an executioner's ax, branding irons, head cages, iron-spiked collars, and "the rack."

Lewis & Clark State Historic Site. One Lewis and Clark Trail; (618) 251-5811; www .campdubois.com. The 14,000-square-foot visitor center is located at the confluence of the Missouri and Mississippi Rivers and is the site of Camp DuBois, where explorers Meriwether Lewis and William Clark wintered before embarking on their great trek westward. There are a number of displays and multimedia presentations on the Lewis and Clark expedition, including a 55-foot keel boat, which is a full-size replica of the Corps of Discovery's vessel. The boat is open on one side, revealing the interior passages, storage compartments, living quarters, and cargo. The center also includes exhibits on the Louisiana Territory and the Native Americans who lived there, the Corps of Discovery's preparations for the trip, and the impact and legacy of the expedition. Watch the 12-minute orientation film, *At Journey's Edge,* to get a good overview of the expedition, and check out the "misquitors" exhibits, which quote extensively from the journals of the two explorers—neither of whom was a spelling champion. Open Wed through Sun.

Mississippi River State Fish & Wildlife Area, West-Central Region. 17836 MO 100 North; (618) 376-3303; http://dnr.state.il.us/lands/landmgt/parks/r4/miss.htm. The Missis- sippi River Area (MRA) spans more than 24,000 acres along 75 miles of two major rivers. The scenic bluffs offer breathtaking views, and the area is an ideal spot for picnics and "leaf peep- ing" during the peak fall foliage season of late Sept and Oct. The MRA also offers prime bald eagle–watching opportunities in Jan and Feb, as the majestic birds travel downriver looking for breaks in the ice floe. Boating and fishing are allowed along the Mississippi River, but certain sections of the MRA are marked as restricted during waterfowl season. Pilots of smaller boats and canoes will probably be better off in the calmer, less trafficked waters of the backwater lakes. Nearly 40 miles of the Mississippi River are available via the Piasa Creek Access Area and Royal Landing, while the Glades, Godar Diamond, Hadley Landing, and Michael Landing provide access to 35 miles of the Illinois River. Camping is prohibited in the entire MRA, but there are plenty of camping opportunities nearby in Pere Marquette State Park.

Pere Marquette State Park. 13112 Visitor Center Ln.; (618) 786.3323; http://dnr.state.il .us/lands/landmgt/parks/r4/peremarq.htm. Pere Marquette is an 8,000-acre nature lover's paradise that's filled with activities and beautiful scenery. Known as an ideal spot for bald eagle watching each winter, the park has spectacular views of the Illinois River. Recreational opportunities abound, including camping, hiking, fishing, hunting, boating, and horseback riding from Pere Marquette Stables. Start your visit with a stop at the visitor center for a look at the 3-D map of the park and a peek at the exhibits about the local history, wildlife habitat, geology, and the Illinois River.

Raging Rivers Waterpark. 100 Palisades Pkwy.; (618) 786-2345; www.ragingrivers.com. The 20-acre family water park located alongside the Mississippi River is open from Memorial Day weekend through Labor Day. Wet and wild attractions include the 4-foot waves at Breaker Beach, Cascade Body Flumes, Treehouse Harbor, Endless River, Shark Slide, Runaway Rafts, and Swirlpool. Itty Bitty Surf City, designed for wee ones under 42 inches tall, has pint-size waterslides and splash pools, a rain tree, tunnel area, and the Fountain Mountain family interactive area.

where to shop

Grafton Country Corner Fudge. 321 E. Main St.; (618) 786-3700; www.graftonfudge .com. If you like fudge, you'll want to savor your way through all 16 flavors of Country Corner's homemade fudge. Choose from amaretto chocolate swirl, rocky road, vanilla pecan, or cheesecake—a confectionary hybrid of vanilla fudge made with cream cheese and a swirl of chocolate fudge. There's also an assortment of other sweet treats on hand, including pecan brittle, cashew crunch, hand-dipped caramel apples, and a full line of premium chocolates.

Grafton's Artisan Village. 15 E. Main St.; (618) 786-4277. The village features more than 20 local vendors who sell handmade items including wood carvings, jewelry, primitive and Americana furniture, paintings, stained glass—there's even a chain saw carving artist. Open Wed through Sun.

Iron Decor & More. 1406 W. Main St.; (618) 786-2343; www.irondecornmore.com. If you're in the market for a whimsical conversation starter, stop by and browse through the unique decorative items created on-site. In addition to handcrafted iron tables, chairs, fencing, and indoor/outdoor sculptures and kinetic wind sculptures, the eclectic shop creates custom pieces, wine bottle trees, tables, and hand-blown glass gazing balls.

where to eat

Aerie's Riverview Winery. 600 Timber Ridge Dr.; (618) 786-8439; www.aerieswinery .com. Perched atop a bluff 250 feet above the confluence of the Mississippi and Illinois Rivers, Aerie's Riverview Winery definitely lives up to its name. Refreshment options include various appetizers, sandwiches, and made-from-scratch gourmet pizzas, along with 20-plus beers and wines. Enjoy live music and homemade barbecue brisket and ribs on the weekends. $–$$.

Fin Inn. 1500 W. Main St.; (618) 786-2030; www.fininn.com. The Fin Inn restaurant has four 2,000-gallon aquariums that feature many species found in the Mississippi River. Other amphibious inhabitants include an assortment of centenarian turtles that weigh in at more than 100 pounds apiece. Catfish is a specialty on the menu, along with a number of other fish dinners, sandwiches, appetizers, desserts, and homemade turtle soup. (Hmmm . . , wonder how the resident turtles feel about that?) There's also a kids' menu for tiny diners under 8 years of age. $$.

The Lodge. 13653 Lodge Blvd.; (618) 786-2331; www.pmlodge.net. The Pere Marquette Lodge offers a full-service dining room that serves standard Midwestern favorites in a rustic yet elegant environment. The centerpiece of the room is a 700-ton stone fireplace, and the Lodge offers beautiful views of the Illinois River. Menu options include hearty breakfast fare, along with an assortment of appetizers, sandwiches, and salads for lunch. At dinner the menu expands to include entrees like Settlers Pot Roast, Oak Trail Shrimp, and the Lodge's Famous Fried Chicken. There's also a wine-tasting room inside the Lodge, which features an appetizer menu that includes escargot, portobello ribbons, breaded calamari, toasted ravioli, and an antipasto plate. $$.

The Mississippi Half Step Restaurant. 420 E. Main St.; (618) 786-2722; www.mississippi halfstep.com. Located in the historic Brainerd House, circa 1885, this casual eatery serves up a selection of pastas, sandwiches, and salads for lunch, and dinner entrees that include steak, grilled scallops, and surf and turf kabobs. There's a modest beer and wine list, and carryout bottles of wine are also available. If the weather's nice, take advantage of the patio dining option. On Sunday try a breakfast egg casserole like the Big Bertha (artichoke hearts, mushrooms, black olives, tomatoes, and feta and Asiago cheese with a basil-infused Greek seasoning) or the Mexicali Blues (jalapeño and red peppers, tomatoes, bacon, and cheese, topped with salsa and sour cream). Open daily, but breakfast is only available Sun. $$.

where to stay

Pere Marquette Lodge. 13653 Lodge Blvd.; (618) 786-2331; www.pmlodge.net. The lodge at Pere Marquette State Park was originally built in the 1930s by the Civilian Conservation Corps. Although the lodge has been expanded and updated, the native stone and rustic tim-bers of the original structure have been maintained. There are 50 guest rooms and 22 stone guest cabin rooms available, along with an on-site restaurant, wine-tasting room, gift shop, indoor swimming pool, whirlpool, saunas, game room, and tennis court. Cabin facilities are also available on-site. Seventeen of the furnished 3-room cabins have a king bed, sleeper sofa, and bunk beds, while the other five cabins have queen or double queen beds and sleeper sofas. All are located approximately 150 feet from the main entrance of the lodge. $–$$.

Pere Marquette State Park Campgrounds. 13112 Visitor Center Ln.; (618) 786-3323; http://dnr.state.il.us. The park's Class A campground has 2 Rent-A-Camp cabins and 80 campsites, including 2 that are wheelchair accessible. The sites have electrical hookups, with a sanitary dump station, drinking water, and shower building available on the grounds. There's also a tent camping area available that offers access to the shower building. Camp-site reservations can be made at www.reserveamerica.com. $.

day trip 02

north

springfield, il

Just two hours northeast of St. Louis is the Illinois state capital of Springfield. While the state of Illinois lays claim to being the Land of Lincoln, Springfield should call itself the epicenter of all things Lincoln. But all of the history around these parts isn't just about the 16th president of the US. Car buffs and fans of the Mother Road will find plenty to explore here as well, as there are still a number of Route 66 related icons in and around Springfield. Foodies can fill up on fun facts as well as delicacies born in Springfield like the corn dog on a stick, the horseshoe sandwich, and Joe Rogers' Original Recipe Chili—even the drive-thru window was born here thanks to the Maid-Rite Sandwich Shop chain. Springfield celebrates its Route 66 heritage every September with the International Route 66 Mother Road Festival.

getting there

From downtown St. Louis, take I-70 East into Illinois for about 19 miles. Continue straight onto I-55 North for 73 miles and make a slight left onto I-55 Business North/I-55 Loop North (signs for I-55 North/6th Street/I-72 West/Jacksonville). Follow it for a little more than 3 miles and make a left onto E. Myrtle Street.

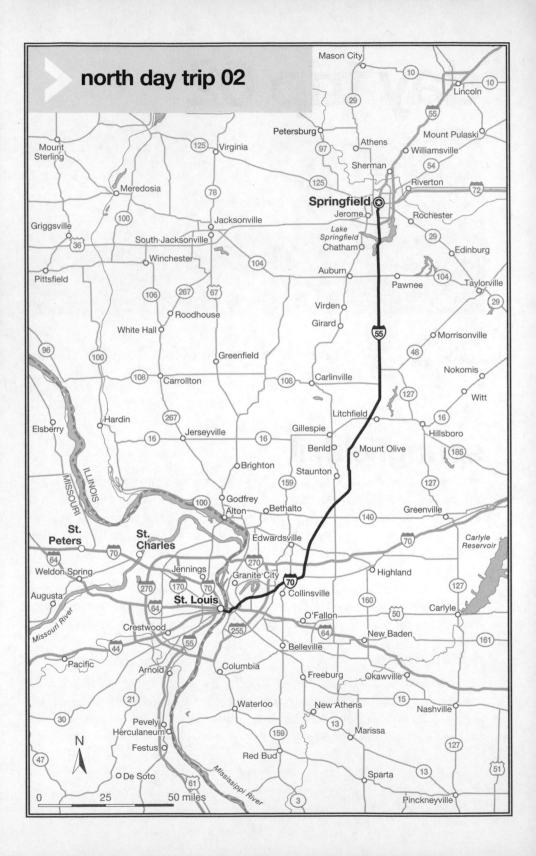

north day trip 02

where to go

Illinois Visitor Center at Union Station. 500 E. Madison St.; (217) 557-4588. Conveniently located across the street from the Abraham Lincoln Presidential Library & Museum. In addition to Springfield information, visitors can pick up Illinois tourism materials and book hotel accommodations and special event packages available across the state.

Abraham Lincoln Presidential Library & Museum. 212 N. 6th St.; (217) 558-8844; www .alplm.org. The museum portion of the complex features several galleries that depict the different segments of Lincoln's life. The Treasures Gallery highlights dozens of actual items that were a part of the Lincolns' lives, including family photos, the clock from Abe's law office, his stovepipe hat, and china and crystal from the White House. Mrs. Lincoln's Attic is a children's play area open to kids of all ages, with activities like playing dress-up with Abe's suit, Mary's dress, or a Civil War soldier's uniform; rearranging the furniture in the Lincoln Home dollhouse; or having a picture taken with life-size cutouts of young Abe Lincoln and his family. The Union Theater features *Lincoln's Eyes,* a theatrical special-effects presentation that offers an overview of Lincoln's life. The Journey One: The Pre-Presidential Years gallery has life-size dioramas representative of different points of Lincoln's pre-presidential life, including the log cabin he lived in and the Lincoln-Herndon law office. Journey Two: The White House Years includes a peek inside the Lincolns' life in Washington, DC, and displays depicting touchstones of Lincoln's presidency and the Civil War. *Campaign 1860* is a contemporary exhibit that brings the presidential campaign to life via video monitors as they spin out a TV news program analyzing the campaign Lincoln ran in his march to the presidency.

The Abraham Lincoln Presidential Library is a public, noncirculating research facility that contains just about anything and everything that details Illinois's history. The Illinois State Historical Library is responsible for collecting and preserving "books, pamphlets, manuscripts, monographs, writings, and other materials of historical interest and useful to the historian, bearing upon the political, religious, or social history of the State of Illinois from the earliest known period of time."

Dana-Thomas House. 301 E. Lawrence Ave.; (217) 782-6776; www.dana-thomas .org. The Dana-Thomas House represents one of Frank Lloyd Wright's finest prairie-style homes and features original furniture and art-glass doors, windows, and light fixtures. The elaborately restored residence was completed in 1904, after Wright was commissioned to renovate the home by Springfield socialite and activist Susan Lawrence Dana.

Illinois State Museum. 502 S. Spring St.; (217) 782-7386; www.museum.state.il.us. The museum includes numerous galleries and changing exhibits covering a wide range of subjects. One of the newest is the Mary Ann MacLean Play Museum, a free hands-on children's gallery where kids ages 3 to 10 can learn what it's like to work at a museum. Activities range from framing and displaying child-friendly art and piecing together a baby mastodon puzzle to exploring the worlds of nature and culture through play. Other galleries include Changes:

Dynamic Illinois Environments; At Home in the Heartland; and Peoples of the Past, which uses life-size dioramas and artifacts to bring Illinois's rich Native American heritage to life. The Anthropology Exhibit focuses on archaeological and ethnographic topics and artifacts, including Native American pottery, basketry, weavings, weapons, and tools.

Knight's Action Park & Caribbean Water Adventure. 1700 Knights Recreation Dr.; (217) 546-8881; www.knightsactionpark.com. This double dose of family fun is one part wet and wild water park action and one part nonstop sports fun. Knight's Action Park features a 50-tee driving range, batting cages, a putting green, and 2 miniature golf courses along with kiddie rides, arcade games, go-karts, and the Big Wheel Ferris wheel–type ride. The Caribbean Water Adventure park offers lots of ways to cool off, including waterslides, a giant wave pool, and the Caribbean Wild River. The water park also has 4-seat pedal boats, bumper boats, and the Seal Bay activity area for wee swimmers up to 48 inches tall. The individual attractions have different hours and seasons. Both attractions are closed Dec through Feb.

Lake Springfield. Lake Springfield Marina, 17 Waters Edge Blvd.; (217) 483-3625; www .lakespringfieldmarina.com. City Water, Light & Power owns and manages Lake Springfield and its surrounding 57 miles of shoreline, which includes several public boat docks and launches. The 4,200-acre reservoir, located just southeast of downtown, is the largest municipally owned lake in Illinois. Anglers can try their luck at catching 15 sport fish species in the lake, including channel and flathead catfish, white crappie, bluegill, largemouth bass, carp, striped bass, and tiger muskie. Public fishing spots are located throughout the lake area, but Illinois fishing licenses are required. The Lake Springfield Marina rents canoes, kayaks, fishing and pontoon boats, Wave Runners, and pedal boats by the day or the half day. Swimming and wading are permitted in designated areas.

Lincoln's Home National Historic Site. 413 S. 8th Street; (217) 492-4241; www.nps .gov/liho. Built in 1839, the home was purchased by the Lincolns in 1844. The National Park Service site features a Lincoln-era neighborhood with a variety of exhibits such as *What a Pleasant Home Abe Lincoln Has* in the Dean House, which focuses on the family's life in Springfield. At the Arnold House, the *If These Walls Could Talk* display focuses on historic preservation, and there are a number of additional exhibits throughout the 4-block historic area. Access to the Lincoln Home is free but it requires a ticket for a specific tour time. Tickets and information are available at the visitor center information desk.

Lincoln's New Salem State Historic Site. 15588 History Ln., Petersburg; (217) 632-4000; www.lincolnsnewsalem.com. Abraham Lincoln spent six years living and working in New Salem, from 1831 to 1837. The reconstructed village features timber houses, shops, and stores, and costumed interpreters assume the roles of people who lived and worked alongside Lincoln more than 150 years ago. Today there are 12 log houses, the Rutledge Tavern, workshops, stores, mills, and a school in the village, and all have been furnished as they might have been in the 1830s. The authentic furnishings, which include many articles actually used by the people of New Salem during Lincoln's time here, include such early 19th-century articles as wheat cradles, candle molds, cord beds, flax hackles, wood cards, and dough and cornmeal chests.

The Oaks Golf Course. 851 Dave Stockton Dr.; (217) 528-6600; www.theoaksgolfcourse .com. The 18-hole regulation-length public course features more than 6,100 yards of golf from the longest tees for a par of 70. The course rating is 68.8, it has a slope rating of 117 on bluegrass, and it features bent grass greens. The signature hole is number 10, which is a 115-yard par 3, requiring a tee shot over a ravine to the green. Amenities include a putting green, teaching pros, and a chipping area.

Old State Capitol. Old State Capitol Plaza, near 6th and Adams Streets; (217) 785-7960; www.oldstatecapitol.org. The Old State Capitol building opened in 1839 as the fifth Illinois statehouse. It's here that Abraham Lincoln and Stephen Douglas battled over slavery's future, and it served as the seat of the state's government from 1839 to 1876. Lincoln was a frequent visitor to the building as a lawyer and served his last term in the Illinois House of Representatives here. In 1858 Lincoln delivered the famous "House Divided" speech here in Representatives Hall, and his body was brought to the capitol to lie in state in May of 1865. The building was designated a National Historic Landmark in 1961 and is listed on the National Register of Historic Places. Today visitors can take a 30-minute interpreter-conducted tour and view a 15-minute orientation video on the building's history.

Piper Glen Golf Club. 7112 Piper Glen Dr.; (217) 483-6537; www.piperglen.com. Built in 1996, the Bob Lohmann–designed public course features bent grass tee boxes and fairways and was designed using the natural terrain. Polecat Creek runs through much of the course, and there are water hazards on 12 holes and a number of sand bunkers that come into play. The greens on the course are undulating, and all of the tees, with the exception of the championship tees, have a slope and course rating for men and women.

Route 66 Twin Drive-In Theater. 1700 Recreation Dr.; (217) 698-0066; www.route66-drivein.com. The Route 66 Twin is one of Illinois's last remaining drive-in theaters. Renovated and reopened in 2002, the throwback theater has 2 screens showing first-run movies on weekends from Apr through Oct, and nightly double features from Memorial Day weekend through Labor Day weekend.

Shea's Gas Station Museum. 2075 Peoria Rd.; (217) 522-0475. Shea's is a favorite stop for Route 66 travelers from around the world—for both its charming and eclectic collection of memorabilia and for its "celebrity" owner, Bill Shea. Shea, who has created a jam-packed museum that pays tribute to the early days of gas stations, is always happy to share stories about his collection and his 50-plus years on the Mother Road. It's free to tour the museum—Bill only asks that all visitors leave their signature in his guest book. The photographs alone are worth the visit. Closed Sun and Mon.

where to shop

The Blue Door. 214 S. 6th St.; (217) 753-0262; www.bluedoorart.com. The shop is a repository for artwork by 60-plus local artists, so the available wares range from watercolors, collages, oils, acrylics, and pastels to one-of-a-kind art pieces and handmade jewelry. There's something for everyone, including kids and even pets in need of a beaded handmade collar.

The Sumac Shop. 301 E. Lawrence Ave.; (217) 744-3598; www.sumacshop.com. Located in the Carriage House behind the Dana-Thomas House, the shop sells items related to the house and the architectural designs of Frank Lloyd Wright. The Sumac Shop collection includes apparel, calendars, jewelry, art glass, prints, stationery, and books about Wright, the prairie style of architecture, and the arts and crafts movement. Proceeds from sales support the education and preservation programs at the Dana-Thomas House.

Tinsley's Dry Goods. 209 S. 6th St.; (217) 525-1825; www.tinsleydrygoods.com. If you can't leave town without some sort of Lincoln-inspired souvenir, Tinsley's Dry Goods is a definite "must" for your itinerary. The renovated storefront claims to have the largest collection of Lincoln busts, along with a host of Abe-related T-shirts, Civil War figures, and tchotchkes. Built in 1840, the shop is located in the heart of historic Springfield, next door to the Lincoln-Herndon Law Office.

Widow at Windsor Antiques. 711 S. 5th St.; (217) 744-3735 or (217) 494-4643; www .widowatwindsorantiques.com. The charming shop, located in a 1920s-era Mediterranean Revival building, offers an eclectic assortment of antiques, architectural elements, and unique finds from Europe and Asia. The Widow also features a variety of vintage, cottage style, and "shabby chic" furnishings. The shop has been named "Best Antique Store" in the Springfield *State Journal-Register*'s Readers' Choice Awards.

where to eat

Augie's Front Burner. 109 S. 5th St.; (217) 544-6979; www.augiesfrontburner.com. Located in downtown Springfield, Augie's offers fine dining and a unique menu of innovative dishes made from locally sourced ingredients. Lunchtime options include salads, sandwiches, and entrees such as the Bunn Farm Steak Salad, the Conrady Farms Elk Burger, and a pan-roasted Chilean salmon. The dinner menu offers entrees like the Maple Leaf Farms Szechuan Half Duckling, the Bunn Farm New York Strip Steak Espagnole, and a pan-roasted quail. There's also a respectable wine list. $$–$$$.

Cozy Dog Drive In. 2935 S. 6th St.; (217) 525-1992; www.cozydogdrivein.com. It's not often that you can eat a piece of history, but you can when you visit the Cozy Dog Drive In. The Route 66 mainstay was created by Ed Waldmire when he introduced the Cozy Dog in 1946, and the rest is culinary history. The famous "hot dog on a stick" is still served at the Cozy Dog six days a week (Mon through Sat), and the diner's colorful decor and Route 66 memorabilia highlight its life along the Mother Road. The menu includes burgers, sandwiches, ice cream, and your standard-issue hot dog, and the diner also serves breakfast. $.

Joe Rogers' Original Recipe Chili Parlor. 820 S. 9th St.; (217) 522-3722; www.joe rogerschili.com. "Having it your way" at a restaurant wasn't just a novelty in 1946—it was revolutionary. But Joe Rogers knew a good thing when he thought of it, so he decided to give diners options when they ordered chili. The same holds true today, as you decide if you want your chili mild, a little hot, medium hot, hot, or firebrand. You also choose between the regular amount of meat or extra meat, regular beans or no beans—you get the idea. Your bowl of chili isn't prepared until you order it. Joe Rogers introduced his secret chili recipe to Springfield in 1946 at the Den Chili Parlor, and the restaurant has continued the tradition well into the 21st century. The eatery was selected by *Bon Appétit* magazine as one of the Midwest's great neighborhood restaurants. Open Mon through Sat, 11 a.m. to 4 p.m. $.

Jungle Jim's Cafe. 1923 Peoria Rd.; (217) 789-6173. Jungle Jim's is a local mainstay and is known for its presentation of a longtime culinary tradition—Springfield's famed horseshoe sandwich. The horseshoe consists of toast on a warm platter smothered with meat, cheese sauce, and french fries, and while the inventor of the hearty sandwich is a bit unclear—there are two or three stories out there—most agree that the key to a great horseshoe is the cheese sauce. $.

Maldaner's Restaurant. 222 S. 6th St.; (217) 522-4313; www.maldaners.com. Established in 1884, Maldaner's is one of the city's finest restaurants and serves up contemporary cuisine in a historic setting. The chef uses seasonal local and regional ingredients influenced by Mediterranean composition and preparation, including heirloom vegetables and humanely raised meats. Menu options for lunch include the organic mesclun salad (greens with toasted walnuts, Gorgonzola, bacon, and balsamic vinaigrette) and sandwiches like dilled Havarti and Maldaner's chicken salad. The dinner menu offers entrees such as beef Wellington, stuffed quail, pistachio-crusted wild salmon, and various pastas. There's also an extensive wine list. $$–$$$.

Norb Andy's Tabarin. 518 E. Capitol Ave.; (217) 670-1024; www.norbandys.com. The folks at Norb Andy's claim to serve the previously highlighted horseshoe sandwich with "The Original Leland Hotel Horseshoe Sauce." And because they also serve up Joe Rogers' Original Recipe Chili—they own the recipe—they created "The Chilishoe," which combines two of the family's favorites. The casual eating and drinking establishment's menu also includes a lineup of standard pub grub and adult beverages. $.

where to stay

The Rippon-Kinsella House. 1317 N. 3rd St.; (217) 241-3367. The Victorian B&B is located in a quiet, tree-lined neighborhood on the north side of Springfield. Built in 1871, the Italianate-style house currently offers 3 guest rooms for overnight accommodations—the Captain's Quarters, the Campaign Room, and the Maid's Room—and is located about 10 minutes from downtown. $–$$.

The Statehouse Inn. 101 E. Adams St.; (217) 528-5100; www.thestatehouseinn.com. An Ascend Collection hotel that's listed on Springfield's register of historic buildings, the Statehouse Inn is located across the street from the Illinois State Capitol complex and about 0.5 mile from the Abraham Lincoln Presidential Library & Museum. Amenities include free parking, free in-room Wi-Fi, and a free full hot breakfast. The property holds the AAA Three-Diamond award. $.

northeast

day trip 01

northeast

kitschy & ketchup:
collinsville, il

collinsville, il

In addition to having the dubious distinction of being the Horseradish Capital of the World, Collinsville is home to the World's Largest Catsup Bottle and is both a Route 66 community and a Route 40 National Road community. The two historic scenic byways run through this town of 25,000 residents that serves as a suburban outpost of St. Louis. Located less than 20 minutes from downtown St. Louis in southwestern Illinois, Collinsville hosts a number of family-friendly events each year, including the Italian Fest (September), the International Horseradish Festival (June), and the World's Largest Catsup Bottle Festival Birthday Party & Car Show (July).

getting there

From downtown St. Louis, take I-70 East over the Mississippi River and take exit 11 to merge onto IL 157 South/N. Bluff Road. Make a left onto W. Main Street and follow it for about 1.5 miles, then turn right onto S. Morrison Avenue. Collinsville is about 12 miles east of St. Louis.

where to go

Brooks Catsup Bottle Water Tower. 800 S. Morrison Ave.; www.catsupbottle.com. Located alongside Route 159 is the World's Largest Catsup Bottle, which stands 170

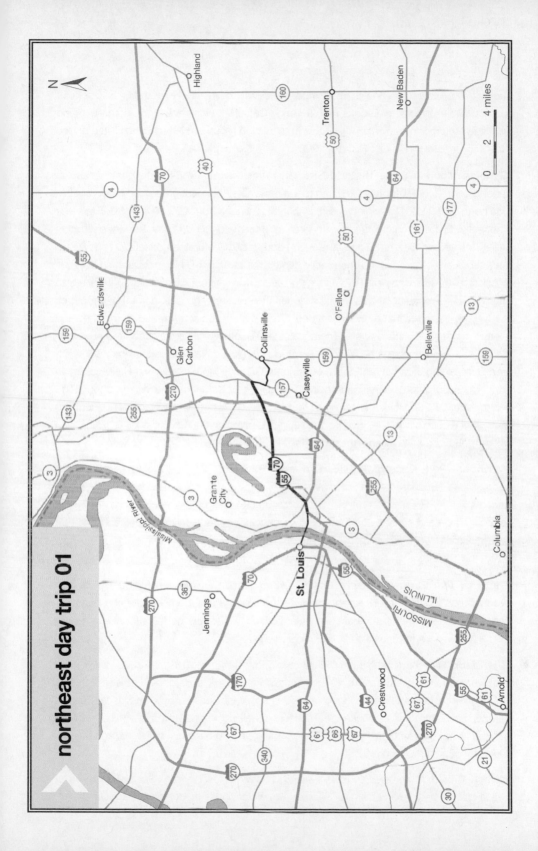

northeast day trip 01

feet tall. The kitschy ketchup-themed water tower was built in 1949 for the G. S. Suppiger bottling plant—bottlers of Brooks Rich & Tangy Catsup. It was saved from demolition and restored to its original splendor by a local preservation group in 1995 and was listed on the National Register of Historic Places in 2002.

Cahokia Mounds State Historic Site. 30 Ramey St.; (618) 346-5160; www.cahokia mounds.org. Cahokia Mounds is home to the remains of the most prehistoric native civilization north of Mexico. The original settlers inhabited the area from AD 700 to 1400. The site is known for its collection of large man-made earthen structures built by an ancient civilization called the Mound Builders. Today the 2,200-acre facility features an orientation show theater, a museum shop, and an interpretive center that gives a 3-D history lesson on how the Mississippian Indian tribe lived more than 900 years ago. Visitors can walk through a life-size diorama of a Mississippian village that includes the stockade, houses, and other structures as well as everyday items such as stone tools, pottery, objects crafted from shell, and clothes made from natural fibers. There's also a Woodhenge solar calendar and an explanation of how the Indian mounds were created. The United Nations Educational, Scientific, and Cultural Organization (UNESCO) designated Cahokia Mounds a World Heritage Site in 1982 because of its importance in helping modern-day historians and visitors understand North America's prehistory. A variety of themed special events takes place throughout the year, so it's best to check in advance to see what's going on during your planned visit. Open Wed through Sun. Donations are suggested.

Fairmount Park Racetrack. 9301 Collinsville Rd.; (618) 345-4300; www.fairmountpark .com. Considered one of the top racetracks in the state, Fairmount was originally established in 1925. Horseracing on the 1-mile oval track is held Mar through Sept. The track is a clay and sand surface and there are two chutes: one for 6-furlong races and one that provides room for 1.25-mile races. On-site restaurants include casual dining at the First Turn Cafe, the Top of the Turf, and the Black Stallion Room.

Gateway Fun Park. 8 Gateway Dr.; (618) 345-7116; www.gatewayfun.com. Kids can work off some of their ever-present energy with miniature golf, bumper cars and boats, or the Water Wars game of skill that uses water balloons. There are go-karts for older children and a kiddie track for ages 4 to 9. Open daily year-round.

J-H Bison Ranch. 10802 Sunnyside School Rd., Trenton; (618) 934-3029; www.jbarh bisonranch.com. Located about 30 minutes outside of Collinsville, the J-H Bison Ranch is a family-run critter farm with a lineup of residents that includes a pony, an alpaca, 10-plus llamas, Sadie the Sicilian donkey, a Tennessee walking horse, and a black bear. Tours include baby bison feeding, herd tours, and photo ops with baby bison, llamas, and horses. Open by appointment only.

Splash City. 10 Gateway Dr.; (618) 346-4571; www.splashcity.org. Get wet and wild at Splash City—there's something for all ages. The water park's most popular attraction is the

FlowRider, which pumps 36,000 gallons of water a minute to create a continuous wave for body boarding and surfing. Monsoon Mountain is a 50-foot-tall water fortress with 5 slides and an assortment of buckets and hoses that kids can use to squirt one another. Every 5 minutes the big bucket on top empties its 500 gallons of water on anyone and everyone underneath it. Adventurous types can try to make it across the pool hanging on to the overhead rope and using the inflated lily pads (it's a lot harder than you think!). Guppy Gully is a good place for toddlers that's not as frenzied as the rest of the park, and there's a manmade sand area outfitted with buckets and shovels for those who want to experience some beach time during their visit. Splash City also features 2 waterslides, the Crystal Creek Lazy River, daily surf lessons for those 48 inches and taller, and swimming lessons for kids ages 3 to 11 in the 4 lane lap pool.

where to shop

Ashmann's Pharmacy. 209 E. Main St.; (618) 344-2300. In addition to your run-of-the mill drugstore needs, Ashmann's is the place to pick up your Brooks Catsup Bottle Water Tower souvenirs, including T-shirts, coffee mugs, magnets, and postcards.

Cahokia Mounds Museum Gift Shop. 30 Ramey St.; (618) 346-5160; www.cahokia mounds.org. The shop has an assortment of handcrafted Native American–made items such as paintings, drawings, ceramics, sculptures, textiles, and jewelry. There's also a selection of books on the history of Cahokia Mounds, archaeology, anthropology, Native cooking, and plant identification, along with some games, arts and crafts items, and logoed souvenirs.

Cross Patches. 110 W. Main St.; (618) 345-3661. Quilters and the people who love them/buy gifts for them will find plenty to explore throughout this 4,000-square-foot shop. Specializing in batik, moda, and hand-dyed fabrics as well as quilting supplies and notions, the shop is also an authorized Bernina sewing machine dealership and service location.

where to eat

Bert's Chuck Wagon Bar-B-Q. 101 E. Main St.; (618) 344-7993. Bert's is a great local hole-in-the-wall eatery with a simple, inexpensive menu of filling fare like burgers, pulled pork barbecue, taco salads, and nachos. The Collinsville mainstay has been serving up a variety of American, Mexican, and Tex-Mex favorites since 1963. Open for lunch and dinner Mon through Sat. $.

Dairy Haven. 112 N. Main St., Caseyville; (618) 345-8866. Classic walk-up and drive-thru ice-cream stand known for its soft-serve "swirl" ice-cream cones and orange sherbet. The menu includes milk shakes and a variety of soft-serve ice-cream flavors in addition to a cheesecake flavored yogurt. Outdoor tables for seating. Open Mar through Oct. $.

Happy Cow. 601 N. Main St., Caseyville; (618) 346-7421. Located just a stone's throw from downtown Collinsville in nearby Caseyville is a tiny eatery that knows how to overdo a theme. But nobody seems to mind. Outfitted with cow decor, figurines, kitsch, and more, the Happy Cow serves up good diner food for breakfast, lunch, and dinner. The menu also features comfort food favorites like meat loaf, mashed potatoes, country-fried steak, burgers, and pie. Generous portions, reasonable prices. No credit cards accepted. $.

The Oatman Haus Restaurant. 501 E. Main St.; (618) 346 2326. The tearoom menu is limited to salads and sandwiches for lunch, but the dinner options expand to include heartier fare and such German specialties as schweineschnitzel, jägerschnitzel, and sauerbraten. The restaurant is located in a historic Gothic Revival–style home that was built in 1875. $.

Porter's Steakhouse. 1000 Eastport Plaza Dr.; (618) 345-2400. Located in the Doubletree Hotel, Porter's is one of Collinsville's most upscale restaurants. Specialties include peppered tenderloin sliders, bone-in filet mignon, pork porterhouse, tuna mignon, and Porter's grilled pepper loin. The restaurant also features a very nice wine list. $$–$$$.

Ravanelli's. 6 Collinsport Dr.; (618) 343-9000; www.ravanellisrestaurants.com. Family-friendly eatery that serves brick-oven-baked pizzas and pastas, 1-pound tossed pasta bowls, Fritz's Famous Pressure-Fried Chicken, sandwich plates, appetizers, and salads. They even offer a vegan pizza (roasted red pepper, red onion, black olives, artichokes, olive oil, balsamic vinegar, and baby spinach). Open for lunch and dinner. There are two additional locations in nearby Granite City and O'Fallon, IL. $–$$.

day trip 02

northeast

suburban style:
edwardsville, il; glen carbon, il

Edwardsville and Glen Carbon are two dynamic, family-friendly communities within the greater St. Louis area. The region was originally settled in 1805 when southwestern Illinois was taken under control by the American colonies during the Revolutionary War. Today both towns offer all the comforts of an American suburban lifestyle, with good schools, convenient shopping, restaurants, and access to collegiate life at Southern Illinois University's Edwardsville campus.

edwardsville, il

Edwardsville is named for Ninian Edwards, who was appointed territorial governor in 1809 when the Illinois Territory was established. It's the third-oldest city in Illinois and has retained 39 buildings that have been designated as historic landmarks. Two of the town's historic districts—the Brick Street and St. Louis Street districts—were built in the 1880s and '90s. Today more than 25,000 residents call Edwardsville home.

getting there

From downtown St. Louis, take I-70 East into Illinois and continue for about 19 miles. Continue straight onto I-55 North, then take exit 20B to merge onto I-270 West toward Kansas City and follow it for about 3 miles. Take exit 12 for IL 159 North toward Collinsville/

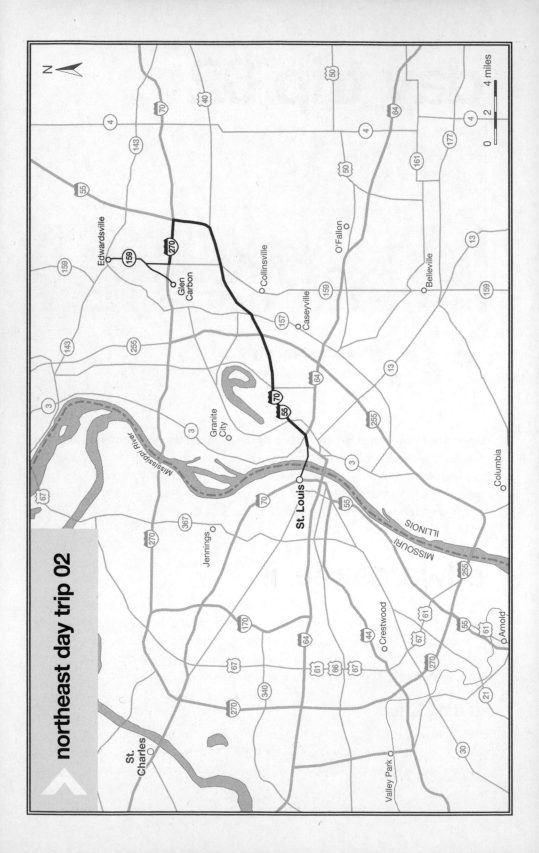

northeast day trip 02

Edwardsville and make a right onto IL 159 North/Troy Road. Follow Troy Road about 3.5 miles and continue onto S. Buchanan Street.

where to go

Colonel Benjamin Stephenson House. 409 S. Buchanan; (618) 692-1818; www.stephen sonhouse.org. Built in 1820, the Stephenson House was constructed in the Federal style and its history links Edwardsville to the earliest days of the Illinois Territory. Listed on the National Register of Historic Places, much of the home's original millwork and architectural features have been preserved. The tour offers insight into how the area's upper class lived in the early to mid-1800s. Open Thurs through Sun.

Wildey Theatre. 252 N. Main St.; (618) 307-2053; www.wildeytheatre.com. Located in the heart of downtown, the newly renovated and reopened Wildey originally opened in 1909 as an opera house. Resurrected in 2011, the venue now screens films and hosts live music concerts, theatrical and dance presentations, and children's events.

where to shop

Afterwords Books. 231 N. Main St.; (618) 655-0355. This family-owned and -operated used bookstore offers a broad selection of fiction, nonfiction, biographies and memoirs, children's books, and science fiction titles. Free Saturday-morning book readings for kids.

Bead it & Main Street Art Gallery. 237-239 N. Main St.; (618) 655-9990; www.beadit-art .com. Design and create your own jewelry masterpieces at Bead it. The store staff will help you make beaded earrings, bracelets, or necklaces. They also stock supplies for crocheting and knitting, and the art gallery features works by local artists. Closed Sun and Mon.

Edwardsville Crossing. 6655 Edwardsville Crossing Dr.; (618) 692-1937. Located at Governors Parkway and New Route 159, the shopping center is home to local shops as well as major retailers like Old Navy, Best Buy, Books-A-Million, Michael's, and Office Depot. The center also features the locally owned upscale grocery store Dierberg's and Phillips Furniture.

The Goshen Market. Next to the Courthouse on St. Louis St.; (618) 307-6045; www .goshenmarket.org. The open-air farmers' market features fresh locally grown produce and homemade baked goods as well as juried fine-art products. Live entertainment and demonstrations keep the place lively. Open Sat mornings only from mid-May through mid-October.

Heroic Adventures. 1031 Century Dr.; (618) 659-0099; www.heroic-adventures.com. If your idea of settling in with a good book involves a comic book or a graphic novel, this is your mecca. They have the largest selection in town, as well a spate of board and card games, miniatures, and unique toys, and they host weekly gamer events for Warhammer

40K, Magic TCG, Pokemon, World of Warcraft minis, and others. They're also an authorized retailer for Games Workshop, Wizards of the Coast, and Upper Deck products.

Lost Arts & Antiques. 254 N. Main St.; (618) 656-8844; www.lostartsandantiques.com. Located in the historic Wildey Theatre, the shop displays and sells works by artists from the region along with national artists. They proudly sell only American-made furniture, artwork, and decor and gift items.

Red Barn Antiques. 3616 Edwardsville Rd./IL 143; (618) 659-0145. Browse the Barn's selection of collectibles and primitive furniture, as well as an assortment of crocks, quilts, baskets, gardening items, farm tables, and country-style items. Located inside a 100-year-old barn, the 1,000-square-foot shop features antiques from 10 dealers.

where to eat

Bully's Smokehouse. 1035 Century Dr.; (618) 659-1802; www.bullyssmokehouse.com. Bully's specializes in Southern-style barbecue, and the menu also includes a variety of sandwiches, salads, burgers, steaks, and a couple of fish options (fried catfish and Creole tilapia). But people come here for the barbecue—choose from St. Louis–style ribs, beef, chicken, and pulled pork sandwiches and plates. $.

Erato Wine Bar on Main. 126 Main St.; (618) 307-3203; www.eratoonmain.com. Enjoy a large selection of boutique wines, international beers, 100-plus spirits, and a menu of tapas. Choose from small plates like lobster cakes, seared marlin, or a chicken pot pie and such "slightly larger small plates" as lamb rib chops, a wasabi-rubbed petite filet, or seared scallops. Other wine- and beer-friendly foodstuffs available are the candied bacon nachos (roasted red pepper, onion, chive, and borson cheese) and the bread crumb–encrusted risotto with mozzarella and pesto aioli. $$–$$$.

Global Brew Tap House & Lounge. 112 S. Buchanan St., Ste. 1; (618) 307-5858; www .globalbrewtaps.com. Okay, so there's no food menu here, but beer is considered sustenance in some arenas, and this pub is full of sustenance. There are 50 beers on tap and an international selection of more than 200 bottled craft beers. Try a Beer Shot—a 4-ounce mix of different brews like the Pink Elephant (Belgian strong ale and raspberry lambic), Wit Chocolate (chocolate stout and witbier), or the Hi-C (citrus wheat beer, flavored cider, and witbier). Open daily. $.

Northside Dairy Haven. 1902 N. Main St.; (618) 656-9233. The Midwest loves its frozen custard, and the Northside Dairy Haven serves up an array of tasty shakes, sundaes, and concretes (frozen custard blended with fruit, candies, or other sweet treats). Northside also offers a limited snack bar–style food menu that includes kid-friendly staples like corn dogs and grilled cheese. Cash only. $.

Sacred Grounds Cafe. 233 N. Main St.; (618) 692-4150. The menu is all vegetarian, but carnivores will enjoy it anyway. Known for its sandwiches and soups, the cozy coffeehouse is a popular breakfast spot on weekends. They can also make most of their dishes vegan upon request. $.

Wang Gang Asian Eats. #4 Club Centre Dr.; (618) 655-0888; www.wanggangasian.com. Chef-created Thai, Chinese, and Vietnamese cuisine including MSG-free spring rolls, pad thai, and the usual lineup of noodle-based dishes served in a nicer atmosphere than your typical Asian food eatery. Plenty of vegetarian dishes available as well as a gluten-free menu. The drinks menu includes the Yum Yum Boom Boom (an Asian margarita with tequila, sour apple liqueur, and freshly squeezed lime) and the Ginger Island Tea (ginger liqueur, tequila, vodka, triple sec, and sweet and sour). Located "sort of behind the Moto Mart on I-157." Open daily for lunch and dinner. $–$$.

glen carbon, il

The village of Glen Carbon was originally referred to as the "Land of Goshen." A Virginia Baptist minister passed through the area in 1799 and compared it to the biblical Land of Goshen because of its flourishing vegetation. In 1801 Colonel Samuel Judy was given 100 acres of land in the area as a military grant and became the area's first settler. Modern-day Glen Carbon was named one of *Money* magazine's top 100 places to live in 2009, and it is currently home to approximately 12,500 residents.

getting there

From Edwardsville, head south on S. Buchanan Street toward E. Park Street for about 0.5 mile, then continue onto Troy Road for a little more than 2 miles. Turn right onto Glen Carbon Road and follow it for 1.7 miles, then continue onto S. Main Street.

where to go

Glen Carbon Heritage Museum. 124 School St.; (618) 288-7271. The museum includes displays of memorabilia that reflect daily life in Glen Carbon's early days, in addition to various books on local history, artifacts from the Middle Woodland Village site, and items discovered during an archaeological investigation at the Yanda Log Cabin site. Open Tues, Thurs, and Sat.

Yanda Log Cabin. 148 Main St.; (618) 288-7271. Part of the Glen Carbon Heritage Museum site, the cabin was built around 1853 by William Yanda, a blacksmith who immigrated to the area from Bohemia Austria. He and his wife, Annie, raised 10 children in the cabin, and it was passed down through the family over the years. In 1989 the village of Glen

Carbon purchased the homesite and completely renovated the cabin. Open Tues, Thurs, and Sat.

where to shop

Karma. 164-A South Main St.; (618) 924-4427. This juniors' boutique sells brand-name, slightly worn clothing at deeply discounted prices. The mother-daughter owned and operated resale shop includes a variety of T-shirts, jean shorts, jeans, tops, pajamas, accessories, and jewelry in sizes ranging from extra small to extra large. Closed Sun and Mon.

day trip 03

northeast

old national road:
vandalia, il; altamont, il; effingham, il

In 1839 America's first interstate highway the National Road—was completed as far as Vandalia, IL. The road was built to link the Eastern Seaboard with the cities and towns west of the Allegheny Mountains. Authorized by Congress in 1806, road construction began in Cumberland, Maryland, in 1811. Today the National Road features plenty of rolling countryside, prairie fields, and an abundance of small towns and cities with a variety of charms and historic significance.

vandalia, il

Vandalia's most historic claim to fame is that the town served as the state capital from its founding in 1819 until the capital was moved to Springfield in 1839. Today the white Federal-style building that served as the Illinois state capitol from 1836 to 1839 is still impressive, with its high ceilings, tall windows, and vintage furnishings. Abraham Lincoln began his political career in the senate and house of representatives chambers, and the building is the oldest Illinois state capitol in existence.

Located in Fayette County, Vandalia is on the Kaskaskia River about 69 miles northeast of St. Louis. The city occupies just less than 6 square miles and is situated on US 40, which is also known as the National Road. Also called the "Road That Built the Nation," the byway was created in 1806 by legislation signed by President Thomas Jefferson. The road was designed to provide a route from Maryland through Pennsylvania, West Virginia, Ohio,

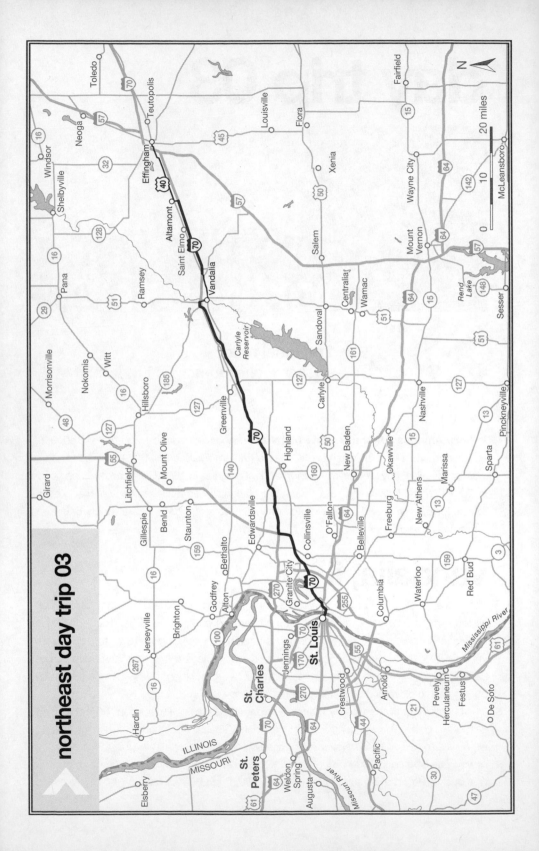

northeast day trip 03

Indiana, and Illinois. Unfortunately, federal funding was discontinued before the road was finished, and construction stopped at Vandalia. Today the Illinois National Road stretches more than 160 miles from Marshall to East St. Louis.

getting there

From St. Louis, take I-64 East/I-70 East over the river and follow the ramp to Louisville/St. Clair Avenue. Continue on I-70 East, following the signs for Indianapolis, for approximately 48 miles, then take exit 63 for US 51 toward Vandalia/Pana.

where to go

Vandalia Tourist Information Center. 1408 N. 5th St.; (618) 283-2728; www.vandalia illinois.com. The Tourist Information Center can provide insight into local lodging options and tales, community events, restaurants, and historic site information. Open Mon through Fri.

Archway Skydiving. RR 3, Box 602; (618) 283-4978; www.archwayskydiving.com. Take a flying leap! Archway Skydiving has been in business since 1999, and the outfit averages more than 12,000 skydives per year, including more than 1,200 first-timers. They say they have the fastest turbine jump airplane in the area, and their on-the-ground amenities include a spectator area with picnic tables and barbecue pits as well as an indoor game room and lounge for friends and family members who are on hand merely for moral support.

Evans Public Library. 215 S. 5th St.; (618) 283-2824. The public library houses a collection of Lincoln books, pamphlets, pictures, and other items, but what's unusual is the life mask of Abraham Lincoln that's housed in a glass display case. A Springfield resident donated the life mask to the library's collection because Vandalia was where Lincoln started his legislative career. It's one of only a few copies made from the original mask, which was made for a statue of Lincoln in 1860 just after he was elected president of the US. The original mask remains part of the Smithsonian Institution's collection.

Madonna of the Trails statue. Southeast corner of the Old State Capitol site. The 17-ton monument to pioneer women was dedicated on October 26, 1928, and features a woman holding a baby with a small child clutching at her skirt. It is one of a series of 12 monuments created by sculptor August Leimbach commissioned by the National Society of Daughters of the American Revolution. The monuments are dedicated to the spirit of American pioneer women and were placed in 12 different states along the National Old Trails Road, which was established in 1912.

National Road Interpretive Center. 106 S. 5th St.; (618) 283-2728. The center tells the story of the surveyors, laborers, and travelers of the National Road, which is often called the Cumberland Road or National Pike. In addition to information about the road's history, the center doubles as a museum with hands-on activities for kids like loading up a Conestoga wagon—the semitrailer of the era. Open Wed through Sat.

Old State Capitol. 315 W. Gallatin St.; (618) 283-1161. The white Federal-style building was finished in 1836 and is the oldest of the Illinois state capitols. It served as the capitol from 1836 to 1839. Displays include vintage furnishings, copies of documents from the state's early days, and the senate and house of representatives chambers where Abraham Lincoln began his political career as a state representative. Admission is free. Closed Sun and Mon.

where to shop

Tiger Lily Florist Gift & Art Gallery. 131 N. 5th St; (618) 283-8748. The gallery provides an outlet for local and out-of-town artists to display and sell their watercolor paintings, pottery, silks, wood turning, and other media. The shop also offers a variety of home decor items, including wind chimes, Demdaco frames, and floral arrangements. Closed Sun.

where to eat

Chuckwagon Cafe. 704 Janette Dr.; (618) 283-2220. Chuckwagon serves up simple food, including hearty breakfasts, large stacks of pancakes, delicious omelets, grilled sandwiches, and soups. The decor is "vintage" but the place gets high marks for the fried fish, pork tenderloin sandwiches, and friendly staff. $.

The Copper Penny Bar & Grille. 125 S. 4th St.; (618) 283-2200. The lively eatery offers an array of appetizers, sandwiches, burgers, and salads along with entrees like fried shrimp, marinated chicken breast, and fried walleye. Try some fried pickles as an appetizer then dive into a Horseshoe Burger, which is served on Texas toast and smothered with an order of cheese fries. There are also lots of drink specials and an assortment of draft beer, wine, and spirits. $–$$.

Vandalia Whistle Stop. 615 W. Gallatin St.; (618) 283-9140. The menu features filling, stick-to-your-ribs goodies like chili cheese fries, shrimp po' boys, prime rib sandwiches, the giant Big Whistle burger, and the El Diablo burger (topped with two onion rings stuffed with jalapeño, covered with melted pepper jack cheese, and topped with homemade BBQ sauce). They also serve gyros, hot dogs, and salads like the Tangled Up in Bleu (a garden salad with black olives, hard-boiled egg, ham, bacon, turkey, and blue cheese crumbles). $.

altamont, il

Another town you'll run across on the Old National Road is Altamont, a small community with a population of 2,300. Located in Effingham County on US 40, the city is midway between St. Louis and Terre Haute, IN. First organized as an actual town in 1871, Altamont was settled by early German immigrants coming from the "Faderland" on the banks of the Rhine by way of Pennsylvania and Ohio.

getting there

From Vandalia, take IL 185 East/US 40 East about 4.5 miles, then turn right to merge onto I-70 East toward Effingham and follow it for approximately 15 miles. Take exit 82 for IL 128 toward Altamont, then turn right onto IL 128 North/CR 25 for a little less than a mile. Continue onto S. Main Street into Altamont.

where to go

Ballard Nature Center. 5253 US 40 East; (618) 483-6856; www.ballardnaturecenter.org. Commune with Mother Nature along the walking trails; explore the various woodlands, prairies, wetlands, and savannas; or picnic at one of the large pavilions outfitted with electricity, picnic tables, and running water. There's also a kids' fishing pond and wheelchair-accessible trails, pavilions, and a fishing pier. The center also has an exhibit room with interactive displays, a bird-watching window, and a non-lending library with scientific publications, children's books, videos, and photo journals. Open year-round; closed Sun from Nov through Feb.

Ben Winters' Steam Engine Museum. 1815 E. 900th Ave,; (217) 342-5310. In addition to housing 15 steam engines, the museum features a number of gas and oil engines, steam-driven tractors, and a large stationary steam engine. There's a model train layout in the loft, and kids can ride a miniature train through the orchards. Winters' collection also includes an assortment of antiques such as Victrolas, the *Altamont News*'s old Linotype machine, and a playable pipe organ from St. Paul Lutheran Church. Open mid-April through mid-October.

Dr. Charles Wright House. Corner of N. Main St. and W. Jackson Ave.; (618) 483-6397; www.wrightmansion.org. Listed on the National Register of Historic Places, the Wright House was designed in the Second Empire (Mansard) style with Italianate-style influences. It features a Mansard roof with a patterned slate; dressed stones on the exterior corners of the buildings, which are known as quoins; and tall windows on the first story. Tours of the mansion take place on Sun from 2 to 4 p.m. during the months of June, July, and Aug. Other tour times can be arranged upon request.

effingham, il

Called the "Crossroads of Opportunity," Effingham traces its roots back to 1814 when the first pioneers settled along the Little Wabash River. Today the town of approximately 35,000 residents has become a regional trade and transportation center, offering central Illinois families an idyllic spot to live and work.

getting there

Effingham is only a 10-minute drive from Altamont—just follow CR 1250/US 40 East for about 11 miles and turn right onto W. Fayette Avenue.

where to go

Effingham Convention & Visitors Bureau. 1505 Hampton Dr.; www.visiteffinghamil.com. Stop in for details on area eateries, overnight accommodations, attractions, concerts, and special events.

The Effingham Performance Center. 1325 Outer Belt West; (217) 540-2788; www.the-epc.org. Effingham's 1,500-seat theater hosts about 50 performances a year, ranging from local and regional artists to national headliners like Foreigner, Tim Conway & Friends, Sara Evans, Brian Regan, Kenny Rogers, and REO Speedwagon. The Performance Center also hosts jazz, dance, and classical performances.

My Garage Museum. 1 Mid-America Pl.; (217) 347-5591; www.mygaragemuseum.com. In Route 66 country the Corvette is king, so this collection of Chevy's favorite muscle car is a must-see for car nuts. The museum showcases classic and one-of-a-kind models, including Indy 500 pace cars, a '54 Pennant Blue, a '62 big tanker race car, a Lemans Blue 427 CID L-88, and a 1989 Challenge version. Plus there's tons of Corvette, Porsche, and Volkswagen memorabilia and a restored 1910 gas station that was moved to the site. Open daily.

Teutopolis Monastery Museum. 110 S. Garrott St.; (217) 857-6404. Begun in 1858, the museum building originally served as the Franciscan friars' home and now includes a collection of articles and books used by the friars during the novitiate year, along with various items used by early Teutopolis pioneers such as farm tools, furniture, quilts, toys, and household items. Tours include the mausoleum and St. Francis of Assisi Church, which contains stained-glass windows that depict events throughout the life of St. Francis. The museum is open only on the first Sun of the month from Apr through Nov.

Tuscan Hills Winery. 2200 Historic Hills Dr.; (217) 347-WINE; www.effinghamwinery .com. Experience a taste of Tuscany and sip some local wines while enjoying the view at this picturesque winery northeast of Effingham. Located on an old farmstead, circa 1860, the winery usually has live entertainment on weekends and occasional special events like a harvest grape crushing. Try the white sangria, with tropical fruits and a hint of ginger, or the red sangria, with a host of raspberry and citrus flavors. Tuscan Hills also produces 3 whites, 3 reds, and 3 blush wines, along with a unique Glühwein, or mulled wine. Served hot, this spicy German wine is an ideal treat in front of the fire during the colder months. The menu also features a number of specialty beers and seasonal brews along with soft drinks and fruit juices. Open daily.

where to shop

Downtown Effingham. Visit the 25-plus specialty shops offering everything from arts and crafts, gifts, and decor to clothing for women and children. The downtown shops also offer designer jewelry, furniture, pet supplies, and collectibles.

Legacy Harley-Davidson. 1315 Althoff Ave.; (217) 342-3494; www.legacyhd.com. Hog fans won't want to miss "The Harley Barn." Legacy's showroom, parts and service area, merchandise, and "motor clothes" shop are all located within the giant barn structure. Rides are scheduled most Saturdays, weather permitting, and if you don't know how to ride, they offer regular classes during warm-weather months. Closed Mon.

Samuel Music. 908 W. Fayette Ave.; (217) 342-0221; www.samuelmusic.com. Samuel offers new and used brand-name musical instruments and gear, including Fender, Yamaha, Epiphone, Marshall, Peavey, Boss, Pearl, and Zildjian. Listed by *Music Trades* magazine as one of the top 200 music retailers in the US, Samuel also sells sheet music, rents equipment, offers music lessons, and has Musikgarten classes for kids up to 9 years old. Open-mic nights are held every Wed. They also have stores in Springfield and Champaign.

day trip 04

northeast

double the fun:
bloomington-normal, il

bloomington-normal, il

Located in the heart of Illinois just 155 miles northeast of St. Louis, the Bloomington-Normal area is a lively community of more than 165,000 residents. The region offers the youthful exuberance of a college town, thanks to the rotating influx of students from Illinois State University and Illinois Wesleyan University, and the corporate presence of company headquarters like State Farm Insurance, COUNTRY Financial, and Beer Nuts. Bloomington-Normal features an eclectic mix of big-city options that have been seasoned with small-town charisma and friendliness.

getting there

Hop on I-70 East from St. Louis and follow it into Illinois for about 19 miles, then continue straight onto I-55 North for about 137 miles. Take exit 157A-B for I-55 Business Loop North/Veterans Parkway/I-74/US 51 toward Decatur/Indianapolis, then take exit 157B on the left for I-55 Business North/Veterans Parkway. Merge onto I-55 Business Loop North/S. Veterans Parkway and follow it for about 2 miles. Take the US 51 Business/Main Street ramp and make a left onto S. Main Street, following it for a little more than a mile, then continue onto S. East Street.

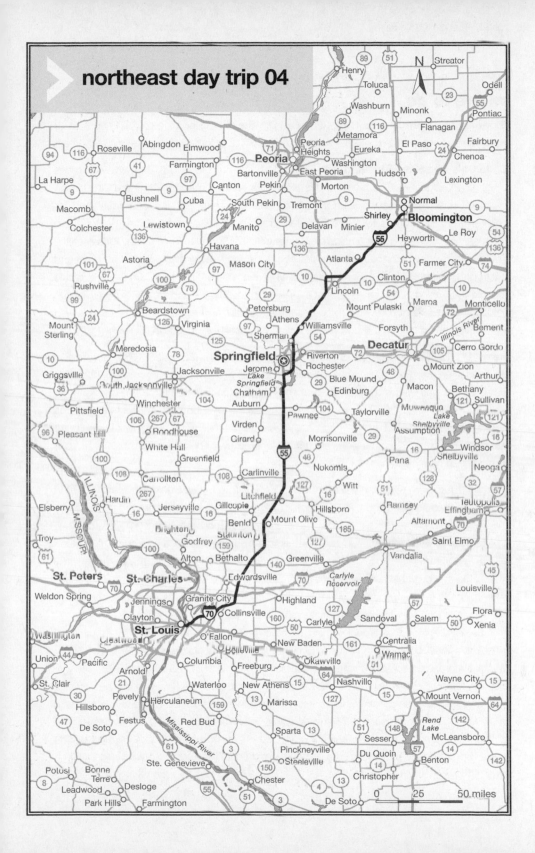

where to go

Bloomington-Normal Area CVB. 3201 Cira Dr., Ste. 201, Bloomington; (309) 665-0033; www.bloomingtonnormalcvb.org. Friendly folks and lots of info on the greater "B-N" area.

Children's Discovery Museum. 101 E. Beaufort, Normal; (309) 433-3444; www.childrens discoverymuseum.net. The museum has 3 floors of hands-on exhibits that are fun enough to make kids forget they're learning. Educational programs and activities designed for children from 12 months to 13 years old include Toddler Backyard, Water Works, Train Express, and Inside Me, which helps explain how the body works. The Healthy Kids–Healthy Future gallery offers informational activities about making healthy choices in what to eat and the importance of the great outdoors to overall health. Visit the Dig It Pocket Garden, tackle the Dig It Climbing Wall, and see what's shaking in the Dig It Wind Power exhibit. The Oh Rubbish display includes a walk through a talking landfill, and AgMazing engages kids with information about what it's like to live and work on a 21st-century farm. Open daily.

David Davis Mansion. 1000 E. Monroe St., Bloomington; (309) 828-1084; www.david davismansion.org. This 19th-century mansion was the home of US Supreme Court Justice David Davis, who was a mentor of Abraham Lincoln's as well as his campaign manager. Built in 1872, the mansion combines Italianate and Second Empire architectural features and is known as Clover Lawn. When Lincoln became president, he appointed Davis to the Supreme Court in 1862. Interpretive tours are offered every half hour from 9:30 a.m. to 4 p.m. Closed Mon and Tues.

Funks Grove. 5257 Old Route 66, Shirley; (309) 874-3360; www.funksgrove.org. Located a little less than 10 miles southwest of Bloomington is Funks Grove, a compound owned by the Funk family since the mid-1800s. The attractions include the Funk Prairie Home, built by Marquis de LaFayette Funk in 1864 with timber from Funks Grove and containing much of the family's original rosewood and walnut furniture. All 13 rooms of the home are fully decorated and available for viewing. Also on-site is the Gem & Mineral Museum, which contains minerals from around the world as well as collections of fossils, central Illinois Indian artifacts, Chinese soapstone carvings, seashells, and corals.

Funks Grove is the largest remaining intact prairie grove in the state of Illinois, and portions of the 1,000 acres have been designated a National Natural Landmark. The Sugar Grove Nature Center, also located on-site, is stocked with interpretive exhibits, sensory displays, a few live animals, and a wildlife-viewing area that offers a way to see native birds and other wildlife in an up-close-and-personal kind of way. Admission to the nature center is free. During Feb and Mar at the Pure Maple Sirup Store (they use the old-fashioned spelling of the word *syrup*), visitors can enjoy a guided tour that shows how maple syrup is made in the "boiling down" process. The gift shop is stocked with syrup year-round, along with a smattering of Route 66 memorabilia.

McLean County Museum of History. 200 N. Main St., Bloomington; (309) 827-0428; www.mchistory.org. Located in downtown Bloomington, the museum got its start back in 1904. Permanent displays include Encounter on the Prairie and 4 galleries examining the different aspects of life in McLean County: People, Farming, Politics, and Work. The Harriet Fuller Rust Pioneer Neighborhood/Discovery Room is an experiential display where visitors are encouraged to participate in activities from the past like pushing a steel plow, beating a rug, fetching a little water then scrubbing some clothing clean, and doing some arithmetic homework on a slate. The nationally accredited museum is housed in a historic courthouse that's listed on the National Register of Historic Places.

The Prairie Aviation Museum. 2929 E. Empire St., Bloomington; (309) 663-7632; www.prairieaviationmuseum.org. The 2,400-square-foot facility's displays include information about various segments of aviation history, including WWII aircraft carriers, Charles Lindbergh, Edwin A. Link's pilot trainer, and the 20-plus astronauts from the state of Illinois. There are also permanent and rotating exhibits and static outdoor displays of historical aircraft and vehicles. The highlight of the tour is "getting behind the wheel" of a flight simulator for some virtual flight time. Visitors can view or take a ride in the restored DC-3, the only flying exhibit on the National Register of Historic Places.

Upper Limits Rock Climbing Gym. 1304 W. Washington St., Bloomington; (309) 829-TALL; www.upperlimits.com/bloomington. The indoor gym offers individual and family climbing packages. They've got all of the gear, plus 65-foot-tall silos, a main climbing area of overhanging terrain, an outdoor boulder, a 110-foot-tall outdoor wall, and 6 auto belays. Upper Limits has a number of classes available and can accommodate any skill level from beginner to experienced.

White Oak Vineyards. 8621 E. 2100 North Rd.; (309) 376-3027; www.whiteoakvineyards inc.com. Family-run winery set amidst 8 acres of vineyards in central Illinois. Enjoy a glass or a bottle inside the comfortable tasting room, step outside and grab a seat on the wrap-around porch, or take it "to go" down by the pond. The winery produces a Seyval Blanc named after their golden retriever, Maxi, and a Bernese Red named for their Swiss Bernese mountain dog, Mortiz, as well as a Norton, Vignoles, Riesling, Steuben, and Cayuga White. Closed Mon.

where to shop

A. Gridley Antiques. 217 E. Front St., Bloomington; (309) 829-9615. Located across from Central Station, treasure hunters can sift through 2 floors of furniture, rugs, lamps, artwork, and bric-a-brac. Open Fri and Sat only. No credit cards accepted.

Beer Nuts Company Store. 103 N. Robinson St., Bloomington; (309) 827-8580. Headquartered in Bloomington, Beer Nuts are still manufactured using the original 1837 recipe.

Stop in the store and pick up some Beer Nuts gear and some salty snacks for the ride home.

Downtown Bloomington. 106 W. Monroe St., Bloomington; (309) 829-9599; www.down townbloomington.org. Shop and stroll through downtown and visit the more than 35 retailers offering goods and services ranging from art and antiques to tailoring and tattooing. There are also a number of restaurants, coffee shops, clubs, and entertainment options available.

Eastland Mall. 1615 E. Empire St., Bloomington; (309) 663-1340; www.ishopeastlandmall .com. Major shopping mall with national retailers like Aeropostale, Express, Express Men, Gap, Gap Kids, Hollister Co., JCPenney, Macy's, Sears, Talbots, Victoria's Secret, and Zales Jewelers.

Par's Rug Warehouse. 229 E. Front St., Bloomington; (309) 828-1336; www.rug101 .com. The shop offers antique rugs and fine Persian and Oriental rugs. Featured collections include Heritage Hall, Nourmak, Saffira, Nourison 2000, and Nourison 2003.

The Shoppes at College Hills. North Veterans Pkwy., Normal; (309) 862-3761; www .theshoppesatcollegehills.com. The open-air shopping plaza features top-name stores like Ann Taylor Loft, Bath & Body Works, Chico's, Gordman's, Coldwater Creek, Jos. A. Bank, Lane Bryant, Target, Tuesday Morning, Von Maur, and Yankee Candle.

Uptown Normal. 108 Beaufort St., Normal; (309) 433-3420; www.uptownnormal.com. The eclectic retail district offers an array of services, specialty shops, bookstores, coffeehouses, and casual restaurants. It's also home to attractions like the Normal movie theater and Children's Discovery Museum.

where to eat

DESTIHL Restaurant & Brew Works. 318 S. Towanda Ave., Normal; (309) 862-2337; www.destihl.com. A self-described "gastrobrewpub" that serves eclectic artisan food that goes well with (or without) beer. Menu specialties include rustic flatbreads, stone-oven pizzas, entree salads like the Brewmaster's (ancho chicken, andouille sausage, ale onions, mozzarella, smoked Gouda, and chipotle espresso BBQ sauce), hand-breaded cheese curds (with roasted garlic and tomato sauce), spicy Thai shrimp pasta, and the Dopple Chop (beer-brined double bone-in pork chop, roasted red pepper, ale onions, maple glaze, sweet potatoes, and andouille sausage). The restaurant features a wide variety of handcrafted beers as well as a very good selection of wine and spirits. Open for lunch and dinner, and they offer a weekend brunch on Sat and Sun. $$.

Gene's Dairy Delight. 1019 S. Main St., Bloomington; (309) 829-6022; www.genes icecream.com. Tiny, old-fashioned ice-cream stand serving soft-serve cones, sundaes, shakes, and banana splits. Gene's is a local tradition—no matter what the weather is like, people line up for cold treats whenever the stand is open. Open daily from late Feb to Sept. $.

Kelly's Bakery & Cafe. 113 N. Center St., Bloomington; (309) 820.1200; www.kellys bakeryandcafe.com. Open for breakfast and lunch, Kelly's serves fresh soups, salads, and cafe and grilled sandwiches like the Black Russian (Angus roast beef, turkey, and provolone cheese with homemade Russian dressing on pumpernickel rye) and the Twisted Turkey (fresh-cut turkey, raspberry-jalapeño spread, and smoked Gouda or provolone cheese). The bakery offers fresh-baked muffins, scones, cream cheese puffs, cinnamon rolls, caramel brownies, and the house specialty, decorated butter cookies. $.

Lancaster's Fine Dining. 513 N. Main St., Bloomington; (309) 827-3333; www.lancasters restaurant.com. Lancaster's offers seasonal menus with items like the Lobster BLT (lobster salad, bacon, tomato, and mesclun mix on a croissant) and Irish Duck Nachos (spicy roasted and shredded duck breast, fresh black bean and corn salsa, pickled jalapeños, lettuce, and *queso blanco* sauce over fresh-fried potato chips), along with steaks, pasta dishes, seafood, and an impressive wine list. Live music on most Fri nights. $$.

Lucca Grill. 116 E. Market St., Bloomington; (309) 828-7521; www.luccagrill.com. Established in 1936 by the Baldini brothers, the eatery was named for their hometown of Lucca, Italy. House favorites include Lucca's Famous Chicken Livers, lasagna, Pizza a la Baldini (sausage, pepperoni, ham, onions, mushrooms, green peppers, and pepperoncini), and sandwiches like the Lois (roast beef with grilled onions and green peppers, topped with Swiss cheese) and the Dago Steak (ground chuck served on a hoagie roll). $–$$.

Medici. 120 North St., Normal; (309) 452-6334; www.medicinormal.com. Elegant decor and contemporary ambiance with a menu of fresh seasonal foods and upscale pub grub. Choose from an array of salads, sandwiches, and Gastroburgers (served on a cornmeal-dusted challah bun), along with specialty pizzas and delicacies liked the smoked Gouda mac and cheese, truffle-braised mussels, smoky IPA rib eye, and Puget Sound vegetable couscous. Open daily for lunch and dinner, along with Sunday brunch. $$.

Reality Bites. 414 N. Main St., Bloomington; (309) 828-1300; www.realitybitesinc.com. A contemporary tapas restaurant and bar with a menu of salads, cold plates, hot plates, and specialty plates like Baja fish tacos, sesame-encrusted salmon, and the drunken chicken (pan-roasted chicken breast, sautéed green beans, garlic mashed potatoes, and dark rum reduction). There's a good selection of wines, artisan beers, and cocktails. Closed Sun and Mon. $$.

Rosie's Pub. 106 E. Front St., Bloomington; (309) 827-7019; www.rosiesbloomington .com. Rosie's offers a casual, intimate dining experience with a menu of grilled flatbreads, burgers, sandwiches, and appetizers. Try the Rosie's Red Eye (Bloody Mary–marinated

8-ounce flatiron steak topped with a fried egg) or a chipotle black bean burger. There is also an extensive specialty martini selection. Open for lunch and dinner. $–$$.

Station 220. 220 E. Front St., Bloomington; (309) 828-2323; www.station220.com. Housed within the Central Fire Station, built in 1902, Station 220 is a complete "Farm to Fork" restaurant. Offering food that's "globally influenced and locally produced," the eatery serves a lunch menu of soups, sandwiches, salads, and a few entrees. The dinner menu expands to include such dishes as filet Oscar, lamb shank, schnitzel, mahi mahi, and shrimp and mussels. $$$.

where to stay

Burr House Bed & Breakfast. 210 E. Chestnut St., Bloomington; (309) 828-7686; www .burrhouse.com. This Civil War–era brick home, built in 1864, is located in Bloomington's historic district. Six rooms are available, including a suite called the Queen Anne. The home still has the original black walnut floors and woodwork, as well as its ornate plaster ceilings and 4 marble fireplaces. Breakfast available from 6 to 9 a.m. $.

Vrooman Mansion. 701 E. Taylor St., Bloomington; (309) 828-8816; www.vrooman mansion.com. Nestled in the residential neighborhood of Dimmitt's Grove, the home was originally built in 1869. Today the B&B offers 5 comfortable guest suites that are decorated with antique period furniture and outfitted with creature comforts like down pillows, high-quality bed linens, and free Wi-Fi. Enjoy a full gourmet breakfast in the formal dining room or on the side porch, weather permitting. $–$$.

east

day trip 01

east

>>>

go outside & play:
carlyle lake, il

carlyle lake, il

Administered by the US Army Corps of Engineers, Carlyle Lake is the largest man-made lake in Illinois, containing more than 26,000 acres of water and 11,000 acres of land. Located just 50 miles east of St. Louis, the lake's beaches prove to be a popular weekend getaway spot for area residents in need of some sand between their toes.

getting there

From downtown St. Louis, merge onto I-64 East and continue onto I-70 East into Illinois. Make a slight right onto I-64 East/IL 3 North (the signs will say Louisville/St. Clair Avenue), follow I-64 East for about 16 miles, and take exit 19B to merge onto US 50 East/Air Mobility Drive toward Carlyle. Continue on US 50 East for about a mile, then turn right to stay on US 50 East and follow it for about 4 miles. Turn left onto S. Madison Street, then turn right onto US 50 East/Federal Aid Secondary 1780/E. St. Louis Street. Continue to follow US 50 East for 24 miles, then turn left onto IL 127 North. Take the first right onto CR 1840 East/ William Road and continue onto CR 1840 East. Continue straight onto Sunrise Hill and turn left onto Carlyle Dam Road. The lake will be on the left.

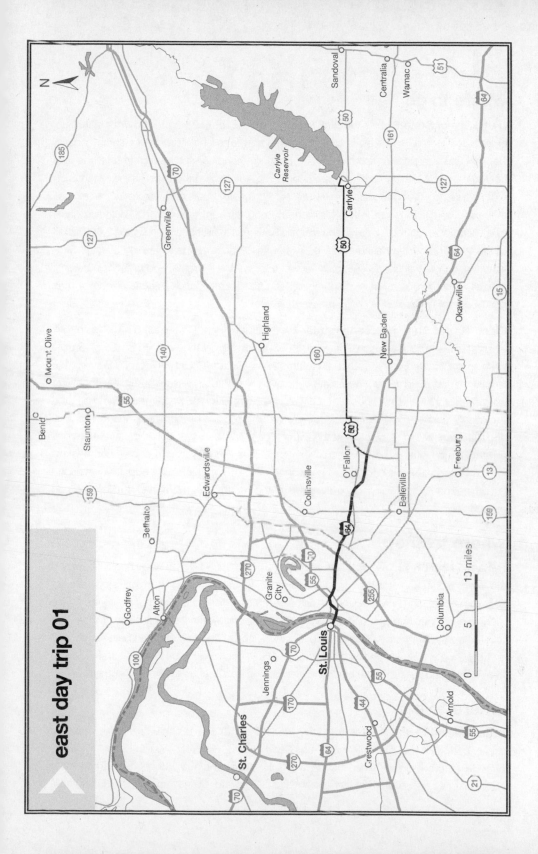

east day trip 01

where to go

Carlyle Lake State Fish & Wildlife Area. RR #2; (618) 452-3533; http://dnr.state.il.us. In addition to giving you a place to cool off with a swim on hot Midwestern summer days, Carlyle Lake is a popular spot for fishing, boating, camping, and sailing. In fact, the lake hosted the 1994 US Olympic Festival Sailing Competition, and there are sailing regattas on most weekends during the summer. However, all types of boats and watercraft can access the lake. There's excellent fishing for more than 30 different types of fish, including bass, bluegill, crappie, catfish, walleye, and sauger. Fishing is available on more than 2,000 acres of the lake and on the Kaskaskia River, which has 2 boat ramps for fishing access. Bird-watchers can see ducks, geese, bald eagles, ospreys, cormorants, and great blue herons, as well as numerous species of shorebirds and songbirds. Carlyle Lake is also known as one of the top waterfowl hunting areas in the state.

Eldon Hazlet State Recreation Area. 20100 Hazlet Park Rd.; (618) 594-3015; http://dnr.state.il.us. The recreation area is a 3,000-acre site on the western shore of Carlyle Lake that's located 2 miles east of Route 127 in Clinton County. Eldon Hazlet has the largest campground in the Illinois state park system, with 328 Class A campsites that have 30- and 50-amp electrical hookups, 36 Class C campsites for walk-in tent camping, and 2 rustic cabins for rent. Campsites occupy about 1.5 miles of the Carlyle Lake shoreline, and many are within easy reach of the water. There are 3 shower buildings and numerous privy toilets on-site, along with recreational amenities like playground equipment, basketball and sand volleyball courts, and horseshoe pits. The area is also a popular destination for fishing, hunting, picnicking, bird watching, and hiking, with more than 9 miles of hiking trails in the park.

where to shop

Henkel's Hook & Arrow. 951 12th St. (Rte. 127); (618) 594-4818; www.henkelshookandarrow.com. Stock up for your trip into the wilds of Carlyle Lake with a pit stop here for bait, jigs, bows, and knives. Henkel's carries AMS bow-fishing kits and accessories, Strike King spinner baits and jigs, and Geno's Stink Bait, along with natural baits like chicken and rooster livers, mealworms, night crawlers, and minnows. The fully stocked bait, tackle, and archery shop is a Bowtech, Diamond PSE, and Hoyt dealer, and you can pick up everything from hooks and nets to rods, reels, lines, and stringers. Open daily except holidays.

where to eat

Bretz Wildlife Lodge & Winery. 15469 Rte. 127; (618) 594-8830; www.wildlifelodgeandwinery.com. Located about 2 miles from Carlyle Lake, the Bretz Wildlife Lodge & Winery offers a relaxing dining experience in a South African–themed atmosphere. The dinner menu features appetizers like nachos and fried pickles and a variety of entrees ranging from shrimp and frog legs to prime rib and catfish. On Sunday the restaurant offers a breakfast buffet and a separate brunch buffet. Enjoy complimentary wine tasting in the Kudu Room. Open daily. $–$$.

The LuBar & Bistro. 911 Fairfax St.; (618) 594-6333; www.thelubar.com. Located in the nearby town of Carlyle, the LuBar serves up a full-service lunch and dinner menu of wraps, salads, burgers, pasta dishes, and pizzas along with comfort food specialties like chicken-fried steak, chili mac, and open-faced roast beef sandwiches. On weekends the eatery offers a breakfast menu that includes omelets, waffles, and pancakes. They also offer gluten-free options. The downstairs bar is open until midnight Tues through Thurs and until 2 a.m. on Fri and Sat. $.

where to stay

Hickory Shores Resort. 21925 Dove Ln.; (618) 749-5288; www.hickoryshoresresort.com. The camping resort features 200 full hookup and tent sites as well as 18 themed cabins that can accommodate anywhere from 4 to 16 guests. The Redneck Cabin, inspired by country singer Gretchen Wilson (a former area resident), houses 4 folks, and the Dove's Landing accommodates 16 guests. All cabins have a stove/oven, refrigerator and microwave, linens, satellite TV, air-conditioning, a fire ring, and a picnic table. Hickory Shores features 2 fishing ponds, shuffleboard courts, horseshoe pits, 2 swimming pools, 3 playgrounds, and additional recreational facilities, as well as the Jamaican Bamboozle nightclub. $.

day trip 02

east

hit the lake:
mt. vernon, il; rend lake, il;
whittington, il

mt. vernon, il

Located about 90 minutes from downtown St. Louis, Mt. Vernon is the business, financial, cultural, and entertainment center of Jefferson County, IL. Mt. Vernon was founded in 1817, but there wasn't a real road into town until 1820 or 1821, when an enterprising local built a bridge over Casey Creek, southeast of town. From there the first road was built, and in 1823 another road was constructed that connected the town to Vandalia, which was then the Illinois state capital. Because of the bridge and the new road, the town was now literally "on the map" and soon captured most of the traffic westward.

Today Mt. Vernon is home to just over 15,200 residents and the city proper covers about 11 miles. It's located on high ground between Casey Creek and the Big Muddy River, which join south of the town in what is now called Rend Lake. Area residents and visitors can enjoy a variety of outdoor activities available nearby at Rend Lake and in the Wayne Fitzgerrell State Recreation Area, including fishing, boating, hiking, hunting, and camping. And for those who prefer to stay on the city side of things, Mt. Vernon has shopping and cultural offerings to keep you occupied for the day.

getting there

Take I-70 East across the Mississippi River and continue for about 3 miles, then make a slight right onto I-64 East/IL 3 North (signs for Louisville/St. Clair Avenue). Continue to follow

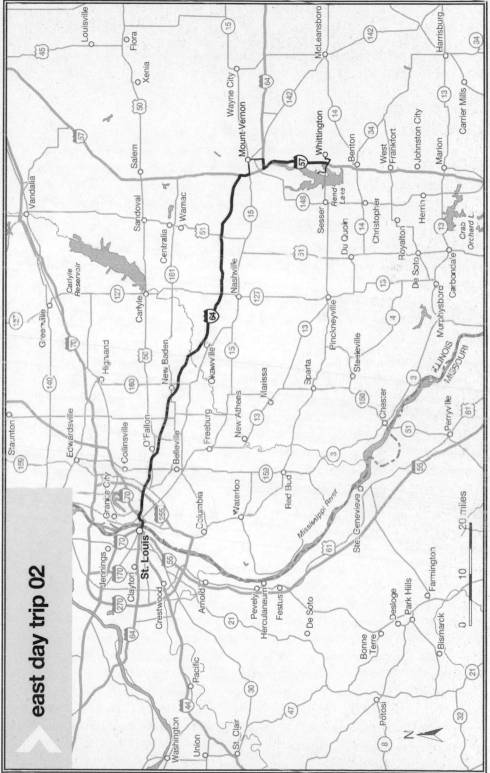

east day trip 02

I-64 East for 72 miles, then take exit 95 for IL 15 toward Mt. Vernon/Ashley. Make a left onto IL 15 East/Broadway Street and follow it for about 3 miles.

where to go

Appellate Courthouse. 14th and Main Streets; (618) 242-3120. The historic courthouse was built around 1857 in the Greek Revival style, and its courtroom features walnut benches and other period furnishings. Abraham Lincoln argued cases here, including a tax case where he represented the Illinois Central Railroad. Today the courthouse houses the Fifth District Appellate Court for the State of Illinois. Tours are free and available Mon through Fri, but you'll need to call in advance to schedule one.

Cedarhurst Center for the Arts. 2600 Richview Rd.; (618) 242-1236; www.cedarhurst .org. In addition to presenting a variety of visual and performing arts programs, the facility is home to Cedarhurst Sculpture Park, an outdoor gallery with more than 60 large-scale sculptures, and the Mitchell Museum's contemporary art exhibitions. Check out the Children's Gallery and the collection of American painters like Mary Cassatt, Maurice Prendergast, and Childe Hassam.

Fire Museum of Southern Illinois. 42nd and Broadway Streets, Times Square Mall; (618) 244-4560. Hosted by the Mount Vernon Professional Firefighters (MVPF) organization, the museum is located inside the Times Square Mall. It contains one of the most comprehensive collections of historical firefighting equipment and photos in the region, including photos of various firefighting apparatuses, personnel, and fires from as far back as 1819. There are display cases with antique equipment and historic examples of the firefighters' tools of the trade, as well as the MVFD's original 1939 Diamond T fire engine. The museum is open the same hours as the shopping mall. Admission is free.

Jefferson County Historical Village. 1411 N. 27th St.; (618) 246-0033. Located near downtown Mt. Vernon, the village offers a look back in time to what life was like when the early settlers first arrived in the region. In addition to authentic log cabins and an interpretive center, the museum and village include artifacts that reflect life in Jefferson County from the mid-19th century to more modern times. The village features original buildings and restorations from the late 1800s through the early 1900s, such as an operating printing shop, a log church, a blacksmith shop, an 1820 calaboose (jail), and a windmill and gristmill. Furnished buildings showcase items like merchandise in the general store and medical equipment ranging from a foot-treadle dentist's drill to a Civil War amputation kit. The Schweinfurth Museum contains a variety of exhibits ranging from cameras and clocks to a display of bridal attire, and there are 2 trails that offer a different type of trek through area history. One of the nature trails winds though a wooded area beside a stream and the Old Union Cemetery, where many early settlers are buried, and the second is a grassland trail outfitted with markers that integrate local history into world events of the time.

where to shop

Made in Mt. Vernon. 200 Potomac Blvd.; (618) 242-3151. This specialty shop offers such works by local artists as jewelry, candles, paintings, and mosaics, as well as porcelain, metal, and wood items. There's also a selection of Mt. Vernon logoed merchandise for the ultimate souvenir.

Rend Lake College Market Place. 200 Outlet Ave.; (618) 244-9525. The 100,000-square-foot Market Place features a large golf outlet store plus the Lone Star Steakhouse, Shoe Stop, BrassWerks, Kountry Depot Crafts, a coffee shop, and a salon.

Times Square Mall. 42nd and Broadway Streets; (618) 244-4560; www.thetimessquare mall.com. Major shopping mall with such retailers as Bath & Body Works, JCPenney, Sears, Kirlin's Hallmark, Hibbett Sports, GNC Live Well, and Claire's. Two casual restaurants are also on-site—Subway and China Buffet—along with a full-service hair salon and a liquor store.

where to eat

Bugsy's Chicago Dog. 311 Broadway St.; (618) 242-0647. Sure, Chicago is a couple of hours away by car, but Bugsy's offers authentic Chicago-style hot dogs for downstate Illinois. The menu also includes a number of Greek options and daily vegetarian-plate specials like dilled spinach with rice, fresh vegetables, and feta cheese, with a tomato balsamic salad and grilled pita bread. $

9th Street Grill. 222 S. 9th St.; (618) 244-1190; www.9thstreetgrill.com. A friendly, casual eatery with a lunch menu of soups, sandwiches, bison burgers, pizzas, and calzones as well as wraps on Mediterranean flatbread like the Casbah (chunks of grilled chicken tossed in homemade hummus with pickle, onion, tomato, and romaine) and the Capri (chunks of fresh mozzarella, tomato, and basil leaves with pesto spread and pine nuts). For dinner the menu expands to include pasta dishes like lobster-stuffed ravioli and the Gambit (grilled chicken, spicy browned sausage, shrimp, red and green bell peppers, and onion tossed with extra-hot Cajun cream sauce over whole-wheat penne), along with steak, fish, and chicken entrees. Try the ginger pork chops (grilled French-cut, bone-in pork chops served with an Asian-inspired ginger sauce). Beer and wine list also available. Closed Sun and Mon. $–$$.

Silver Streak Inn. 201 Broadway St.; (618) 244-1749. Don't let the exterior fool you—the Silver Streak Inn is a highly recommended, friendly, locals kind of restaurant that serves up steaks, ribs, pulled pork barbecue sandwiches, and a variety of side dishes like the tasty twice-baked potatoes. Try the broccoli cheddar bites as an appetizer, and opt for the home-made Thousand Island or ranch dressing on a salad. There is full bar service as well. $–$$.

The Tavern on 10th. 224 S. 10th St.; (618) 244-7821. Enjoy standard pub grub and domestic brews in a casual neighborhood tavern. Open for lunch and dinner Mon through Sat, and local bands play on Fri and Sat nights. $.

where to stay

Inglenook Farm Bed & Breakfast. 10882 E. Richview Rd.; (618) 244-6282; www.ingle nookfarm.com. Originally built as a summer home by Norman A. Piercy, a prominent Mt. Vernon lawyer, the spacious Victorian home has been turned into a B&B by Piercy's grandson. And keeping things all in the family, the 5 guest rooms of varying sizes are named for women in the Piercy family. $–$$.

rend lake, il

The Rend Lake reservoir was created when the US Army Corps of Engineers dammed the Big Muddy River in order to provide a dependable water supply to Franklin and Jefferson Counties in the 1960s. Rend's lakeshore covers more than 160 miles, and part of the area is preserved as the Wayne Fitzgerrell State Recreation Area. Hunting, fishing, camping, and getting in tune with Mother Nature are the popular diversions around these parts, but surrounding towns like Mt. Vernon and Whittington offer cultural attractions and dining experiences for those who aren't ready to abandon civilization completely.

getting there

From Mt. Vernon, take IL 37 South/S. 10th Street about 3 miles, then merge onto I-64 West toward East St. Louis. Take exit 78 on the left and merge onto I-57 South toward Memphis and continue for about 14 miles. Take exit 77 for IL 154 toward Sesser, then turn right onto IL 154 West and make a right. Then take the first right, then the first left, and then a slight right—whew, you're there!

where to go

Rend Lake Visitor Center. 12220 Rend City Rd.; (618) 724-2493; www.rendlake.com. Get the lay of the land—and the lake—and find out about the recreational opportunities available in the area. The center also offers an interactive computer station and a variety of exhibits detailing the flora and fauna that call Rend Lake home. There's a 250-gallon aquarium filled with Rend Lake fish species, a herpitat with live snake specimens, a wetland and wildlife demonstration garden, as well as a working demonstration beehive.

Rend Lake Resort. 11712 East Windy Ln.; (618) 629-2211; www.rendlakeresort.com. Located within Wayne Fitzgerrell State Recreation Area, the Rend Lake Resort offers fishing, boating, swimming, biking, tennis, horseback riding, skeet and trap shooting, and 27 holes of golf. Quench your thirst at Reilly's Lounge, or grab some ice cream at the Blue Heron General Store.

Rend Lake State Fish & Wildlife Area. 10885 E. Jefferson Rd.; (618) 279-3110; http://dnr.state.il.us. The Rend Lake area, located between Mt. Vernon and Benton, includes a 19,000-acre reservoir and 20,000 acres of land ideal for outdoor recreation. Rent a boat at the Rend Lake Marina; swim; fish for largemouth bass, crappie, bluegill, and channel catfish; go hiking or biking; or just explore the nature trails. The area is also known as one of the better waterfowl hunting areas in the state for both ducks and geese. The sub-impoundment dams located across the Big Muddy River and Casey Creek and the upstream areas they impound are flooded for optimum waterfowl hunting. Each day a drawing is held on-site to determine the allocation of goose pits at the Whistling Wings Access Area and staked locations at the Casey Fork Sub-impoundment Dam. For those who just want to watch the wildlife, Rend Lake provides habitat for a variety of birds, including great blue herons and various species of shorebirds. Camping facilities include both primitive and developed campsites at Wayne Fitzgerrell State Recreation Area and the Corps of Engineers campgrounds on Rend Lake. If you aren't into roughing it along the lake, the Rend Lake Resort in nearby Whittington has waterside rooms that allow you to enjoy all of the scenery from the comfort of a climate-controlled room.

where to stay

Benton KOA Campground. 1500 N. Duquoin St.; (618) 439-4860. A full-service campground located 1.5 miles from all of the Rend Lake water activities. There's a pool, pavilion, grocery store, RV supplies, and laundry on-site; modern hookups are available as well. The campground has 20 shaded tent sites in addition to its RV sites. $.

Rend Lake Cabins in the Woods. 12767 Woodland Dr.; (618) 927-7796, www.rendlakecabins.com. The 2 rental cabins are located less than 5 minutes from Rend Lake's 2 beaches, picnic areas, and 13-plus miles of continuous hiking and biking trails. Each cabin includes a full kitchen complete with a stove/oven, full-size refrigerator, microwave, service for 6, cooking utensils, pots and pans, dish detergent, and salt and pepper. There are 2 bedrooms and a full bath in each cabin as well as towels, washcloths, and bed linens. Each cabin has a TV, alarm clock, washer and dryer, fire pit, and barbecue grill. Sit and swing a spell on the front porch swing while communing with Mother Nature. $$.

whittington, il

Perched along the eastern edge of Rend Lake, Whittington is an unincorporated community that serves as the headquarters of Wayne Fitzgerrell State Recreation Area. The tiny outpost exists only because of the outdoorsy visitors who trek through on their way to the lake or the recreation area.

getting there

From Rend Lake, take IL 154 East across the lake for about 2 miles, then turn left onto IL 37 North and follow it for about a mile. Make a right onto Ewing Road and continue for a little less than 0.5 mile.

where to go

Pheasant Hollow Winery. 14931 IL 37; (618) 629-2302; www.pheasanthollowwinery .com. Nestled on the eastern shore of Rend Lake, the winery is set among 5 acres of scenic woodlands. Sit and sip on the outdoor deck and sample an array of finely crafted fruit and table wines. Pheasant Hollow produces 4 red wines—Cabernet Sauvignon, Ringneck Red, Concord, and Black Gold—along with 5 whites and 3 blush wines. The winery also offers 7 fruit wine varieties, including Red & Blue, a semisweet with an ultra-rich cherry and blueberry flavor, and the signature Black & Blue, which is a rich blueberry wine with a blackberry finish. Open daily.

Rend Lake Shooting Complex. 17738 Conservation Ln.; (618) 629-2368; www.rend lakesc.com. If your trigger finger is itching but it's not hunting season, head for the Rend Lake Shooting Complex. Here you'll find a 400-acre facility that offers trap, skeet, and five-stand shooting, along with picnic facilities, a shooters' pro shop, and a 3-D archery range. (By the way, no animals will be harmed in the making of this recreational opportunity.)

Wayne Fitzgerrell State Recreation Area, South Region. 11094 Ranger Rd.; (618) 629-2320; http://dnr.state.il.us. Overlooking the US Army Corps of Engineers' 19,000-acre Rend Lake reservoir, the Wayne Fitzgerrell State Recreation Area is a paradise for folks interested in hiking, horseback riding, picnicking, bird watching, and viewing wildlife. It also offers ample opportunity for water sports, including pleasure boating, fishing, and water-skiing. Hikers and bikers can enjoy the newly constructed 4-mile trail that runs from the day-use areas through the campgrounds to Rend Lake Resort and connects to the Rend Lake College Bike Trail.

Dedicated in 1975, the site is named in honor of Wayne Fitzgerrell, a state representative from nearby Sesser, IL, who was an advocate for the construction of Rend Lake. The park encompasses 3,300 acres of former farmland leased to the Department of Natural Resources by the US Army Corps of Engineers. About 2,000 acres have been developed for picnicking, camping, and other activities, while another 1,000 acres have been set aside for hunting, field trials, wildlife observation, and hiking. The majority of the site's perimeter is Rend Lake shoreline, so the park's varied topography offers excellent habitat for various upland and woodland wildlife, including waterfowl, shorebirds, and raptors.

In addition to the lodging facilities at Rend Lake Resort, which is located at the park, Wayne Fitzgerrell has 40 tent sites to accommodate primitive campers who are looking for a truly rustic outdoor experience. Those who aren't looking to "rough it" quite as primitively can use one of the 240-plus modern campsites that offer electrical hookups and sanitary facilities. Three shower buildings are available for campers. No reservations are accepted, as the campground remains available on a first-come, first-served basis in order to give everyone an equal opportunity to get a campsite.

where to shop

Rend Lake Antique Mall. 301 Ina Ave.; (618) 437-5801. Located just 4 miles north of Whittington, the Rend Lake Antique Mall is a 12,000-square-foot facility that specializes in antiques. There are 80 vendors located on site, and all but a handful of them sell genuine antique items and collectibles. You'll find lots of primitives as well as a variety of accent items. The management prides itself on renting the majority of its spaces to vendors who offer authentic antiques; however, in an effort to have an assortment of items that will appeal to almost everyone, they have included a minimal number of merchants that sell items such as homemade candles and handmade dolls.

Southern Illinois Art & Artisans Center. 14967 Gun Creek Trail; (618) 629-2220; www .museum.state.il.us/Ismsites/so-il. This 15,000-square-foot facility features works by more than 850 juried Illinois artisans and hosts numerous workshops, demonstrations, and seasonal festivals annually. Choose from one-of-a-kind items like textiles, jewelry, ceramics, and baskets that are reasonably priced and beautifully made. The Illinois Artisans Member Exhibitions Space in the Artisans Shop also offers changing exhibits and artist receptions throughout the year.

where to eat

Gibby's on the Green. 12476 Golf Course Rd.; (618) 629-2454. It's not terribly fancy, but Gibby's offers a full service menu for breakfast, lunch, and dinner. The lunch menu is pretty straightforward with sandwiches and such, but the dinner entrees include such delicacies as shrimp scampi, prime rib, baked salmon, Chicken Ala Oskar, and Jack Daniel's Ribeye. $–$$.

Windows Restaurant. 11712 E. Windy Ln.; (800) 633-3341; www.rendlakeresort.com. Rend Lake Resort's full-service restaurant is open for breakfast, lunch, and dinner. Specialties include themed dinner buffets like BBQ on Wed, Cajun Day on Thurs, a seafood buffet on Fri, and the prime rib and pasta bar buffet on Sat. $–$$.

where to stay

Gun Creek Campground. Gun Creek Trail; (618) 629-2338. The facility offers 100 campsites, all with electrical hookups, and it's ideal for RV or tent camping. Amenities include a dump station, hot showers, a boat ramp, and playgrounds. The campground is located within walking distance of the Seasons Lodge Restaurant, Rend Lake Golf Course, and the Southern Illinois Art & Artisans Center. $.

Rend Lake Resort. 11712 E. Windy Ln.; (618) 629-2211; www.rendlakeresort.com. Stay in one of the modern waterside cabins or spend the night in a "Boatel." Each of the floating Boatels has a private deck overlooking the lake, and you can choose from a contemporary loft unit with a wet bar and fireplace, a single-level unit with 2 queen-size beds, or a double-decker unit with a queen-size bed in the loft and a trundle bed downstairs. There's an outdoor pool and children's playground on-site. $$–$$$.

Seasons Lodge. 12575 Golf Course Rd.; (618) 629-2600; http://rendlake.org/oldsite/lodging-dining. The lodge features nicely appointed guest rooms and amenities like an outdoor pool, a sundeck with a whirlpool, free Wi-Fi access, an outdoor spa under a gazebo, and complimentary use of bicycles in case you want to take a spin on the nature trail. $–$$.

day trip 03

east

>>> amish country:
arcola, il; arthur, il; tuscola, il

These three towns are all located within the largest Amish settlement in Illinois, and the surrounding countryside is full of scenic farmlands. East-central Illinois is home to approximately 4,000 Amish scattered throughout Douglas, Moultrie, and Coles Counties, which results in an abundance of handcrafted wood furniture and accessories. Things move a little slower around here, and the friendly townspeople are usually willing to share a story or offer suggestions for the best place to grab a bite or pick up a unique keepsake to take home.

arcola, il

In addition to its role as the epicenter of all things Amish, Arcola is known as the Broomcorn Capital of the World and the birthplace of Johnny Gruelle, creator of Raggedy Ann and Andy.

getting there

From St. Louis, take I-70 East to Effingham, IL, then follow I-57 North to exit 203 at Arcola.

where to go

Arcola Depot & Welcome Center. 135 N. Oak St.; (217) 268-4530; www.arcolachamber .com. Stop in and gather some info about the area. Located inside the historic Illinois

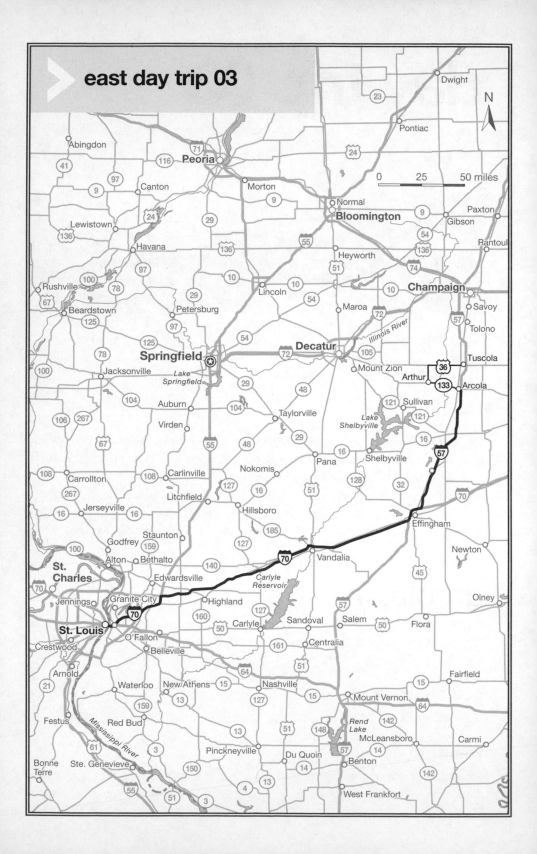

east day trip 03

Central train depot, circa 1885. In addition to details about where to go and what to see, there's a small museum that contains railroad memorabilia, a Raggedy Ann doll collection, and an assortment of antique brooms and brushes.

Illinois Amish Interpretive Center. 125 N. CR 425 East; (888) 45-AMISH; www.amish center.com. Stop here for some background on the Amish and get a feel for what you'll experience on the many tour opportunities available. There's an 18-minute introductory video about the Amish as well as permanent exhibits about Anabaptist and Amish history, quilting, homes, and technology. This is the place to set up tours of Amish homes, farms, and woodworking shops and the chance to enjoy a meal in an Amish home, plus there are a number of Amish gift items available in the gift shop.

Rockome Gardens. 125 N. CR 425 East; (217) 268-4106 or (888) 45-AMISH; www .rockome.com. This longtime Arcola mainstay is known for its unique rock creations and themed gardens that contain tens of thousands of flowers and plants. Activities and attractions within Rockome include a children's petting zoo, a blacksmith shop, the Old Hickory Railroad, and buggy rides. Rockome Garden Foods offers insight into where a number of foods come from, thanks to an on-site cheese factory where visitors can watch the cheese being made, and a bakery and candy shop where you can see the treats being created. You can watch a gristmill grind corn, wheat, and oats into meal and flour, and see honey being made through an observatory window into an active beehive. All of the products made here are available for purchase.

World's One & Only Hippie Memorial. 135 N. Oak St. Located next door to the historic Illinois Central train depot, the hippie memorial was created by the late Bob Moomaw. When he wasn't painting messages such as "America you're turning into a nation of minimum-wage hamburger flippers. Rebel. Think for yourself. It works!" on the side of a building he owned, the Arcola resident used the 62-foot-long piece of artwork to express how he felt about major events and eras throughout his life, including the Great Depression, World War II, and the Reagan years.

where to shop

Marcella's Corner—The Official Raggedy Ann & Andy Shop. 125 N. CR 425 East; (217) 268-4106; www.marcellasraggedyann.com. Located within Rockome Gardens, the shop offers official Raggedy Ann and Andy dolls, books, charms, and just about everything else you can imagine. All items bear the signature of Joni Gruelle, granddaughter of Raggedy Ann and Andy creator Johnny Gruelle. Open May through Oct.

My Favorite Things. 124 E. Main St.; (217) 268-3576. If you're looking for a unique gift or something to splurge on for yourself, take a look at this shop's selection of Camille Beckman body products, Village candles, and an assortment of charms, baskets, and home decor. They also stock gourmet foods, coffees, and teas.

Olde Brick Wall. 122 E. Main St.; (217) 268-4793; www.oldebrickwall.com. Tucked inside an old hotel building in the heart of town, the Olde Brick Wall features a collection of tinware, light fixtures, candles, folk art, and primitives along with upholstered and early American reproduction painted wood furniture. In addition to the furniture and artwork, the shop carries paint, curtains, pillows, rugs, chandeliers, shelves, Boyd's Bears, florals, candles, and a full line of country furnishings and accessories. Open daily.

The Primitive Goose. 107 East Main St.; (217) 268-4800. The shop specializes in primitive decor along with a collection of home and garden furnishings, folk art, and antiques.

Simply Amish. 401 E. CR 200 North; (217) 268-4504; www.simplyamish.com. Simply Amish offers heirloom-quality solid-wood bedroom sets, living room furniture, desks, dining room sets, storage pieces, and office furniture in a variety of styles like Mission, classic, traditional, Shaker, country, contemporary, and transitional.

Vyverberg's. 119 E. Main St.; (217) 268-3646. Don't miss the chance to visit this unique shopping experience from days gone by. Vyverberg's is an old-school family department store that handles everything from custom window treatments and Alfred Dunner ladies sportswear to Raggedy Ann merchandise like dolls, books, and T-shirts. If you like to collect obscure high school football team merchandise, you'll want to pick up an Arcola Purple Riders T-shirt or hat. They also sell general gift items and Hallmark cards. Open daily.

Yoder's Homestead Furniture. 117 E. Main St.; (217) 268-3841; www.yodershomestead furniture.com. Located in downtown Arcola, Yoder's storefront looks like something straight out of an old Western movie. Inside you'll find locally crafted Amish furniture made from walnut, oak, cherry, hickory, and maple, along with handmade quilts and quilted purses. The store also stocks an assortment of Amish delicacies like jams, jellies, and popcorn.

where to eat

The Dutch Kitchen. 127 E. Main St.; (217) 268-3518. Serving Dutch-style home cooking for breakfast, lunch, and (early) dinner, the restaurant is also known for its homemade coconut, peanut butter cream, Dutch apple, cherry crumb, and shoofly pies, along with homemade bread and Amish apple butter. Plate lunches are a specialty, and they feature locally produced beef, pork, chicken, turkey, sausage, and fish, served with mashed potatoes and gravy, dressing, vegetables, and bread. There's also a salad bar that includes homemade items like corn relish, pineapple salad, and pea salad. Open daily. $.

Monical's Pizza. 528 E. Springfield Rd.; (217) 268-4141; www.monicals.com. The central Illinois restaurant chain is famous for its crispy, thin crusts and offers a variety of pizza choices—including pan crust and gluten free—along with sandwiches, pasta dishes, and salads. Open daily for lunch and dinner. $.

where to stay

Arcola Flower Patch B&B and Diamond House Bed & Breakfast. 225-229 E. Jefferson St.; (217) 268-4876; www.arcolaflowerpatch.com. Located next door to one another, the Flower Patch and Diamond House are two family-run B&Bs in one. The Flower Patch, which offers 5 guest rooms, is known for its elaborate gardens and 7-course breakfast served on fine china. The Diamond House has 6 rooms available, including the largest—and most secluded—the Diamond Room. $$.

arthur, il

Located in the heart of Amish country, Arthur is a quiet small town that's surrounded by picturesque countryside and recreational activities. The settlement got its start in 1850 when the Illinois Central Railroad created two lines from Chicago across the prairies of central Illinois. In 1872 the railroad discovered the need for another passing switch and water tank in the area, and the switch and tank became the nucleus of what would be called Arthur. The first Amish families came to the area in 1865, when the families of Moses Yoder, Daniel Miller, and Daniel Otto arrived from Summit Mills, Somerset County, Pennsylvania. Bishop Joseph Keim arrived in 1865 as well and organized the first Amish church in the region. Today there are more than 4,000 Amish living in the Arthur area.

getting there

Arthur is less than 10 miles west of Arcola via IL. 133 West/E. Springfield Road. Just follow IL 133 West, turn right onto CR 000 East/S. Vine Street, and you've found it.

where to shop

Downtown Arthur. Arthur's downtown business district offers a number of places to shop for locally made crafts, clothing, furniture, and gifts. And when it's time to take a break from shopping, stop in at Dicks Pharmacy for an old-fashioned soda or pick up something sweet at Aunt Sarah's Fudge inside the Arthur Flower Shop. Look for additional ideas at www.illinoisamishcountry.com.

Homestead Bakery. RR1, Box 102; (217) 543-3700; www.the200acres.com. The bakery features made-from-scratch breads, chocolate chip cookies, angel food cake, cinnamon-raisin bread, and sticky pecan rolls, along with homemade salsas, pumpkin butter, and an assortment of mustards, pickled vegetables, relishes, jams, jellies, and fine candies and fudge. In the spring the shop stocks the Homestead Seeds line of heirloom cucurbit seeds, and there's always a collection of items culled from area auctions and garage sales. Open May through Dec; closed Sun.

The Woodloft. 138 S. Vine St.; (888) 321-9663; www.woodloft.com. This shop specializes in handcrafted, custom-made Amish furniture in Mission, country, Queen Anne, and Shaker styles. You pick the hardwood, the stain, the style, and the size and their craftsmen do the rest.

where to eat

Dicks Pharmacy. 118 S. Vine St; (217) 543-2913; www.dicks-pharmacy.com. Belly up to the marble counter at this old-fashioned soda fountain and order up a cold and frosty treat from yesteryear. In addition to malts and shakes, Dicks serves Green Rivers, floats, and phosphates. Check out the soda pop bottle collection. $.

The Kitchen of Doris Yoder. RR 1, Box 19; (217) 543-3409. Reservations are required for this only-in-Amish-County experience, where diners enjoy dinner in an Amish home. Meals are served family style, and it's an all-you-care-to-eat affair. $$$.

Roselen's Coffees & Delights. 1045 E. Columbia St./IL 133; (217) 543-3106; www .roselens.net. Don't let the Dollar General sign fool you. Roselen's—"the only Amish-owned coffee shop in the state of Illinois"—serves up a variety of espresso-based drinks, chai tea, deli sandwiches, muffins, breakfast sandwiches, and more than 20 ice-cream flavors. Closed Sun. $.

Yoder's Kitchen. 1195 E. Columbia St./IL 133; (217) 543-2714; www.yoderskitchen.net. Voted "Best Family Restaurant" in the 2010 Official Best of Illinois poll, Yoder's serves up traditional Amish and Mennonite cooking along with American favorites. A hearty breakfast menu includes the traditional Haystack (similar to a taco salad) and the Casualty (scrambled eggs mixed with hash browns, cheese, and bacon or ham). The lunch and dinner menu includes broasted chicken as a specialty, along with sandwiches, salads, and an all-you-can-eat buffet. Closed Sun. $.

tuscola, il

Tuscola was originally settled in 1834, and the feisty small town now boasts a population of around 4,500 folks. Tuscola, which is a Cherokee word that means "digging in many places," is home to high-end shopping and charming one-of-a-kind corner stores in its historic downtown.

getting there

From Arthur, follow CR 000 East/S. Vine Street toward W. Illinois Street for approximately 5 miles, then turn right onto US 36 East/CR 950 North for 10 miles. Turn left onto S. Niles Avenue and continue for about 0.5 mile until you reach N. Central Avenue East. Make a left and you're there.

where to shop

Amish Country Heirlooms. Amishland Red Barn, 1304 Tuscola Blvd., Unit 14; (217) 253-9200; www.shopach.com. Located in the Amishland Red Barn next to the Tanger Outlet Mall, the store has baby furniture, rockers, bedroom and living room furniture, entertainment centers, inspirational decor, and more. They feature brands such as P. Graham Dunn, Brookside Furniture, Amish Mills, Weaver & Sons Wood Products, E&S Wood Creations, Millcraft Handcrafted Furniture, Streamside Wood Shop, Schwartz Woodworking, R. H. Yoder Woodworking, Hoosier Crafts, and Simply Amish.

Amishland Red Barn. 1304 Tuscola Blvd.; (217) 253-9022. It's hard to miss this place—the name is as descriptive as it is quaint, The 72,000-square-foot red building features a variety of Amish items and foods all under one roof. The indoor village of shops includes antiques and collectibles, Amish hardwood furniture, locally produced crafts, quilts, seasonal decor, and Amish jams and jellies, as well as assorted fashion and travel accessories from names like Vera Bradley. There's also a Cheese & Meat Shop that sells locally produced sausages and bacon. Open year-round.

Art Glass Creations. Amishland Red Barn, 1304 Tuscola Blvd.; (217) 253-9022. Browse the in-store display of stained and art glass, or have local artist Karen Good produce custom designed glass panels for doors, windows, and cabinets. Good also offers classes in stained glass and painting on occasion.

Country Heritage Gallery. Amishland Red Barn, 1304 Tuscola Blvd.; (217) 253-9022. The big red barn houses a gallery with more than 90 canvas and paper prints from the "Painter of Light," Thomas Kinkade, known as "the country's most collected living artist" before his death. The gallery also features works from contemporary nature and wildlife painter Terry Redlin; a selection of music boxes, plates, and nightlights; and a collection of Sarah's Angels. There is also an assortment of home and garden items on the gallery's porch that includes benches, wind chimes, and light-catching pieces.

Dogtown Artworks. 704 N. Main St., Ste. 102; (217) 689-4575; www.dogtownartworks .com. Fun and whimsical "dogs as people" photos by a husband-and-wife team of photographers. The gallery features their dog art, where they take pictures of dogs and superimpose the dog's head onto a human body. There's an on-site photo studio where they will photograph your dog and turn him or her into a custom "dog person." The human duo's work has appeared in two books, *Happy Tails: The Call of Nature* and *Happy Tails: Earl and Pearl on the Farm.*

Just Vintage. 306A E. Southline Rd.; (217) 549-8883. Specializing in retro, vintage, mid-20th-century, and "shabby chic" home decor, jewelry, furniture, and accessories from the 1930s through the 1970s, this fun and funky store has a little bit of everything. Even if you don't buy anything, it's worth the trip down memory lane. Open Thurs through Sat and occasionally on Sun.

Paddy Wagon Antiques. 101 E. Southline Rd.; (217) 253-9150. The well-stocked store features primitives, collectibles, lamps, coins, and antiques as well as various musical instruments. If you're looking for deals on furniture, Paddy Wagon offers quality antique armoires, beds, chests, rockers, and dining sets.

Tanger Outlet Mall. D400 Tuscola Blvd.; (217) 253-2282; www.tangeroutlet.com/tuscola. The mall is home to more than 40 stores, including outlets for Old Navy, Famous Footwear, Lane Bryant, Gap, Gymboree, VF, Zales, and Coldwater Creek, as well as factory stores for Nike, Coach, and Polo Ralph Lauren.

Winterberry Store. 116 W. Sale St.; (217) 253-6250; www.winterberrystore.com. The downtown Tuscola shop features 18th-century gifts and home furnishings like furniture, lamps, bedding and quilts, rugs, framed artwork, and other assorted treasures. They also carry bath products and have an assortment of seasonal decor items.

where to eat

Amishland Bakery. Amishland Red Barn, 1304 Tuscola Blvd.; (217) 253-9022. Start off your morning here, and you'll be almost overwhelmed with the smell of fresh-baked Amish-style breads and cinnamon rolls. The bakery specializes in made-from-scratch cookies and pies using farm-fresh ingredients. $.

Country Restaurant. Amishland Red Barn, 1304 Tuscola Blvd.; (217) 253-9022. If you're looking for a heartier meal, you've still come to the right place, as the Amishland Red Barn also offers a restaurant featuring home-style foods that are made using real, farm-fresh ingredients. The all-you-can-eat lunch and dinner buffet is available daily, beginning at 11 a.m. Fried chicken is one of the house specialties. $–$$.

Flesor's Candy Kitchen. 101 W. Sale St.; (217) 253-3753; www.flesorscandy.com. The candy shop and bistro is run by two sisters who reopened their family's soda fountain and confectionary business in downtown Tuscola. The bistro menu features sandwiches, salads, and daily specials, but what sets the place apart is the soda fountain. Enjoy an old-fashioned banana split, sundae, ice-cream soda, float, or phosphate, then pick up a box of hand-dipped chocolates and candies made from the family's generations-old recipes. Try the chocolate-covered honey salted caramels or Devon's Divine Divinity. Sugar-free options are also available. $.

southeast

day trip 01

southeast

beautiful city across the river:
belleville, il

belleville, il

Belleville, which means "beautiful city" in French, is one of the oldest cities in Illinois and was named a 2011 All-America City. The suburban outpost of St. Louis was first settled after the Revolutionary War by veterans who received land grants. Today the city boasts a population of more than 45,000, and the military tradition continues with Scott Air Force Base, which is the area's largest employer.

getting there

From St. Louis, take I-64 East/I-70 East over the Mississippi River and into Illinois for approximately 10 miles to IL 159. Take IL 159 for about 6 miles and follow the signs toward Belleville/Collinsville.

where to go

Eckert's Millstadt Fun Farm. 2719 Eckert Orchard Ln.; (800) 745-0513; www.eckerts .com. Eckert's Millstadt Fun Farm, located about 15 minutes outside of Belleville, offers city kids a taste of life on the farm. In addition to pick-your-own apples, pumpkins, peaches, and whatever else is in season, the Millstadt farm offers an array of kid-friendly activities like the Barnyard Petting Corral, Billy Bob's Pig Races, miniature golf, the Jack O'Lobber Pumpkin Cannon, the Pedal-Push Tractor Path, pony rides, and the 70-foot Mine Shaft Slide. On

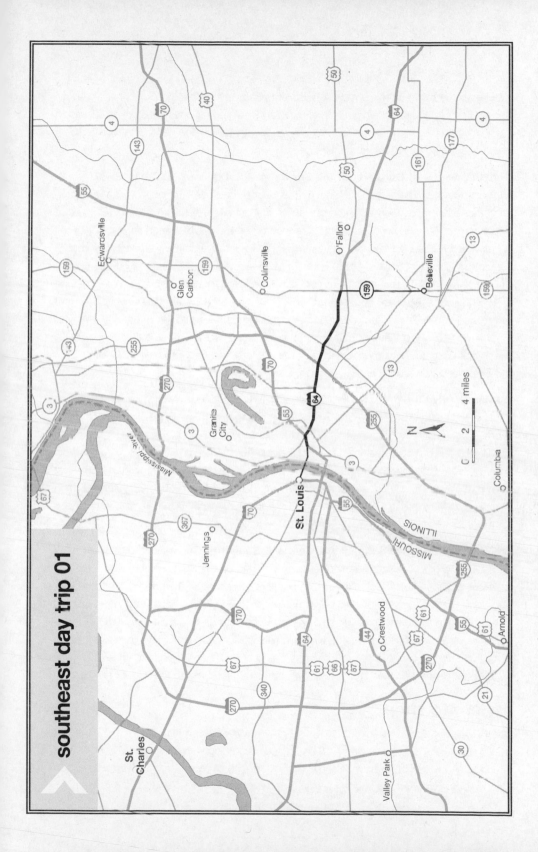

southeast day trip 01

weekends there's live entertainment with Eckert's Barnyard Follies Show, and in the early fall the activities extend into the night with bonfires and haunted hayrides. This Eckert's location is more about the "farm," whereas the Eckert's Country Store—located in Belleville itself—is more about the fruits of the farm's labor.

National Shrine of Our Lady of the Snows. 422 S. De Mazenod Dr.; (618) 397-6700; www.snows.org. The Snows is one of the largest outdoor shrines in North America, encompassing more than 200 acres. Part of the outreach of the Missionary Oblates of Mary Immaculate, the shrine attracts more than one million visitors each year and features 13 devotional areas: Agony Garden, Annunciation Garden, Children's Memorial Playground, Church of Our Lady of the Snows, Father's Memorial Wall, Guild Center, Lourdes Grotto, Main Shrine/Amphitheatre, Millennium Spire, Mother's Prayer Walk, Our Lady of Guadalupe Hill, Resurrection Garden, and Way of the Cross. The grounds are open every day, and admission is free. During the winter holidays, thousands drive through the facility's Way of Lights display, which features more than one million lights, statues, and electro-art sculptures that illustrate the story of Christmas. Masses are held daily, and there is a restaurant on-site, along with a hotel and a gift shop.

Skyview Drive-In. 5700 N. Belt West; (618) 233-4400; www.skyview-drive-in.com. Originally opened in July 1949, the Skyview has changed with the times and now offers an updated drive-in movie experience. Movies are broadcast in FM stereo via your car radio, and both screens show double features of first-run flicks. For kids with a little extra preshow energy, there's a lighted playground that's open until 5 minutes before the start of the first movie. Skyview's summer season runs from late Mar/early Apr through Oct. They're open nightly mid-May through Labor Day, and Fri through Sun nights before and after those dates.

William and Florence Schmidt Art Center & Sculpture Gardens. 2500 Carlyle Ave.; (618) 222-5278; www.schmidtartcenter.com. Located on the Southwestern Illinois College campus at Belleville, the Schmidt Art Center offers more than 400 art and cultural artifacts, including a variety of sculptures, paintings, photographs, lithographs, and monographs. The collection includes works by such renowned artists as Salvador Dali, Ansel Adams, Rembrandt van Rijn, Robert Motherwell, and Claus Moor. On Saturdays the center hosts Creative Kids Art Classes for children ages 5 and up. Kids and their parents take a quick tour of the center and then create their own artwork that relates to the current exhibits.

where to shop

Don Rodgers. 6727 W. Main St.; (618) 398-2421; www.donrodgersltd.com. Don Rodgers offers upscale apparel, including a full line of men's clothing with dress shirts by Forsyth of Canada and suits from Hardwick and Palm Beach. The store also carries women's casual and dressy attire, handbags, and jewelry from designers like Hugo and Ethel & Myrtle.

Eckert's Country Store & Garden Center. 951 S. Green Mount Rd.; (618) 233-0513; www.eckerts.com. The shelves are stocked with such old-fashioned country favorites as pickled vegetables, apple butter, jams, and preserves, as well as various coffee blends, specialty teas, and gourmet boxed mixes. There's also fresh produce and fresh-baked pies, breads, cookies, and muffins available, along with more than 200 wines. You can also take a cooking class—there are some for adults as well as kids—or sign up for a course to learn more about wine or beer.

Peace by Piece. 132 W. Main St.; (618) 233-1519; www.peacebypiececo.com. This specialty boutique, offering only American-made products, specializes in unique fashion accessories such as men's and women's TOMS shoes, unique handcrafted jewelry created by local artists, and Harvey's Seatbeltbags. Items in the store's bath and body selection are handmade in Belleville by Sea Street Soap Works.

St. Clair Square. 134 St. Clair Square; (618) 632-7567; www.stclairsquare.com. St. Clair Square is one of the area's major shopping malls and features many of the big-name chain stores, including Banana Republic, Abercrombie & Fitch, Jos. A Bank, Gymboree, Cardinals Clubhouse Shop, Victoria's Secret, Talbots, Champs, Dillard's, JCPenney, Macy's, and Sears.

where to eat

Acropolis. 200 W. Main St., (618) 234-5883. This small family-owned restaurant serves up freshly made Greek specialties, including shish kobab, *pastistio, mazithra,* and *souvlaki* plates and Greek country salads. Desserts are just as good, with honey-dripped homemade baklava, *kourabiethes* (Greek wedding cookies), and *koulourakia* (Greek Easter cookies). Beer and wine are available, including Greek Mavrodaphne wine. Open for lunch and dinner Mon through Fri and dinner only on Sat; closed Sun. $–$$.

Castletown Geoghegan Authentic Irish Pub & Restaurant. 104 W. Main St.; (618) 233-4800; www.ctgpub.com. Specialties include shepherd's pie, Irish nachos (potato chips topped with beef and cheddar cheese sauce or shredded Monterey Jack), the Mediterranean Burger (handmade veggie burger of feta cheese, millet, sun-dried tomatoes, bread crumbs, baby spinach, minced garlic, and spices), and the Cloughaneely Chicken (breaded chicken breasts sautéed in virgin olive oil and a slightly sweet Irish liqueur). House-made desserts include Irish Cream Cheesecake and Guinness Chocolate Cake. Enjoy traditional Irish music live and in person on Tues, Fri, and Sat. Closed Sun. $–$$.

HyHo Cafe. 20 S. Belt West; (618) 235-1269. It ain't fancy, but it's great for simple, quick, and affordable diner food. You can have breakfast anytime, or select from the menu of sandwiches, salads, and home-style specials like the half-pound BLT, homemade chicken and dumplings, or sweet Bourbon-glazed chicken wings. $.

Mariachi's Mexican Restaurant & Cantina. 400 S. Illinois St.; (618) 236-9492; www .mariachismexfood.com. Offering a casual atmosphere and affordable made-from-scratch Mexican food, Mariachi's menu has the usual lineup of burritos, quesadillas, and the like. Some of the eatery's selected favorites include the Milanesa (breaded chicken or steak cooked on a flat grill) and Mariachi Loco Fajitas (with steak, chicken, and shrimp). $–$$.

Maxwell's Restaurant. 923 W. Main St.; (618) 277-4799; www.maxwellsrestaurant.com. Maxwell's is a downtown Belleville dining mainstay that's known for its cozy atmosphere and a hearty menu of pizzas, pastas, seafood, and steaks. Specialties include the Potato Nachos (baked, deep-fried, thinly sliced potatoes covered with cheddar cheese, bacon, and hot peppers); the Moo, Oink & Cluck (more than a pound of smoked beef, pork, and chicken breast with barbecue sauce); and the Texas Longhorn pizza (barbecue sauce, ground beef, onions, jalapeños, and cheddar cheese). $$.

The Pie Pantry. 310 E. Main St.; (618) 277-4140; www.thepiepantry.com. In addition to the 15 pie varieties on the menu—including chocolate chip cheese, Black Forest cherry, rhubarb, pecan, lemon meringue, and banana cream—the quaint eatery offers salads, sandwiches, soups, daily home-style breakfasts, and Sunday brunch. There's a fresh breakfast buffet on weekend mornings, with homemade cinnamon rolls, muffins, and fruit turnovers. $.

Rachel's Garden. 3917 Frank Scott Pkwy. West; (618) 234-9355; www.rachelsgarden .com. This family-owned and -operated lunch spot features a menu of salads, sandwiches, soups, and quiches. The in-store bakery makes the restaurant's cheesecakes, cakes, and pies, and whole desserts are available with advance notice. They also have a selection of homemade cookies, specialty cupcakes, and muffins. Closed Sun. $.

Shenanigan's Restaurant & Sports Bar. 6401 W. Main St.; (618) 398-6979; www .shenanigansinfo.com. A friendly sports bar with a full menu of appetizers, soups, salads, hand-cut steaks, sandwiches, wings, pizzas, and half-pound burgers like the Hot 'n Spicy Buffalo Cheeseburger and the Nightmare Burger ("buried under an avalanche of chili, then showered with a cheese sauce and additional shredded mozzarella and cheddar"). $.

day trip 02

southeast

>>> **roughing it along the wine trail:**
carbondale, il; makanda, il; alto pass, il;
pomona, il; cobden, Il; anna-jonesboro, il

Located in the picturesque Shawnee Hills just south of Murphysboro and Carbondale, Il., is the Shawnee Hills Wine Trail. There are 12 family-owned and -operated wineries along the trail, which stretch along a 30-mile "horseshoe" route through Jackson and Union Counties. Each vineyard or winery offers a unique experience and assortment of wines. These are the towns along the trail, which are listed in order starting in Carbondale and heading to the south. Get more info about the Shawnee Hills Wine Trail from the Southernmost Tourism Bureau at (800) 248-4373 or via www.shawneewinetrail.com.

carbondale, il

In addition to being home to Southern Illinois University's Carbondale campus, the city of 26,000 serves as the entrance to the Shawnee Hills Wine Trail. Carbondale was recently named by *Outdoor Life* magazine as one of the top 200 towns for sportsmen, thanks in part to its proximity to Shawnee National Forest and Giant City State Park and the region's scenic lakes, hiking and biking trails, and other recreational opportunities.

getting there

Cross over the mighty Mississippi River via the Martin Luther King Bridge and merge onto I-64 East. Continue on I-64 East and take exit 50 for IL 127 toward Carlyle/Nashville.

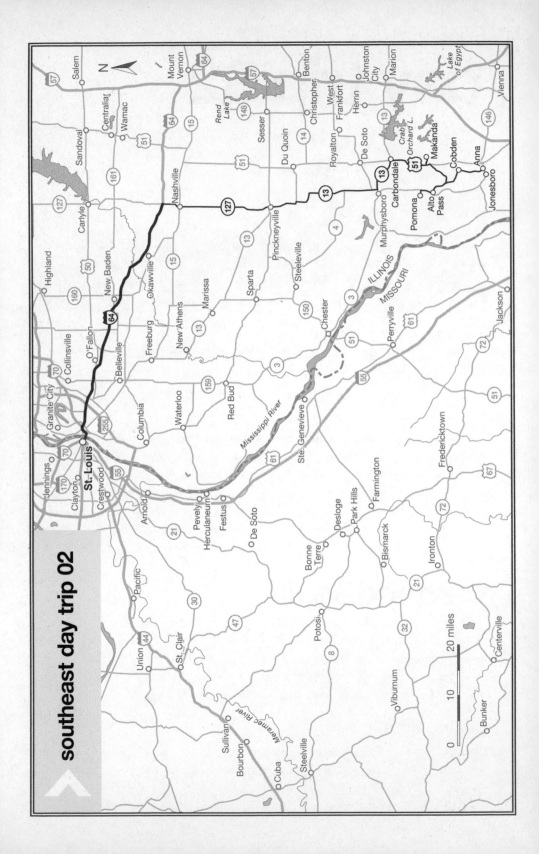

Continue to follow IL 127 and make a left onto Walnut Street. Follow IL 13 East into Carbondale. The drive is a little over two hours.

where to go

Hickory Ridge Golf Course. 2727 W. Glenn Rd.; (618) 529-4386. Hickory Ridge is a city-owned and operated course designed by William J. Spear, ASGCA. The course, which opened in 1993, is an 18-hole parkland course with tree lined fairways and water in play on 7 holes. It features 6,863 yards of golf from the longest tees for a par of 72. The course rating is 73.3, and it has a slope rating of 137 on zoysia grass. It's one of 5 courses on the Southern Illinois Golf Trail. Open year-round.

Honker Hill Winery. 4861 Spillway Rd.; (618) 549-5517; www.honkerhillwinery.com. Located on the highest point in Williamson County, the Shawnee Wine Trail's newest addition to the wine-making family is surrounded by the Crab Orchard Fish and Wildlife Refuge and Shawnee National Forest. Honker Hill's wines are made from fruit grown on-site in their vineyard, and the grounds include 5 ponds. Guests are encouraged to enjoy the vino and the view from the patio or in the tasting room.

Kite Hill Vineyards. 83 Kite Hill Rd.; (618) 684-5072; www.kitehillvineyards.com. A boutique winery located on 26 scenic acres, including 4 acres of vineyards and a small lake. The winery offers a Traminette, Chardonel, Chambourcin, Chambourcin Reserve, White Chambourcin, Sweet Rose, and Proud Port. Open Apr through Oct and by appointment Nov through Mar. Kite Hill also features an on-site bed-and-breakfast.

where to eat

Mary Lou's Grill. 114 S. Illinois Ave.; (618) 457-5084. A downtown Carbondale staple, tiny Mary Lou's Grill serves up generous portions of good old-fashioned diner food like flapjacks, eggs, hash browns, and fresh cream pies. The biscuits and gravy are a "must have." Friendly staff, homey atmosphere. Cash only. $.

Newell House Bistro Cafe. 201 E. Main St.; (618) 549-6400; www.thenewellhouse.com. This fine-dining restaurant, housed in a historic building completed in 1872, is open for lunch and dinner. The extensive lunch menu has a variety of upscale salads, sandwiches, soups, and burgers like the Drunken Bull (a beef patty covered in melted blue cheese, sautéed mushrooms, caramelized onions, crispy prosciutto, and a Cabernet reduction) and the Thai Chicken Burger (a ground chicken patty topped with Thai peanut sauce, coconut milk, and green papaya slaw). For dinner the choices include shared appetizers like smoked trout and wild rice pancakes (mini wild rice pancakes, smoked trout spread, and field greens, rimmed with rich maple-vanilla gastrique), seafood, pasta dishes, and an array of steaks including the Stuffed Manhattan (a crumb-encrusted 8-ounce filet stuffed with Gorgonzola, sautéed onions, spinach, and prosciutto, drizzled in a mushroom demi-glace). Reservations are recommended. Closed Sun. $$–$$$.

where to stay

Cabin on the Hill. 145 Cabin Hill Rd.; (618) 529-5667; www.cabinonthehill.com. Located on 80 private acres of woods and hills, each of the 3 cabins sits on a hillside overlooking the owner's hobby farm. If you're traveling with kids—or if you just really like animals—you can visit the farm's four-legged inhabitants, which include horses, miniature donkeys, potbellied pigs, pygmy goats, peacocks, and turkeys. There's also a walking trail that runs through the owner's 40-acre forest. The cabins have a hot tub, stone gas fireplace, outdoor fire pit, gas grill, satellite TV, DVD player, phone, dishwasher, washer and dryer, stove, refrigerator, toaster, coffeemaker, central heat and air, kitchen utensils, dishes, cookware, towels, and linens. Cabins 1 and 2 each can accommodate 4 people, the Premier Cabin sleeps 8, and the Little Red Barn sleeps 4. Dogs are allowed to stay in Cabin 2 and the Little Red Barn. $$.

Hundley House Bed & Breakfast. 601 W. Main St.; (618) 457-2170; www.hundleyhouse .net. Located in a historic home that was built in 1907, the Hundley House offers 3 guest rooms and a home-cooked breakfast every morning. They offer additional services to spice up a romantic getaway, including candles and a rose petal sprinkling service. Oh—and they also have NFL Sunday Ticket for football fans who can't stand the thought of getting completely away. $$.

makanda, il

The tiny village of Makanda—home to about 400 residents—is known for its laid-back attitude and its appreciation of the arts. If hippies still roam the earth, they will be able to appreciate the day-to-day vibe in Makanda, which is located about 10 miles south of Carbondale.

getting there

From Carbondale, take US 51 South about 8 miles, then turn left onto CR 29/Makanda Road and continue for approximately 2 miles. Turn right to stay on CR 29/Makanda Road.

where to go

Blue Sky Vineyard. 3150 S. Rocky Comfort Rd.; (618) 995-WINE; www.blueskyvineyard .com. Anchoring the eastern edge of the Shawnee Hills Wine Trail, Blue Sky presents a Tuscan-style ambiance complete with hilly views and an elaborate tasting room outfitted with 200-year-old Portuguese tiles, hand-carved doors, and vintage windmill ceiling fans. Blue Sky's wine list features more than 20 varieties of dry, semidry, sweet, and port wines, including Cabernet Franc, Chardonnay Gold, Norton, Papa's Rosa, Misterioso, Niagara, Rocky Comfort Red, and Cream Sherry.

Giant City State Park Visitor's Center. 235 Giant City Rd.; (618) 457-4836; http://dnr .state.il.us. Check out the information center for a comprehensive look at everything there is to see and do in the park and pick up some brochures about other nearby parks, activities, and attractions. In addition to the center's displays of the park's natural, cultural, and geological features, there's an informative 10-minute film about Giant City and a Discovery Corner for kids to explore. Open daily.

Giant City State Park. The 4,000 acres of Giant City State Park offer breathtaking natural beauty and scads of outdoor recreational activities. Located just south of Carbondale, the park is an ideal retreat for picnicking, hunting, fishing, camping, rock climbing and rappelling, and horseback riding. Part of Shawnee National Forest, the area got its name from the massive sandstone structures throughout the park. The landscape was created by eons of geological faulting and folding, which resulted in such iconic edifices as the Giant City Streets, formed 12,000 years ago by huge bluffs of sandstone. Giant City also includes lush vegetation, including hundreds of species of wildflowers and more than 75 varieties of towering trees. One of the most popular parks in southern Illinois, Giant City's natural splendor attracts more than 1.5 million visitors annually.

Picnic areas are available throughout the park, and each includes covered picnic tables, playground equipment, pit toilets, and charcoal grills. Some of the picnic areas have electricity and/or running water. All are available on a first-come, first-served basis. There are 8 hiking trails of varying length through the park, and all of them are open from dawn until dusk year-round except during hunting season. Take a horseback ride along the equestrian trails—you can rent a horse at Giant City Stables (618-529-4110) in case you didn't bring one with you. They offer guided horseback trail rides, riding lessons, and pony rides for pint-size cowpokes. The stables are open mid-Mar through Oct. Closed Tues.

Orlandini Vineyard. 410 Thorn Ln.; (618) 995-2307; www.orlandinivineyard.com. Orlandini offers beautiful scenery atop one of the highest ridges in southern Illinois and a variety of award-winning dry, sweet, and semisweet wines, including a Chambourcin, Vignoles, Rosso Gustoso, White Chambourcin, and the Saluki White, named for the mascot of Southern Illinois University. Closed Mon and Tues.

Stone Creek Golf Club & Resort. 503 Stone Creek Dr.; (618) 351-4653; www.stone creekgolf.com. Stone Creek is a public 18-hole, par-72 championship golf course that features manicured Bermuda fairways and bent grass greens. Designed by Jerry Lemons, there are 4 sets of tees on each hole and total yardages range from 5,402 to 6,796 yards. On-site amenities include a putting green, a driving range, a full-service pro shop, and a PGA Class A golf professional on staff available for golf instruction. There's also an on-site restaurant and 11 cabins available for rental.

where to shop

Makanda Boardwalk. Situated in downtown Makanda, the historic Boardwalk features unique shops and galleries inside restored storefronts that date back to the 1890s. It's sometimes called the "Valley of the Arts" because of the collection of artists and crafts-people here who work in glass, bronze, clay, wood, and more.

Makanda Trading Company. 520 Makanda Rd.; (618) 351-0201. Features incense, jewelry, locally and internationally produced artwork, Native American items, and locally made organic hemp-seed oil soaps by Hemple. The owner is a world traveler, so when he goes to other countries and sees something he likes, he buys it in quantity and sells it at the store.

RainMaker Art. 530 Makanda Rd.; (618) 457-6282; www.davedardis.com. Bronze and copper sculptures, pendants, fountains, and custom-made artwork by local artist and free spirit Dave Dardis. His whimsical sculptures and fountains range from tabletop designs to those large enough to demand center stage in a backyard garden or courtyard. Custom designs available.

where to stay

Giant City Lodge. 460 Giant City Lodge Rd.; (618) 457-4921; www.giantcitylodge.com. Opened in 1939, the Giant City Lodge is the result of President Franklin D. Roosevelt's Civilian Conservation Corps (CCC). The spacious main lodge, which features the Bald Knob dining room, was built using native materials such as multihued sandstone and white oak timber. There are a number of lodging options within the facility. The 12 original CCC-built cabins, located just south of the main lodge, are 1-room cabins equipped with a full bathroom, telephone, television, clock radio, and independent heat/AC unit. There are 18 larger Prairie cabins north of the lodge that have queen-size beds and a Murphy bed in the living room. The 4 larger and more scenic Bluff cabins have 2 queen-size beds in the bedroom and a cot. Both the Prairie and the Bluff cabins have added amenities like satellite TV, a small refrigerator, coffeemaker, hair dryer, and iron and ironing board. There are also electric fireplaces in the Bluff cabins. The lodge's season is the first Fri of Feb to the middle of Dec. $–$$.

alto pass, il

Alto Pass is located in southern Illinois's Union County, just southwest of Mt. Vernon between Anna and Murphysboro. The area's rich cultural heritage includes the Native Americans who first used the region's resources, as well as French and English explorers who traveled the Ohio and Mississippi Rivers in their first journeys into the wilderness. Today the small towns represent civilization to visitors who opt to "rough it" in the wilds of nearby Shawnee National Forest. The area's Shawnee Hills Wine Trail was the first in the state to receive recognition as an American Viticultural Area for its distinctive wine-making properties.

getting there

From Makanda, take CR 29/Makanda Road for about 2 miles and continue onto Old US 51. Turn left to stay on Old US 51 and follow it for a little more than a mile, then continue onto Old US 51 North and continue for 3 miles. Turn right onto Jamestown Road and follow it for about 2 miles, then make a slight right onto Skyline Drive and continue onto Main Street.

where to go

Alto Vineyards. Hwy. 127; (618) 893-4898; www.altovineyards.net. The oldest winery along the trail is run by the third generation of the wine-making Renzaglia family. Choose from whites like the Oak Chardonel, Wiener Dog White, and Shawnee Gold, or opt for the Rosso Classico, Dawg House Red, Cherry Berry, Nona Mia Sangria, or one of the 17 other wines.

Kosmic Acres Stables & Rentals. Prospect St. off Hwy. 127; (618) 893-2347. Take a ride along the trails and see Shawnee National Forest on horseback. You can rent a mighty steed or BYOH (bring your own horse) and enjoy a scenic trail ride by yourself or in small groups of up to 6 people. The national forest offers miles of equestrian trails of varying terrains, creeks and streams, and spectacular scenery. Kosmic Acres is located on the River to River Trail, which is part of the American Discovery Trail, and they offer year-round riding.

Hedman Vineyards. 560 Chestnut St.; (618) 893-4923; www.peachbarn.com. Enjoy a glass of one of 11 locally produced, award winning wines made from grapes grown on the property, or sip some Swedish Glögg, a mulled, warm red wine. They also offer a variety of alcohol-free alternatives. There's a Scandinavian gift shop on-site as well as the Swedish-themed Peach Barn Cafe. The winery is open Wed through Sun from Apr through Dec, and Fri through Sun from Jan through Mar.

where to eat

Hedman Vineyards' Peach Barn Cafe. 560 Chestnut St.; (618) 893-4923; www.peach barn.com. Who would expect to find Swedish cuisine in the middle of southern Illinois? Well, when the restaurant/winery owner is from Sweden, it's not such a stretch. The Peach Barn Cafe is located in the winery's restored/converted peach barn and the menu offers such entrees as Swedish meatballs, fish au gratin, beef tenderloin on cedar plank, artichoke chicken in a creamy Villard Blanc sauce, and a daily vegetarian special. Outdoor seating in the pavilion is also available when the weather cooperates. $$.

Northwest Passage Root Beer Saloon. #4 Main St.; (618) 893-1634. The kitschy eatery—touted as the "World's First Root Beer Saloon"—serves up 3 microbrewed root beers on tap, along with Orange Dream and cream soda. If you're hungry, they've got a line of gourmet deli croissant sandwiches, including soft-shell crab, Cajun crawfish, mango duck, and honey-orange pheasant. The gift shop offers smoked salmon, botanical extracts, assorted gourmet candies and chocolates, Italian specialty oils, and spice baskets from the West Indies. $.

pomona, il

Located in Shawnee National Forest about 10 miles south of Murphysboro, Pomona is an unincorporated community deep in the hills of southern Illinois.

getting there

Take IL 127 North from Alto Pass for approximately 3.5 miles, then turn left on Pomona Road and left onto 1st Street.

where to go

Hickory Ridge Vineyard & Winery. 1598 Hickory Ridge Rd.; (618) 893-1700; www .shawneewinetrail.com/UCW/hickoryridge.html. Specializing in dry red wines, Hickory Ridge only uses grapes grown on the premises, like the relatively new varietal, Cabernet Franc. In 2010 the winery won the Illinois Governor's Cup for the best rosé, and it was awarded Illinois' Best in Show for its Norton variety in 2009.

Pomona Winery. 2865 Hickory Ridge Rd.; (618) 893-2623; www.pomonawinery.com. Specializing in wines made from locally grown fruits other than grapes, the winery produces 7 table wines and 3 fortified dessert wines. All are handcrafted and hand-bottled. Try the Kir, which is made from a blend of black currants and apples; Once In A Blue Moon Blueberry Dessert Wine; or the award-winning Golden Oak Aged Reserve, made from Golden Delicious apples and aged with toasted American white oak.

Von Jakob Vineyard. 1309 Sadler Rd.; (618) 893-4500; www.vonjakobvineyard.com. Located just 4 miles apart, this vintner actually offers 2 locations: the original winery—Von Jakob Vineyard—in Pomona, and Von Jakob Orchards in Alto Pass. Tasting rooms and special events are available at each. Choose from 4 honey meads, 8 whites, 3 ports, 7 reds, and 2 blush wines.

where to shop

Whipple Creek Guitars. 57 Jerusalem Hill Rd.; (618) 559-2317; www.whipplecreekguitars .com. Custom handcrafted acoustic guitars made with incredible attention to detail, such as projection, clarity, and balanced tone in all ranges. Owner Terry Whipple builds the instruments, including Dreadnoughts, Triple-Os, OMs, and a custom design called the Maybelle.

cobden, il

Cobden is a village of about 1,100 residents in the heart of southernmost Illinois who appreciate good wine, good music, and a diverse assortment of art and artists.

getting there

From Pomona, turn right onto IL 127 South and continue for about 3.5 miles. Make a slight left onto Main Street and follow it onto Skyline Drive. Turn right on Oak Street and continue to N. Front Street for about 2 blocks, then turn left on E. Maple Street.

where to go

Honey Bee Stables. (618) 638-8059; www.honeybeestables.com. You can rent a horse at Honey Bee Stables—in fact, you can even take it camping. In addition to half-day and daylong rides, the stable offers trips that include two days' worth of horseback riding and an overnight camping experience. Or you can try something a little more extreme—rock climbing and rappelling along area rock walls. All activities are by reservation only. Call for information and directions. No credit cards are accepted, so bring your bankroll.

Owl Creek Vineyard. 2655 Water Valley Rd.; (618) 893-2557; www.owlcreekvineyard .com. An artisanal family winery that offers 4 whites, 4 reds, and 2 dessert wines. Bring Fido and the family for a picnic—Owl Creek is decidedly dog-friendly—and enjoy live folk and bluegrass music during spring and fall weekends.

Rustle Hill Winery. 8595 US 51; (618) 893-2800; www.rustlehillwinery.com. Rustle Hill features a number of Chambourcin varieties as well as a rosé, 2 Seyval Blancs, a Vidal Blanc, a Traminetto, and a Chardonel. The winery is home to an on-site restaurant, cabins, and an outdoor amphitheater with live concerts Fri through Sun.

StarView Vineyards. 5100 Wing Hill Rd.; (618) 893-WINE; www.starviewvineyards.com. Ninety percent of the wine made here comes from the 7 varietals of native American grapes and French-American hybrids grown on-site. Starview's Chardonel and SuperNova garnered bronze medals at the 2010 World Wine Championships. Try a Venus, Concord, or SilverStar wine slushy on those hot summer days (for adult consumers only).

where to shop

Anthill Gallery & Vintage Curiosities. 102 N. Front St.; (618) 457-7641; www.anthill gallery.com. The gallery houses works by the two owner-artists and features fine color photography of urban and rural landscapes by Bob Hageman and original stained-glass art panels by Linda Austin. Anthill also hosts regular showings of other southern Illinois artists throughout the year. Closed Mon through Wed.

The Velvet Hammer. 1210 Union Springs Rd.; (618) 893-2216; www.velvethammerltd
.com. A "decorative blacksmithing" shop that creates one-of-a-kind fireplace set tools,
sculptures, music stands, stools, and wine racks. Artist Roberta Elliot also makes some of
the most beautiful and unique lamps you'll find. Appointments are required.

where to eat

The Blue Boar Restaurant. 820-920 Kratzinger Hollow; (618) 833-5858. The Blue Boar is
a casual restaurant with a menu that includes prime rib, crawfish, shrimp étouffée, catfish or
shrimp po' boys, and barbecue. They also serve a made-to-order breakfast on Sun beginning at 8 a.m. Live music every weekend. $–$$.

The Palace Pizzeria. 215 S. Appleknocker Dr.; (618) 893-4415; www.thepalacepizzeria
.com. Casual pizzeria serving thick, thin, and double-crust pizzas as well as beer and wine
from area wineries. Live entertainment on weekends. $.

Trails End Lodge Steakhouse & Saloon. 1425 Skyline Dr.; (618) 893-6135; www.trails
endlodgecobden.com. After you've worked up an appetite doing all of that hiking and communing with nature, stop by the Trails End Lodge for a big ol' juicy steak. The comfortable,
western-style lodge features live entertainment, indoor and outdoor dining, and a menu of
steaks, burgers, and assorted appetizers. The lodge itself isn't visible from Skyline Drive, so
watch for the sign—don't blink or you'll miss it! $.

Yellow Moon Cafe. 110 N. Front St.; (618) 893-CAFE; www.yellowmooncafe.com. Open
for breakfast and lunch, the Yellow Moon utilizes local or sustainable products whenever
possible. Breakfast specialties include an Italian baked omelet and a cured wild Alaskan
salmon platter. Lunch options are mostly salads and sandwiches, and an appetizer/light
dinner menu is offered on Fri and Sat nights, along with live music. $.

where to stay

The Cabin at Mountain Glen. 886 Mountain Glen Rd.; (618) 833-5807; www.winetrail
cabins.com. A luxurious 2-bedroom cabin set among 60 acres of pristine woods, pasture,
and prairie. The cabin has a full kitchen, a vaulted great room with fireplace, a laundry, and
a master bedroom and bath with a custom 2-person shower and Jacuzzi tub. The second-
floor bedroom loft includes a half bath and a view that overlooks 20 acres of pasture and
wildlife. $$.

Shawnee Hill Bed & Breakfast. 290 Water Valley Rd.; (618) 893-2211; www.shawnee
hillbb.com. This small, quaint B&B features 3 rooms on 200 acres of Shawnee National For-
est. There are 3 stocked ponds on the grounds, plenty of trails to wander along, a nearby
cave where Daniel Boone carved his name in 1766, blacksmith shops, and a circa 1860
barn that's been turned into an antiques shop. $–$$.

anna-jonesboro, il

Located about 10 minutes from Cobden, the dual tiny town threat of Anna-Jonesboro is adjacent to Shawnee National Forest and just south of the Shawnee Hills Wine Trail.

getting there

From Cobden, take Old US 51 North about 4 miles to W. Vienna Street, then turn right onto S. Main Street.

where to go

Trail of Tears State Forest, South Region. 3240 State Forest Rd.; (618) 833-4910; http://dnr.state.il.us. Situated in western Union County just 5 miles northwest of Jonesboro, Trail of Tears State Forest is a multiuse site managed for timber, wildlife, ecosystem preservation, watershed protection, and recreation. The forest contains abundant wildlife and plenty of unique vegetation. There are 4 picnic shelters in the main picnic area, and each spot contains a table and grill with privies and drinking water nearby. A number of trails pass through the forest—including one designed for cross-country running—and the fire trails remain open for hiking year-round. Horseback riding is permitted along designated horse trails May through Oct, though the trails may close temporarily in the event of heavy rains during the riding season. Call ahead for an update on trail conditions or to request a detailed map of the horseback trails. Tent camping (with vehicle access) and backpacking camping sites are available, including some locations with log shelters and adjacent privies.

where to eat

Brick House Grill. 308 S. Main St., Anna; (618) 833-5367. Located in downtown Anna, this cozy family-owned-and-operated eatery offers upscale yet casual dining in an inviting atmosphere. The lunch menu has a variety of salads, appetizers, and sandwiches like the grilled Italian sandwich (fresh mozzarella, homemade pesto, and tomatoes) and the half-pound burger. In addition to a spate of homemade desserts, specialties on the dinner menu include cashew-crusted chicken with sesame-ginger aioli, Thai grilled salmon, and grilled rib eye covered with caramelized onions and wild mushroom gravy. $–$$.

where to stay

The Davie School Inn. 300 Freeman St., Anna; (618) 833-2377; www.davieschoolinn .com. The Winstead Davie School, built in 1910, has been transformed into one of the largest bed-and-breakfasts in the state. It features 11 suites of varying sizes, sleeping anywhere from 2 to 5 occupants each, and all have been outfitted with such modern conveniences as a whirlpool tub and air-conditioning. The old schoolhouse vibe is still intact, as each room has one of the original chalkboards and a bookcase, and the hardwood floors still show the marks made by the students' desks. And you don't have to trek down to the old cafeteria for breakfast—it's served to you in your suite. $$–$$$.

Rustic Hideaway Cabins. Off State Pond Rd. on Rustic Ln., Jonesboro; (618) 833-4860; www.rustichideawaycabins.com. Located next door to Shawnee National Forest and just a few miles outside of Anna, these anything but rustic cabins are located on 10 private, wooded acres. Both have 2 bedrooms and offer approximately 850 square feet of space. Each cabin contains a hot tub and gas fireplace. Cabin 1 has an extra half-bath in the loft area and can sleep up to 6 people, thanks to the family room couch that makes into a bed. $$.

Trail of Tears Lodge & Resort. 1575 Fair City Rd.; (618) 833-8697; www.trailoftears.com. The 6,000-square-foot lodge features 7 guest rooms and such family-friendly activities as horseback riding through Shawnee National Forest, a sporting clays gun range, miniature golf, an outdoor pool, and an indoor pool table. An on-site restaurant serves American favorites on Fri and Sat nights. $.

day trip 03

southeast

>>> **into the woods:**
shawnee national forest

shawnee national forest

Located in the rough, un-glaciated areas known as the Illinois Ozark and Shawnee Hills, the forest is nestled between the Mississippi and Ohio Rivers. The Shawnee National Forest land, which was first set aside in the early 1930s, features a landscape that includes everything from rolling hills and open lands to lakes, creeks, and rugged bluffs. In addition, more than 500 wildlife species call Shawnee National Forest home, including 48 mammals, 237 birds, 52 reptiles, 57 amphibians, and 109 species of fish. There are 7 federally listed threatened and endangered species crawling, swimming, and flying around the forest, as well as 33 species that are considered regionally sensitive.

getting there

From St. Louis, take I-64 East/US 40 East to I-70 East into Illinois. Take a slight right onto I-64 East/IL 3 North and continue along I-64 East for 75 miles. Make a slight right onto I-57 South and follow it for 20 miles. Take exit 71 for IL 14 toward Benton/Christopher, then turn left onto IL 14 East/W. Main Street for 0.8 miles. Turn right toward IL 34 South/East Main Street and take the second right onto IL 34 South/East Main Street. Follow IL 34 South for 32 miles. Turn left onto E. Poplar Street, then make a right onto South Commercial Street and continue for about a mile. Turn left onto IL 145.

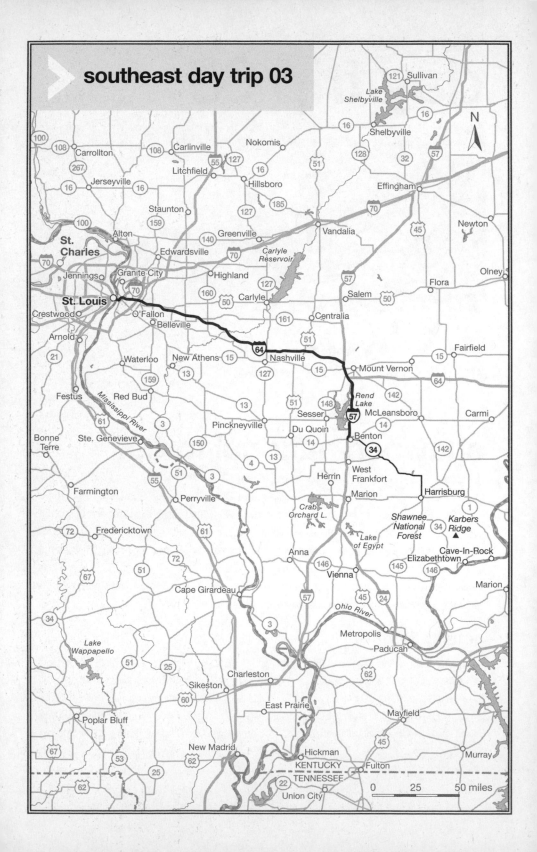

southeast day trip 03

where to go

Shawnee National Forest, Hidden Springs Ranger District. 602 N. 1st St./Rte. 45 North; (618) 658-2111; www.fs.fed.us/r9/shawnee. The Hidden Springs Ranger District encompasses the eastern half of the forest and includes such scenic areas as Bell Smith Springs, Lusk Creek, Garden of the Gods, Lake Glendale, and the Ohio River National Scenic Byway. Stop in for route suggestions, topographical maps, and up-to-date information.

Shawnee National Forest. Shawnee National Forest Headquarters, 50 IL 145 South, Harrisburg; (618) 253-7114. Located in the southern tip of Illinois, the forest covers parts of 10 counties and more than 278,500 acres. There is a diverse collection of outdoor recreational opportunities in the forest, such as fishing, hunting, horseback riding, rock climbing and rappelling, camping, boating, and hiking. Shawnee National Forest features a system of 400 miles of equestrian and hiking trails and 17 picnic areas. Some "must-see" highlights of the region include the Garden of the Gods, whose magnificent rock formations and majestic bluffs make it quite obvious as to how the area got its name; Cave-In-Rock State Park, located along the Ohio River in the eastern section of the forest; the Little Grand Canyon Trail, featuring a 365-foot climb from the canyon floor that results in a panoramic view of the Big Muddy River and the Mississippi floodplain; and Pomona Natural Bridge, a 90-foot-long natural bridge carved out of sandstone. The bridge was formed by the forces of erosion over millions of years. It is accessible via a short (0.3 mile) dirt trail that loops through a forest of mature oak, hickory, and beech trees. The Johnson Creek Recreation Area offers a variety of recreational activities, including camping, swimming, hiking, biking along the area's scenic roads, and horseback riding.

Garden of the Gods. Off Road #17, Karbers Ridge; (618) 658-2111. Garden of the Gods features spectacular rock formations, cliffs, and trails, and it's the most visited site in Shawnee National Forest. There are 5.5 miles of interconnecting trails in the recreation area, including 2 main trail systems—the Observation Trail and the River-to-River Trail. The Observation Trail is the more popular route, following a 0.25-mile stone path that leads to spectacular overlooks of the Garden of the Gods Wilderness Area. It's considered a trail of average difficulty and has occasional educational signs detailing the region's history and geology. The River-to-River Trail enters the east end of the park from High Knob, just below the camping area, and heads west and south below the rock formations. It veers westward again and continues 8 miles to Herod. Other trails lead to places like Indian Point, Anvil Rock, Mushroom Rock, and Big H, and all are interconnecting. Maps are available at the park, which is open year-round.

Cave-In-Rock State Park. #1 New State Park Rd., Cave-In-Rock; (618) 289-4325. The heavily wooded park, perched high atop the bluffs overlooking the Ohio River, is named for the 55-foot-wide cave carved out of limestone rock thousands

of years ago. There are a number of trails located along the riverbank and 2 established hiking trails of moderate difficulty. In addition, a number of unmarked trails
run through the park for those who want to explore the forest areas on their own.
The park is home to a fishing pond, and access is available to the Ohio River for
fishing, boating, and recreational water sports. The north side of the park features
camping accommodations with 34 Class A sites that are equipped with electricity. The sites can accommodate units up to 60 feet long. There are also 25 Class
B/S tent sites available, with showers, restrooms, and dump stations present in
both areas. Wheelchair-accessible sites also are available, and grills are furnished
at each campsite.

Little Grand Canyon Trail. Shawnee National Forest; www.theshawneenational
forest.com. The trail is a 3.6-mile loop through the majestic bluffs of the Little
Grand Canyon. In 1980 it was designated a National Natural Landmark for its
unique ecological and geological features, which contain upland forest, dry hill
prairies, sandstone outcroppings, and an extensive floodplain ecosystem at the
bottom of the canyon. The trail's asphalt and dirt surface offers a moderate to difficult hike, with portions requiring moderate climbing. Along the upper portions of
the trail, the view includes colorful cliffs and the Big Muddy River and Mississippi
River floodplain, and there's a cool and lush bottomland habitat that includes seasonal waterfalls, large sandstone overhangs, and towering beech and sycamore
trees along the canyon floor. One of the trail's unique features is that both the
approach and exit from the canyon is by steps carved into the rocky creek beds.
To get to the trail from Murphysboro, take IL 127 south for 6 miles to Etherton
Road, then go west 5 miles. From Alto Pass, take IL 127 north for 7 miles to
Etherton Road, then go west for 5 miles.

where to eat

Cave-In-Rock State Park Restaurant. PO Box 125, Cave-In-Rock; (618) 289-4545;
www.caveinrockkaylors.com. The family-friendly restaurant offers Southern-style comfort
food with homemade desserts and all-you-can-eat Friday-night fish buffets and Sunday
fried chicken lunch buffets. The menu also includes house specialties like roast beef with
all the trimmings, catfish, shrimp, and steaks. Open daily for breakfast, lunch, and dinner. If
you're looking for an address for your GPS, the owners recommend entering "Main Street,
Cave-in-Rock, 62919." Once you get to Main, you'll see the signs that will lead you to the
restaurant. $.

E'town River Restaurant. 100 Front St., Elizabethtown; (618) 287-2333. Located 12
miles west of Cave-In-Rock State Park, this casual eatery is a floating restaurant on the Ohio
River that's known for its fried seafood and cheeseburgers. Catfish is the house specialty,

served with side dishes of coleslaw, baked beans, and hush puppies. They close early—7 or 8 p.m. during warm-weather months—but are open 7 days a week. Call for winter hours. $.

where to stay

Camp Cadiz. Shawnee National Forest Headquarters, 50 IL 145 South, Harrisburg; (618) 253-7114. Located at the site of an old Civilian Conservation Corps work camp, there are 11 primitive campsites with vault restrooms but no drinking water. From Harrisburg, take IL 13 east for 14 miles, then take Route 1 south for 15 miles. Turn west at the Camp Cadiz sign and continue two miles to the recreation area entrance road. $.

Cave-In-Rock State Park Lodge. PO Box 125, Cave-In-Rock; (618) 289-4545; www.caveinrockkaylors.com. The lodge features 4 duplex guest houses with 8 suites, which can accommodate up to 4 guests. Each suite contains a deluxe bath, dining area, refrigerator and microwave, 2 queen-size beds, satellite TV, and free parking, in addition to a private patio deck that offers a nice view of the Ohio River. Open seasonally. If you're looking for an address for your GPS, the owners recommend entering "Main Street, Cave-in-Rock, 62919." Once you got to Main, you'll see the signs that will lead you to the lodge. $.

Johnson Creek Recreation Area Campground. Shawnee National Forest Headquarters, 50 IL 145 South, Harrisburg; (618) 253-7114. Located on the northwest edge of Kinkaid Lake, Johnson Creek Recreation Area offers 20 campsites with restrooms and dump stations. The area also offers hitching rails and picket lines for equestrian campers, along with tables and fire rings. $.

Pharaoh Campground. Vienna/Elizabethtown Ranger District, 602 N. 1st St., Vienna; (618) 658-2111. The campground is open year-round and includes 12 sites with restrooms and drinking water. Additional facilities include picnic tables and fire pits. Sites are available on a first-come, first-served basis. Overnight parking for backpackers is located at the backpackers' parking lot, which is the first road on the left as you enter the park. $.

River Rose Inn Bed & Breakfast. 1 Main St., Elizabethtown; (618) 287-8811; www.riverose inn.com. Built in 1914, the River Rose Inn is about 12 miles west of Cave-In-Rock State Park on the banks of the Ohio River. Furnished in antiques, the inn's 4 guest rooms include satellite TV, queen-size beds, and private bathrooms. The Magnolia Cottage, located behind the main house, also has a whirlpool tub for two, a gas log fireplace, and a private porch overlooking the river. There's also an in-ground pool and a riverside Jacuzzi on-site. $–$$.

day trip 04

southeast

going golfing:
marion, il

marion, il

Incorporated in 1841, the city of Marion is the county seat of Williamson County, IL. Home to more than 17,000 residents, Marion serves as the largest retail trade center in southern Illinois thanks to its central location along I-57 and IL 13, which is informally referred to as southern Illinois's "Main Street." Marion is also known for the federal penitentiary located just southwest of the city. It's where reputed New York mobster John Gotti was sent to serve his life sentence for murder and racketeering. The penitentiary was built in 1963 to replace San Francisco's Alcatraz prison, which closed that year.

getting there

From St. Louis, take I-70 East into Illinois, then make a slight right onto I-64 East/IL 3 North (signs for Louisville/St. Clair Avenue). Continue to follow I-64 East for 75 miles, then make a slight right onto I-57 South. Follow I-57 South for about 38 miles, then take exit 54A to merge onto IL 13 East/W. Deyoung Street toward Marion/Harrisburg. Continue for about 2 miles and make a right onto N. Court Street, then make a right onto W. Main Street.

where to go

Crab Orchard Golf Club. 901 W. Grand Ave.; (618) 985-2321; www.craborchardgolfclub .com. Located between Marion and Carbondale, this semiprivate 18-hole, par-70 course

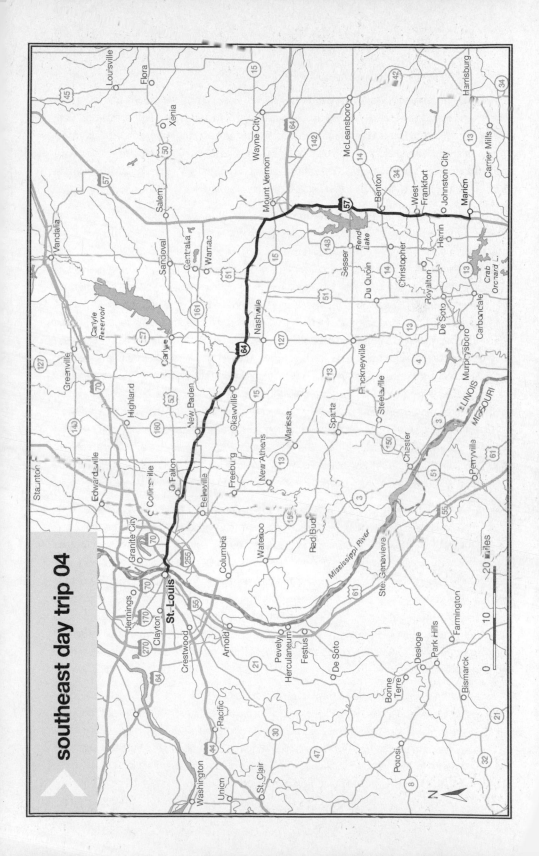

southeast day trip 04

includes a driving range and a large Bermuda practice area with target greens and a bunker. The course features water on 9 holes and lush fairways of Myers zoysia and Westwood Bermuda, as well as zoysia and Bermuda grasses on the tees and fairways with bent grass on the greens. You can choose from 5 sets of tees, and on-site amenities include a full-service golf shop and a clubhouse with a full-service dining room/grill area, bar, and club room. In 2009 Crab Orchard made *Golf Digest*'s "Best Places to Play" list.

Crab Orchard National Wildlife Refuge. 8588 IL 148; (618) 997-3344; http://midwest .fws.gov/craborchard. Located about 5 miles west of Marion, the 44,000-acre wildlife refuge attracts approximately one million annual human visitors and hundreds of thousands of migratory birds utilizing the Mississippi Flyway. The number of wintering Canada geese can peak at 200,000, and more than 245 additional bird species have been documented on the refuge. There are also 700 plant species, 33 mammal species, 63 fish species, and 44 reptile and amphibian species documented on Crab Orchard, as the facility features a wide diversity of flora and fauna. Major habitat types on the refuge include hardwood and pine forests, agricultural land, rolling hills, brushland, wetlands, and lakes. The refuge's western 24,000 acres, which include a 4,050-acre wilderness area, offer a wide range of recreational opportunities, including boating, water-skiing, swimming, hiking, and camping. Duck, goose, turkey, and deer hunting are allowed during specific times of the year. The refuge's 3 man-made lakes are known for their populations of largemouth bass, crappie, catfish, and bluegill, and fishing is permitted from the banks as well as in boats. Periodic interpretive programs offered at the refuge include a wildflower tour along the Rocky Bluff Trail during the spring and bald eagle tours in Jan. Vehicle passes are available at the visitor center.

Kokopelli Golf Club. 1401 Champions Dr.; (888) 746-0887, ext. 2; www.kokopelligolf .com. Kokopelli offers 18 challenging holes of golf spread over 160 acres of beautiful terrain. The daily-fee course and facilities were designed by renowned golf architect Steve Smyers, and Kokopelli was named one of "America's 100 Best Courses for $100 or Less" by *Travel & Leisure* magazine. *Golfweek Magazine* ranked the facility as the No. 3 course in Illinois. There are 5 sets of tees, 96 bunkers, rolling fairways, and open greens that provide golfers with a fair—but challenging—day on the links. Play ranges from 5,400 to 7,200 yards and carries a course rating of 71.6 to 75.2. The facility offers a variety of "stay and play" packages that include unlimited golf and practice range access, meals, and hotel accommodations.

Pirate Pete's Family Entertainment Center. 3000 W. Deyoung St., Ste. 800C; (618) 997-4353; www.piratepetesfun.com. Located in the Illinois Star Centre shopping mall, Pirate Pete's offers such kid-friendly attractions as an arcade full of video games and a 2,000-square-foot laser tag arena. There's also a Parent's Lounge that's outfitted with pool tables, flat-screen TVs, and adult beverages. The food menu is definitely kid-friendly, with options like pizza, hot dogs, tacos, and chicken wings.

Williamson County Historical Museum. 105 S. Van Buren St.; (618) 997-5863; www.the wchs.com. Located in a building that once served as the county jail, the 17-room museum features artifacts, antiques, and records of Williamson County's progress. The brick building, built in 1913, was also home to the county sheriff and his family—steel doors and 13-inch-thick concrete walls separated the prisoners from the family's home. Arrange tours through the Marion Chamber of Commerce (2305 W. Main St.; 618-997-6311).

where to shop

Illinois Star Centre Mall. 3000 W. Deyoung St.; (618) 993-5436; www.llstarcentremall .com. The shopping mall features more than 50 stores and restaurants, including Sears, Lane Bryant, Payless Shoes, Dillard's, Target, GameStop, Bath & Body Works, and Earthbound Trading. Open daily.

Little Egypt Arts Association Art Centre. 601 Tower Sq.; (618) 998-8530; www.little egyptarts.com. The cooperative art center's gallery features rotating shows, and the gift shop sells jewelry, fiber art, paintings, sculptures, and photography by regional artists and artisans. Classes in photography, fiber, sewing, quilting, and painting are offered for adults and children. Open Mon through Sat. Call in advance for hours.

Marion Antique Mall. 501 N. Madison St.; (618) 993-0020; www.marionantiquemall.net. The newly remodeled mall offers an eclectic array of antiques and collectibles, including Fenton Art Glass, baseball memorabilia, beautiful European furniture, jewelry, and an extensive collection of glassware. The 10,000-square-foot mall features wares from more than 30 different vendors. Closed Sun.

where to eat

Jasones B&B Restaurant. 1414 W. Main St.; (618) 997-9450; www.jasones.com. Open for breakfast and lunch, Jasones offers an above-average menu of egg dishes, homemade desserts, soups, salads such as Jason's Oriental (romaine, shredded cabbage, green and red peppers, green onions, sesame seeds, and slivered almonds, topped with homemade Oriental noodles and dressing), and sandwiches like the New York Beef-on-Weck (aged Angus beef, sliced thin, soaked in au jus, and piled high on a kimmelweck roll, served with a side of au jus, ketchup, and horseradish). There's also a kids' menu for diners 12 and under. $.

Koko's—Kokopelli Golf Club. 1401 Champions Dr.; (618) 997-5656; www.kokopelligolf .com. Koko's offers a limited lunch menu of sandwiches and salads for golfers on the go. The dinner menu expands a bit to include appetizers like shrimp, pot stickers, and chicken wings along with such entrees as blackened tilapia, garlic shrimp, beef tenderloin filet, and cheese tortellini with a tomato-basil cream sauce. Cocktails are available at the full-service

Koko's Sports Bar. Lunch and dinner served Tues through Sat, with a lunch buffet offered on Sun. Reservations are recommended. $–$$.

where to stay

Jasones B&B. 1414 W. Main St.; (618) 997-9459; www.jasones.com. The newly renovated and modernized home, which was built in 1906, offers 2 suites and 2 guest rooms. The Tabithian Honeymoon Suite feature a king-size cherry Queen Anne bedroom suite, an adjoining room with his-and-her vanity, and an additional room with a large garden tub and shower, while the Tiffany Suite has a queen-size sleigh bed and marbled shower. Jason's Room offers a cherry Queen Anne bedroom suite, an antique-style wash basin, and a ceramic tile shower, and Danielle's Room features "shabby chic" decor with a full-size antique bed and a marble bath with a ceramic tile shower. Room service is available until 8 p.m. The B&B is also home to Jasones restaurant. $$.

Marion Campground & RV Park. 119 N. 7th St.; (618) 997-3484; www.marioncamp ground.com. Open year-round, Marion Campground & RV Park features 58 full-service sites, including 27 pull-through sites with 50/30 amps, water and sewer hookups, satellite TV, and wireless Internet service available at each. The facility also features an on-site playground, pavilion, pet-walking area, shower and laundry facilities, and mail and fax services. $.

south

>>>

day trip 01

south

>>> **pie town, usa:**
kimmswick, mo

kimmswick, mo

Tiny Kimmswick, MO, was founded in 1859 by Theodore Kimm. The Mississippi River town has been named one of the "100 Best Small-Town Getaways" by *Midwest Living* magazine. A quaint riverside hamlet known for its historic homes, unique shops, and pies from the famous Blue Owl Restaurant and Bakery, Kimmswick is listed on the National Register of Historic Places. Nearly 7 blocks of the old-world town—44 buildings in all—have national historic significance, with most of the restored buildings dating back to the late 19th and early 20th centuries. About 30 of the old structures have been converted into one-of-a-kind gift and specialty shops.

For a unique day trip adventure between St. Louis and Kimmswick, take the *Tom Sawyer* riverboat on the Kimmswick Express Cruise. You'll enjoy a 2-hour river cruise to Kimmswick, have 3 hours to explore the historic town, then take a 30-minute motor coach ride back to the St. Louis riverfront at the base of the Gateway Arch.

getting there

Follow I-55 South from St. Louis for about 21 miles and take exit 186 for Imperial Main Street. Keep left at the fork, following the signs for Imperial/Kimmswick, then make a left onto Imperial Main Street/W. Main Street. Take Imperial Main Street/W. Main Street for about 0.5 mile and continue onto River Street. Turn left onto Highway K, make a right onto

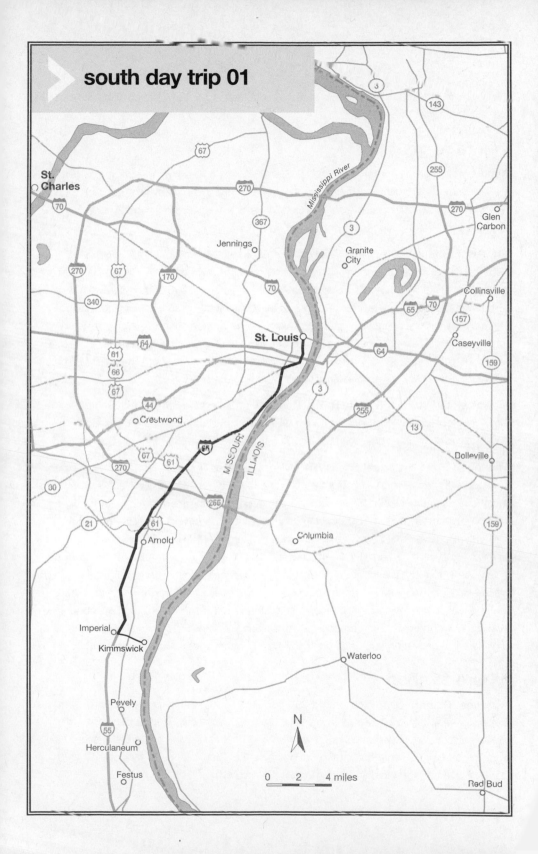

4th Street, then take the first left onto Market Street. Follow Market for about 2 blocks and turn left onto Front Street.

where to go

Kimmswick Visitor Center. 314 Market St.; (636) 464-6464; www.gokimmswick.com. Pick up some free brochures, maps, and tips on all of the local "must-see" stops or do a little shopping for souvenirs. The center sells Kimmswick T-shirts, artisan crafts, cards, and books. Open Tues through Sun from 10 a.m. to 4 p.m.

Anheuser Estate. 6008 Windsor Harbor Rd.; (636) 464-7407 or (636) 464-1698. Built in 1867, the historic 23-acre estate sits at the south end of town near the Mississippi River. It was purchased by the beer barons of the Anheuser family in 1916 and originally used as a summerhouse. The estate includes many of the Anheusers' personal belongings, including family heirlooms, antiques, portraits, furniture, dinnerware, clothing, a large library, and a collection of Westward Ho crystal. There are also hand-carved 1904 World's Fair beds and an original "Feasting Fox" perched on the bluffs overlooking the Mighty Mississippi. The estate is open for walk-in tours every Thurs from noon to 4 p.m.

Kimmswick Historical Society Hall & Museum. 3rd and Vine Streets; (636) 464-8687. Get a quick history of Kimmswick through this collection of memorabilia, historical photographs, artifacts, and maps. Open Sat and Sun from 1 to 4 p.m. Mar through Dec.

Mastodon State Historical Site. 1050 Charles J. Becker Dr.; (636) 464-2976; www.mo stateparks.com/mastodon.htm. The park is home to the Kimmswick Bone Bed, one of the most famous and extensive Pleistocene ice age deposits of fossils. In addition to having a bunch of giant mastodon bones and remnants of other now-extinct animals, the site features interpretative trails, picnic sites, and a museum that tells the story of the Clovis culture, which existed in the area between 10,000 and 14,000 years ago. A full-size replica of a mastodon skeleton highlights the exhibits. In 1979 archaeological history was made here when scientists excavated a stone spear point made by hunters from the Clovis culture. It was the first solid evidence that people coexisted with the giant prehistoric mastodons. Today the 425-acre property preserves this National Register of Historic Places site and provides recreational opportunities on its trails along with a special-use campground.

where to shop

Antiques Galore. 6047 2nd St.; (636) 467-7277; www.antiquesgaloregal.etsy.com. There's literally a little bit of everything here, both old and new. Poke around for some vintage collectibles, housewares, home decor, holiday items, sewing and crafting supplies, books, glassware, linens, and just plain kitschy stuff. They also carry McCall's Country Candles, scented rosehips, and refresher oils. Closed Mon.

Cherrika's. 318 Market St.; (636) 464-8270; www.cherrikas.com. If you're looking for a new decorative garden flag or need to update your current version of Old Glory, this is the place for you. Choose from spring, summer, fall, winter, and holiday designs as well as flags that show your love for dogs, cats, or horses. Cherrika's also carries decorative items like mailbox covers, pottery, linens, baskets, and wind chimes. Closed Mon.

Christmas Haus of Kimmswick. 311 Elm St.; (636) 464-0779. It's Christmas all the time around here, because this is the area's largest year-round Christmas shop and it features more than 40 decorated trees. They have all sorts of ornaments, including Byer's Carolers and Baldwin Brass, as well as a variety of imaginative decorations for the holiday. Closed Mon.

Cozy Cottage. 212 Market St.; (636) 467-3700. Guys—just wait outside on this one. The cottage specializes in "girly fun" through its jewelry, accessories, gifts, and vintage items, and they claim to have the "cutest Madame Alexander doll line ever." So unless you're into that sort of thing, you should probably just have a seat and be patient. Closed Mon.

Karol's Korner. 6061 Front St.; (636) 464-4680. Located in a former bakery, circa 1880, the shop offers something old and something new with its selection of antique and reproduction furniture, china, glassware, and antique kitchen items. Karol's also carries decor items and handmade products, including Missouri-made lye soap and soy candles. Closed Mon.

Mississippi Mud Gallery. 6050 2nd St.; (636) 464-3360; www.mississippimudgallery .com. Featuring works by local artists, including metal and glass bead jewelry, prints, fused glass ornaments, pottery, art glass, wood, baskets, and quilts. The shop also carries Ne'Qwa hand-painted ornaments, Lolita wine and martini glasses, La-Tee-Da! fragrance lamps, and Herbaria handcrafted soap. Closed Mon.

The Purple Pickle. 100 Market St.; (006) 464-6144; www.thepurplepickle2.com. Whimsical gift shop offering crystals, incense, and handmade bracelets and jewelry, along with witch balls, agates and geodes, birdhouses, bird feeders, wind chimes, candles, and candleholders. Closed Mon.

Savannah Rose. 6101 Front St.; (636) 467-7101. The self-described "shabby chic" boutique specializes in unique seasonal giftware and personalized items that can be monogrammed/embroidered on-site. Closed Mon.

Tin Cup. 6025 3rd St.; (636) 464-4747; www.tincupgifts.com. A gift shop offering Chamilia beads, Lampe Berger home fragrances, Aspen Bay soy candles, and Thymes lotions and body washes, as well as jewelry, kitchen gadgets, and handmade soaps. Closed Mon.

The Wild Grey Hare. 116 Mill St.; (636) 467-8099. Carries items like Donna Sharp quilted purses, a custom line of cruise apparel, jewelry, home and garden decor, and assorted antiques. There's also a selection of framed and wall art along with some handmade mosaics. Closed Mon.

where to eat

The Blue Owl Restaurant & Bakery. 6116 2nd St.; (636) 464-3128; www.theblueowl .com. Kimmswick's famous Blue Owl is a family-owned-and-operated eatery known for desserts like their Caramel Pecan Levee High Pecan Pie, German chocolate pie, assorted gourmet cheesecakes, and luscious homemade pastries. Their desserts are simply legendary throughout the region. Sugar-free options are also available, including mini fruit pies, cream pies, and pineapple cream-cheese bars. The Blue Owl's restaurant also serves delicious, hearty breakfasts and country-style lunches with such specialties as the Baked Chicken Salad Pie (chunks of white meat, sliced water chestnuts, celery, onion, cheddar cheese, and sour cream baked in a homemade crust and topped with melted cheddar). Outdoor seating is available. Closed Mon. $.

Dough Depot Cafe & Gifts. 216 Market St.; (636) 464-9339. The Dough Depot is a cozy cafe that offers friendly service and a menu of sandwiches, salads, soups, chili, pizzas, baked goods, homemade candies, and ice cream. Indoor or patio seating is available. Closed Mon. $.

Mary's Sweet Shoppe. 118 Market St.; (636) 464-3900; www.maryssweetshoppe.com. Owned and operated by the folks at the Blue Owl Restaurant next door, Mary's Sweet Shoppe serves up more than 20 flavors of ice cream, 50-plus kinds of homemade candies, and a variety of specialty coffee drinks and hot chocolates. The soda fountain features old-fashioned phosphates as well as malts, shakes, sundaes, and specialties like the Gooey Butter Sensation (crumbled homemade Gooey Butter Cookies, a scoop of vanilla ice cream, and your choice of topping) and the Mississippi Mudd (Mississippi Mudd Cake, a scoop vanilla ice cream, hot fudge, and marshmallow cream). $.

day trip 02

south

ste. genevieve, mo

Perched on the west bank of the Mississippi River, the village was originally settled approximately 2 miles south of its current location during the late 1740s. Devastating floods in 1785 resulted in residents packing up the town and moving it to its present location on higher ground. It was one of several important communities in territory held by France at the time, so many of the earliest residents were French-Canadians who farmed the rich muddy soil adjacent to the village, produced salt, and mined lead.

Ste. Genevieve is an authentic 18th-century French colony that's managed to maintain significant charm and atmosphere thanks in part to the preservation of its many historic buildings and the friendly, laissez-faire attitude of the residents. Ste. Gen kept the narrow streets and fenced gardens surrounding the French colonial buildings made hundreds of years ago in the *poteaux-en-terre* and *poteaux-sur-sole* architectural styles. Modern-day Ste. Genevieve's National Historic District offers visitors an incomparable view into its colonial past and provides a unique set of charming diversions with its quaint shops, cozy eateries, and old-world bed-and-breakfast inns.

getting there

From St. Louis, follow I-55 South for approximately 53 miles to exit 154 for Route O toward Ste. Genevieve. Turn left onto Route O for about 0.3 mile, then turn right onto US 61 South

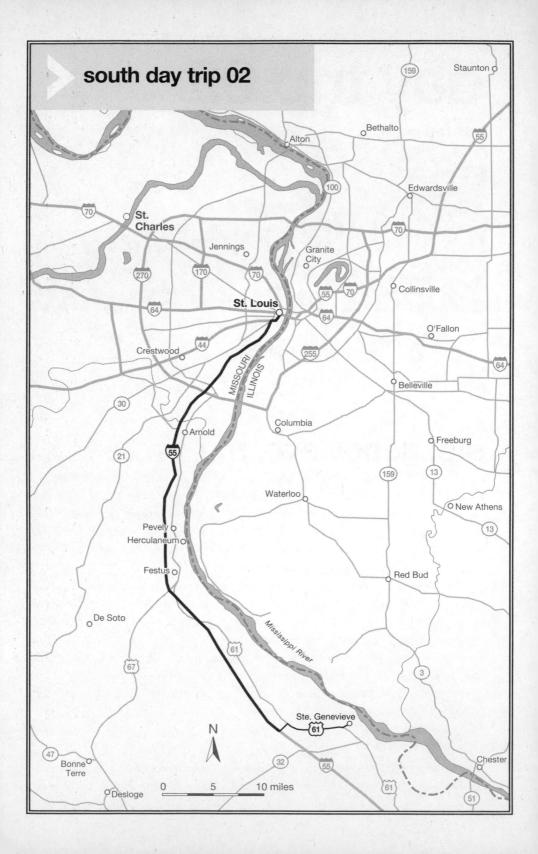

and continue for a little more than 7 miles. Make a left onto Market Street and follow it for about a mile, then turn right onto S. 5th Street.

where to go

Ste. Genevieve Welcome Center. 66 S. Main St.; (800) 373-7007; www.visitstegen.com. Pick up some brochures, maps, and insight into where to go and the best way to get there. The center also has a gallery of Roscoe Misselhorn sketches of Ste. Genevieve and the surrounding area courtesy of the Misselhorn Art Foundation.

Bauvais-Amoureux House. 327 St. Mary's Rd.; (573) 883-7102; www.mostateparks .com/park/felix-valle-house-state-historic-site. Built sometime around 1792 by Jean-Baptiste St. Gemme Bauvais, the historic home features upright cedar log walls that are set directly into the earth. Reminiscent of French-Canadian architecture, the home reflects the rare *poteaux-en-terre* method of construction where heavy hand-hewn timbers form the Norman truss system that supports the steeply pitched roof. Purchased by Benjamin Amoureux in 1852, it's now part of the Missouri Department of Natural Resources' Felix Vallé State Historic Site, which also features a large diorama that depicts the village of Ste. Genevieve as it was in 1832. Open seasonally.

Bolduc House Museum. 125 S. Main St.; (573) 883-3105; www.bolduchouse.com. The complex actually features 3 historic homes—the Louis Bolduc Historic House, circa 1785, and the LeMeilleur House and the Linden House, both built in 1820—and several gardens. The Bolduc House is regarded as the first most authentically restored Creole house in the nation and has been designated a National Historic Landmark by the National Trust for Historic Preservation. Its vertical log walls and heavy oak double-pitched "hip" roof were used to protect the French-Canadian settlers from the elements. The house and grounds display accurately restored 18th-century furnishings. Next door, the LeMeilleur House features a brace frame structure with brick noggins and represents an example of combined French and American influences on local architecture. It has also been accurately restored and furnished with examples of early Federal pieces, and is surrounded by 19th-century-style herb and scented gardens. The Linden House, located across the street from the Bolduc House, doubles as the museum's gallery/gift shop and the headquarters for the National Society of the Colonial Dames of America in the State of Missouri. The home is also listed on the National Register of Historic Places and has been designated a National Historic Landmark. Open daily.

Crown Ridge Tiger Sanctuary. 19620 Rte. B; (573) 883-9909; www.crown-ridge.com. Yep, there are tigers running around the hillsides of Ste. Genevieve. Luckily, they're enclosed within a custom-designed caging system to provide the healthiest and safest possible environment for the four tigers—including a Bengal and a white tiger—as well as the African black-maned lioness and Siberian tiger mix. All of the felines were rescued from abusive or neglectful situations, so they're living the high life these days. They have plenty of room to run and do what comes naturally for them, including jumping in one of their pools and "hunting" for food. Special feeding tours are offered that include a walking tour of the sanctuary, access to the observation deck, assisting in the preparation of the animals' diets, and the chance to participate in feeding the cats. Open Apr through Dec, but special tours can be scheduled during Jan, Feb, and Mar by calling (573) 330-7334.

Felix Vallé State Historic Site. Merchant and 2nd Streets; (573) 883-7102; www.mostate parks.com/park/felix-valle-house-state-historic-site. This state historic site includes several buildings that preserve and interpret different examples of the community's unique architecture and history. Built in 1818 as a mercantile store and residence for the original owner, the Felix Vallé House is made of native limestone. Its Federal-style architecture demonstrates the American influence that infiltrated the community during the decades following the Louisiana Purchase in 1803. The prominent local Vallé family bought the home in 1824, and it became the location of the Menard & Vallé trading firm as well as the residence of Felix and Odile Vallé. Today the home is furnished in the style of the 1830s. Across the street is the Dr. Benjamin Shaw House, built in 1819 as a store house and converted to a residence in 1837. Today the building is used for administrative offices and interpretive exhibits.

Ste. Genevieve's Wine Country. There's a rich wine-making history in Ste. Genevieve County, starting with some of the original French settlers in the early 1700s. The French began utilizing the calcium-rich limestone soil and temperate climate that are ideal for making wines, and they were joined by like-minded German immigrants in the mid-1800s. The Germans brought their own regional styles into the mix to further enrich the art of winemaking in southeastern Missouri, and many of the early pioneers' descendants continue to further the tradition today. With 8 wineries operating in the region, there's no shortage of places to relax and enjoy a glass of vino around here.

Cave Vineyard. 21124 Cave Rd.; (573) 543-5284; www.cavevineyard.com. Nestled in the rolling hills of Ste. Genevieve County, the winery took its name from the saltpeter cave on the property. The family-owned-and-operated winery includes 14 acres of grapes and the somewhat mysterious cave located about 200 yards from the tasting room. The cave doubles as an entertainment area, with seating year-round and live music during the winery's special events. Cave Vineyard produces 5 whites, including the award-winning Chardonel Off Dry and Traminette, and 3 reds. The vineyard's Cave Rock Red was awarded a silver medal in the Missouri State Wine Competition. Enjoy a glass or two and the view from the outdoor pavilion, or order a picnic basket in the tasting room and head off on your own. Open daily.

Charleville Vineyard, Winery & Microbrewery. 16937 Boyd Rd.; (573) 756-4537; www.charlevillevineyard.com. Go west young man—and woman—and enjoy the scenery and the liquid refreshment at Charleville. Located in the Western part of Ste. Genevieve County, the winery offers handcrafted wines and micro-brewed beers in a rustic country setting above the Saline Creek Valley. There are nearly a dozen wines to choose from, along with a variety of seasonal beers that are brewed on-site. Year-round beer options are the Half-Wit Wheat, Hoptimistic IPA, Tornado Alley Amber Ale, and Oatmeal Stout. Nibble on cheese and sausage in the tasting room, or pack your own picnic and take a hike on the nearby trails. A refurbished 1860s log cabin adjacent to the tasting room serves as a 2-room bed-and-breakfast for guests on weekends. Open Wed through Sun.

Chaumette Vineyards & Winery. 24345 Rte. WW; (573) 747-1000; www .chaumette.com. Established in 1990, Chaumette offers a lineup of award-winning wines that are available in the tasting room or at the on-site eatery called the Grapevine Grill. The winery produces more than a dozen wines from grape varieties such as Norton, Chardonel (a hybrid of Chardonnay), Traminette, Chambourcin, and Vignoles. Each year the boutique winery produces up to 6,000 cases of mostly dry wines, along with some semidry and semisweet styles as well as a vintage port and the occasional late-harvest Chardonel. There's also a gift shop, spa, and art gallery on-site, with live music during warm weather months. Open Thurs through Sun Feb, Mar, Nov, and Dec, and Sat and Sun in Jan. The winery is open Wed through Sun April 1 through October 31. Call for hours of operation.

Crown Valley Winery. 23589 Rte. WW; (573) 756-9463; www.crownvalleywinery .com. Great scenery, an abundance of wines to choose from, and an impressive array of handcrafted beers and distilled spirits—what's not to love? In addition to its widely acclaimed Nortons, Crown offers 12 reds, 10 whites, 4 fruit/rosés, and 5 sparkling wines, so there's something for every taste. They even brew their own soft drink—Fizzy Izzy Root Beer. The Bistro offers boxed lunches, sausages, cheeses, and an assortment of gourmet snacks as well as premium cigars such as Cohiba, Dunhill, and Arturo Fuente. Open daily.

Sainte Genevieve Winery. 245 Merchant St.; (573) 883-2800; www.saintegene vievewinery.com. Okay, so there aren't beautiful views or acres of vineyards here, but Ste. Genevieve's oldest winery still produces award-winning varietal wines and an array of fruit wines to enjoy. Located in a 5,000-square-foot, turn-of-the-20th-century home, the winery creates more than 20 handcrafted wines in small lots. The tasting room and their wine-related gift shop are located in the heart of Ste. Genevieve's National Historic District. Open daily.

Sand Creek Vineyard & Winery. 3578 Sand Creek Rd.; (573) 756-9999; www .sandcreekvineyard.com. Sand Creek is the newest member of the Ste. Genevieve wine family, opening their tasting room and large veranda in 2008. They produce 9 wines, including the late-harvest Chardonel, Plank Road Red, and Becky's Blush, one of their most popular varieties. Purchase some of the wine-friendly snacks like sausage, cheese, crackers, and chocolates, or quench your thirst with their selection of draft and bottled beers. Closed Tues.

Twin Oaks Vineyard & Winery. 6470 Rte. F; (573) 756-6500; www.twinoaks vineyard.com. The tasting room literally sits in the middle of the vineyard, so if you're looking to immerse yourself in wine country, this is the spot. Sit and sip on the patio when it's warm, or cozy up around the fireplace when it's not. Twin Oaks produces 2 semisweet varieties—Murphy's Settlement and Sweet Vignoles—along with 2 sweets, 2 dry whites, and 4 dry reds. An assortment of fresh meats, cheeses, crackers, fruits, and chocolates is also available for purchase, along with a few premium beers. Closed Mon and Tues.

Weingarten Vineyard. 12323 Rottler Ln.; (573) 883-2505; www.weingarten vineyard.com. Specializing in 2 Missouri wines—a Norton, which is a deep, dry red wine, and a semidry sweet white Vivant—Weingarten also produces a Chardonel and a Princess Sweet, along with a Weingarten microbrew. The 20,000-square-foot facility also features a deli offering sandwiches, pizzas, cheeses, pastries, and other desserts, and a gift shop with merchandise that includes wine and wine accessories along with home and garden decor, accent dishware, Archipelago body lotions and candles, and artisan crafts. Enjoy the view through the floor-to-ceiling windows of the tasting room or dine alfresco on one of the covered decks. Must be at least 18 to enter. Open Thurs through Sun.

where to shop

European Entitlements. 102 South Main St.; (314) 567-6760. Did somebody say they needed a French puppet? What about some Italian soaps? This shop stocks both of those items along with some of the other finer things in life, including European home decor, French jacquard linens, jewelry from Scotland, German porcelain, English cream ware, Swedish linens, and Irish wools.

Mosart–Missouri Art Studio. 146 S. 3rd St.; (573) 883-3493. Tucked in a garden behind the Southern Hotel is Mosart, a gallery devoted exclusively to juried artists of "The Best of Missouri Hands." It features handmade items such as blown glass, ASL pewter, and Jeff Walker pottery.

Only Child Original. 176 N. Main St.; (573) 883-9682. The shop owner is a local jewelry artist who also stocks "imported" art and craft items—ones not made by him—that he personally selects. Choose from the unique selection of paintings, hanging sculptures, and yard and garden art pieces.

Stained Glass Shop. 252 Merchant St.; (573) 883-5359. In addition to selling custom stained-glass and leaded windows, the shop features pottery, concrete benches, stepping stones, and assorted artwork. The owner doubles as an artist who also does stained-glass repairs and teaches beginning stained-glass classes.

Sweet Things of Sainte Genevieve. 242 Market St.; (573) 883-7990; www.sweetthings stegen.com. Here you'll find fine chocolates and confections as well as candies from back in the day, Jelly Belly products, rock candy, and more. They also offer a variety of gifts such as lotions and soaps by Canus Goat's Milk, gift cards, J. Devlin Glass Art, 1803 Candles, and Carson's Home Accents, including wind chimes, decorative plates, and home accessories.

where to eat

Anvil Restaurant & Saloon. 46 S. 3rd St.; (573) 883-7323. Located in a historic building that once housed a hardware store and gentlemen's saloon, circa 1855, the eatery offers home-style options and comfort food. Anvil is famous for their onion rings, burgers, and generous portions of dishes like the open-faced roast beef sandwich, German liver and sausage dumplings, fried chicken, and pork chops. $.

Big Field Cafe & Wine Bar. 10 S. 3rd St.; (573) 883-9600. Big Field is known for their chicken andouille gumbo, fresh salads, sandwiches, and Cajun-style specialties like their Po' boy Reuben (pastrami, fresh sauerkraut, Cajun remoulade, and melted cheese on French bread) and catfish chowder. Sunday brunch includes such additional menu items as French toast with pecans, homemade pimento cheese spread, and homemade sweet pickles. Open for breakfast and lunch daily, with dinner specials on Fri and Sat. $.

Crown Valley Brewery. 13326 Rte. F, (573) 756-9700; www.crownvalleybrewery.com. Guess what? Everything on the menu here goes really well with beer. Enjoy a sandwich, nachos, or pizza alongside handcrafted brews produced in Crown Valley's state-of-the-art 15-barrel microbrewery. Try the Farmhouse Lager, Wooden Nickel IPA, Worktruck Wheat, Big Bison Ale, or all four. You can buy a 3-ounce beer sample or do a half standard tasting with 4 samples or a standard tasting that has 8 samples. Non–beer drinkers can partake of Crown Valley Winery products or specialty cocktails, or enjoy one of the brewery's 3 ciders: Country Carriage, Strawberry, or Spiced Apple. $.

Old Brick House Restaurant. 90 S. 3rd St.; (573) 883-2724; www.theoldbrickhouse.com. The Old Brick House offers a casual atmosphere and a straightforward and affordable menu of traditional favorites like fried mushrooms, chicken, shrimp, and catfish; toasted ravioli; chopped steak; pork chops; and a few steaks. The restaurant is located in a historic building erected in 1780, and it's the oldest brick building west of the Mississippi River. $–$$.

The Restaurant St. Gemme Beauvais. 78 N. Main St.; (573) 883-5744; www.innst gemme.com. Classic French cuisine at reasonable prices in an elegant atmosphere complete with candlelight and white tablecloths in a historic 19th-century house, the Inn St. Gemme Beauvais. The menu is short—just 4 appetizers and 4 entrees—but it includes such delicacies like *saumon gigondas* (sautéed salmon topped with a butter-flavored red wine, shallots, orange juice, and balsamic vinegar) and *bifteck avec échalotes vinaigrette chaud* (6-ounce filet with a shallot, mustard, and sherry vinegar sauce). The restaurant's wine list includes a selection of award-winning vintages from area wineries. $$.

Sirros Family Restaurant. 261 Merchant St.; (573) 883-5749; www.sirrosrestaurant.com. Super-casual, kid-friendly restaurant with a simple menu of pizzas, salads, appetizers, burgers, "samiches," and pasta dishes. Healthy eaters need not apply. Desserts include funnel cake sticks and Triple Chocolate Tiger Cake (white cake centered between 2 layers of dark and white chocolate butter cream and chocolate cake, "striped" with a chocolate and white butter cream design). $.

Station 2 Cafe. 1 S. Main St.; (573) 883-3600; www.station2cafe.com. Serving lunch inside an old firehouse in Ste. Genevieve's historic district, the Station 2 Cafe features freshly made sandwiches and salads, homemade soups, quiches, coffee drinks, and a variety of pies and pastries. Try the Firehouse Turkey Wrap (turkey, cucumbers, and chipotle slaw) or the Mediterranean Sandwich (chicken breast, roasted red peppers, feta cheese, and pesto on ciabatta). $.

where to stay

Dr. Hertich's House. 99 N. Main St.; (800) 818-5744; www.drhertich.com. Owned and operated by the same people who run the Inn St. Gemme Beauvais across the street, Dr. Hertich's House was built in 1850 and was home to the town's first doctor. There are 4 triple-room guest suites with king-size beds available—the Ste. Genevieve Suite, Family Ties, Memories Suite, and Love Notes—and a smaller, single-room option called the Doctor's Room. Each of the suites has a large whirlpool tub and fireplace, and all of the rooms have a private bathroom. The suites are also equipped with a minifridge, microwave oven, and coffeemaker, and suite guests can opt to have breakfast served in their rooms. $$.

The Inn St. Gemme Beauvais. 78 N. Main St.; (573) 883-5744; www.stgem.com. Constructed in 1848 as a private residence, the Inn St. Gemme Beauvais is the oldest continuously operated B&B in the state and was awarded a Mobil Three-Star rating. All of the rooms have private baths, and guests are treated to a 4-course breakfast with a choice of 8 entrees. There are 6 rooms with queen-size beds and 1 room—the Governor's Chambers—with 2 double beds. The Forever Summer and the Carriage House both feature king-size beds and jetted tubs. Tea time takes places every day at 2 p.m. with teas, breads, and cookies, and the inn offers wine and hors d'oeuvres each evening. $$.

La Dee Marie. 403 Jefferson St.; (573) 883-2232; www.ladeemarie.com. The 1930s-era German brick home is located in the town's National Historic District and offers easy access to cafes, shops, and historic museums and landmarks. There are 3 guest rooms: the queen-size Zelphya's Suite; the smaller Dorothy's Dorm; and Clinton's Closet, which features 2 twin beds in a corner room. Snack on the steady supply of home-baked treats that are available in the dining room throughout the day. Early bird and "sleep in" breakfast times are available. $–$$.

Main Street Inn Bed & Breakfast. 221 N. Main St.; (573) 883-9199; www.mainstreetinn bb.com. The charming B&B is located in the old Meyer Hotel building, which was built in 1882. There are 7 guest rooms, including the 2-room Trope Ricard Suite and the William & Mary Baumstark Room with a 2-person whirlpool tub. Amenities include evening refreshments, triple-sheeted queen-size beds, real feather pillows (synthetic versions are also available), free wireless Internet service, and comfortable shared parlors and porches. $–$$.

The Southern Hotel. 146 S. 3rd St.; (573) 883-3493; www.southernhotelbb.com. The Southern Hotel has been in business as a B&B for more than 25 years and features elaborate—yet tasteful—decor and a large collection of antiques. Housed in a Federal-style brick building that was built in the 1790s as a private home, the B&B features 9 guest rooms, each with a private bath. Eight of the rooms have festively painted claw-foot bathtubs that reflect the decor or theme of the room. The rooms feature full- or queen-size beds, with the exception of the Irish- and English-themed Gentlemen's bedroom, which has a king-size bed. There is a peaceful garden on-site, along with the Mozart art gallery. $$.

day trip 03

south

>>> **going underground:**
bonne terre, mo

bonne terre, mo

Established in 1720 by the French, the settlement was dubbed *La Terre Bonne,* or "Good Earth," in reference to the wealth of minerals in the area. Part of the Viburnum District, the Bonne Terre area was once the largest lead belt in the world. The town was actually formed in 1864 when the St. Joseph Lead Company purchased more than 940 acres of land. During the 19th century the area was host to dozens of mining companies that plunged shafts into the ground looking for seams or drifts of the ore. This was largely a hit-or-miss operation, so numerous shafts were sunk to find the drifts. The Bonne Terre Mine remained in operation until 1962, when it was abandoned. Pumps that kept springwater out of the caves and shafts were turned off when the mining companies left, so the mine filled with billions of gallons of crystal-clear springwater. Today the mine welcomes 30,000 visitors each year who tour the mine on foot, in boats, and via underwater dives.

getting there

Located about an hour from downtown St. Louis, Bonne Terre is an easy 60 miles away. Take I-55 South for about 33 miles, then take exit 174B to merge onto US 67 South toward Bonne Terre/Farmington. Follow US 67 for 23 miles, then take the MO 47 exit toward Bonne Terre/Terre Du Las. Turn right onto MO 47 North and continue for a little more than 0.5 mile, then make a slight left onto Park Avenue.

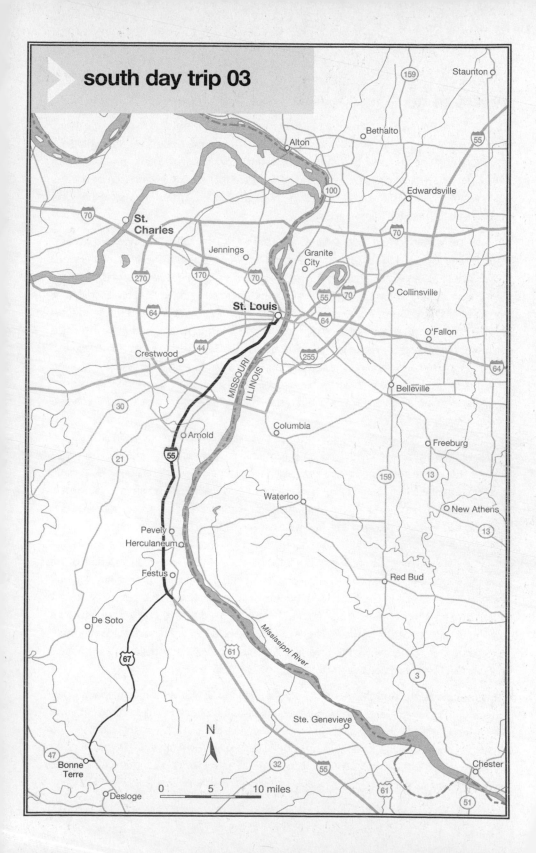

Staunton

159

Bethalto

55

Alton

100

Edwardsville

St. Charles

70

Jennings

Granite City

70

270

170

70

Collinsville

55

70

St. Louis

O'Fallon

64

64

255

Crestwood

44

Belleville

64

30

MISSOURI
ILLINOIS

Columbia

Freeburg

Arnold

55

159

13

21

Waterloo

New Athens

13

Pevely

Herculaneum

Red Bud

Festus

De Soto

61

Mississippi River

3

67

Ste. Genevieve

Bonne Terre

47

32

55

Chester

Desloge

61

51

N

0   5   10 miles

where to go

Bonne Terre Family Fun Center. 111 Old Orchard Rd.; (573) 358-5007; www.bonneterre familyfuncenter.com. The 15,000-square-foot facility is just the place to let the kids blow off steam and use up some of that always-present excess energy. There are 20 bowling lanes, go-karts—electric ones indoors and gas-powered for outside—water bumper boats, 27 holes of miniature golf, batting cages, more than 60 video games, and horseshoe and washers pits. Open Thurs through Sun.

Bonne Terre Mine/West End Diving. 39 Allen St.; (314) 731-5003; www.2dive.com. Bonne Terre Mine is a National Historic Site and the world's largest freshwater dive resort. It was one of the earliest lead mines in Missouri and was once the world's largest producer of lead ore. Mining at Bonne Terre began in 1860 and continued until 1962. Bigger than the town of Bonne Terre, the mine has five levels. The lower three levels combine to form a 17-mile-long underground lake. Water conditions remain constant, and there's visibility of more than 100 feet year-round. Named a National Geographic "Top 10 Adventure," the mine is ideal for diving and is the only inland scuba resort in the country. The location was filmed by legendary oceanographer Jacques Cousteau, and sights include massive architecture, oar carts, scaffolding, grating, staircases, pillars, slurry pipes, and the famed elevator shaft.

You can tour the facilities by foot, by boat, or by diving. Walking tours of the mine's top two layers are available, and they give an idea of what it was like to work in a lead mine during the 1800s. The hour-long guided tours along the old mule trail include huge pillar rooms, Calcite Falls, the Billion Gallon Lake, underground flower gardens, and abandoned mining tools and rail systems. On the boat tours, the Billion Gallon Lake water is so clear, you can see 100 feet deep at any given time, as well as enjoy a spectacular view of the largest parts of the mine. Of course, for certified divers, the only way to see the mine is underwater. Diving conditions remain constant, with a water temperature of 58°F year-round. Depths of the dive tours average between 40 and 60 feet, and 80-cubic-foot aluminum tanks are provided for each diver. Diving is conducted with groups of 10 divers and 2 dive guides on 24 different dive trails that are illuminated from above with more than 500,000 watts of stadium lighting. A number of dive packages are available, and all divers are required to be certified. Children under 18 are allowed to dive only if they are certified and have written parental permission. Dives are coordinated by West End Diving, (573) 358-2148.

St. Francois State Park. 8920 US 67 North; (573) 358-2173; www.mostateparks.com/ park/st-francois-state-park. Fish for smallmouth bass, catfish, and sunfish in the Big River along the park's southern boundary, or pilot a canoe or take a dip in this slow-moving Ozark stream that's ideal for families and novice canoeists. There are 4 hiking trails ranging in length from the 0.4-mile Missouri Trail to the 10.25-mile Pike Run Trail, which navigates through much of the undeveloped 2,200-acre Coonville Creek Wild Area. The Mooner's

Hollow Trail—named for the moonshiners that used to set up stills in the area—and Pike Run Trail provide access to the area, which is covered with woodlands of white oak, black oak, shagbark hickory, and dogwood. The park has more than 160 picnic sites scattered along the Big River and Coonville Creek, with 2 shelters available to rent for family reunions or other large gatherings. Playground equipment, horseshoe pits, and open ball fields are located near the shelters. Campers can access one of more than 100 basic and electric campsites, and the campground offers modern restrooms, hot showers, laundry facilities, and a dump station during the in-season (Apr through Oct). There's also a backpack camp for hikers along the Pike Run Trail. The campground is open and reservable year-round.

where to stay

Bonne Terre Depot B&B. 39 Allen St.; (888) 843-3483. The historic train depot is a 2.5-story frame building that features 4 guest rooms on the second floor and 3 suites in adjacent train cars. Originally built in 1909, the depot was the hallmark of the Mississippi River & Bonne Terre (MR&BT) railway and was owned by St. Joseph's Lead Company. $.

Cherokee Landing. 8344 Berry Rd.; (573) 358-2805; www.cherokeelanding.com. Open for camping on Fri and Sat, Cherokee Landing features primitive sites, sites with water and electricity, and 2 full hookup sites. A number of riverside campsites are available. Facilities include a shower house, restrooms, fire rings, picnic tables, and grills, and there's a common area with volleyball and horseshoes. Dogs are allowed in the camping areas as long as they're on a leash. Weekday camping and float trips are available by special arrangement. $.

day trip 04

south

>>> **cape town:**
cape girardeau, mo

cape girardeau, mo

Founded by an adventuresome French soldier named Jean D. Girardot in 1733, Cape Girardeau was originally established as a remote trading post in a region populated by more than 20 Native American tribes. Girardot chose a rock outcrop overlooking the Mississippi River as the site for his trading post, which became a popular spot for fur trappers and river travelers through the region. The early explorers of the rough and wild forested area soon christened the post "Cape Girardot." Today Cape Girardeau is a regional hub for education, commerce, and medical care in southern Missouri. The city is home to a population of 37,000 residents and to Southeast Missouri State University—or SEMO—which boasts an enrollment of about 11,000 students.

getting there

Cape Girardeau is a quick 2-hour drive from downtown St. Louis, located in what's known as the "Bootheel" region of the state. Follow I-55 South for about 108 miles and take exit 99 for I-55/US 61/MO 34 toward Cape Girardeau/Jackson. Turn left onto I-55 Business Loop South and follow it for approximately 4 miles, then make a left onto Broadway Street.

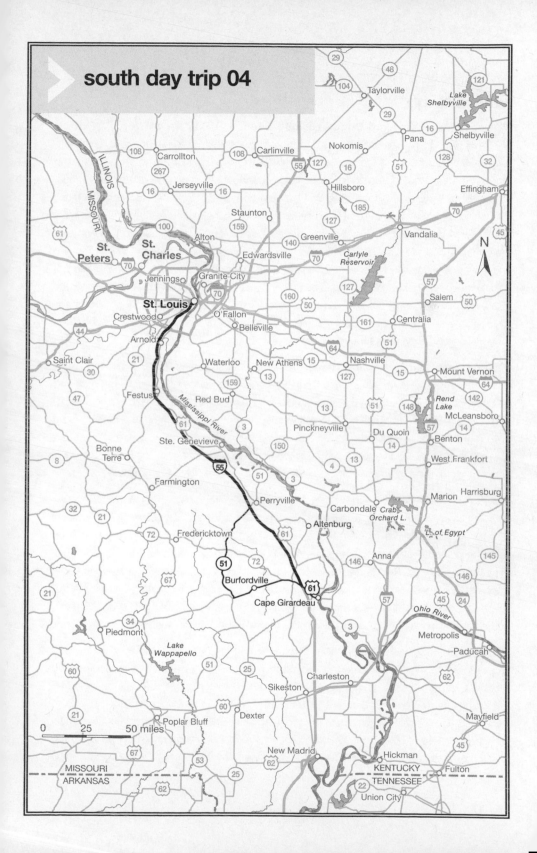

south day trip 04

where to go

Bollinger Mill & Covered Bridge Historic Sites. 113 Bollinger Mill Rd., Burfordville; (573) 243-4591; www.mostateparks.com/park/bollinger-mill-state-historic-site. The massive 4-story Bollinger Mill features exhibits about the evolution of milling in the 19th and early 20th centuries and demonstrations that show how stone-ground cornmeal is made. The restored mill, which is from the Civil War era and on the National Register of Historic Places, is an operating water-powered gristmill that contains examples of milling machinery like separators, scourers, roll stands, millstones, bolters, purifiers, bran dusters, conveyors, and chutes. The site also includes the Burfordville Covered Bridge, one of the four remaining covered bridges in Missouri, along with a shady picnic area, a 0.25-mile section of Whitewater River bank, and a historic cemetery that serves as the final resting place for the man who originally built the mill—George Frederick Bollinger—and members of his family. Special events are held throughout the year, including folk music concerts in June and Sept, and Halloween storytelling around a bonfire each Oct.

Cape Splash Family Aquatic Center. 1565 N. Kingshighway; (573) 339-6343; www.cityofcapegirardeau.org/Parks/Cape-Splash-Family-Waterpark.aspx. The water park has a 700-foot Lazy River, slides, a leisure pool, a spray pad for the kids, a bathhouse, changing facilities, and 23 Funbrellas offering shady spots to get out of the sun. There's also a 140-foot-long enclosed flume, a 177-foot open flume with a 25-foot tower, a 64-foot and 78-foot flume from an 11-foot tower, and a vortex/swirl pool. Cape Splash includes a pavilion/family changing room as well. Open Memorial Day weekend to Labor Day.

Discovery Playhouse: A Children's Museum. 502 Broadway; (573) 335-7529; www.discoveryplayhouse.org. This 7,500-square-foot educational playground of interactive exhibits is a great place to play and learn for kids 11 years old and younger. Hands-on exhibits include Grandma Ruth's Farm, Busy Bodies Fitness Park, Arts Zone, Sand Table, and Velcro Ball Fall. There's also a fire truck you can climb on, a bank that teaches about money, and a dental clinic and grocery store. Kids can splash around in the Secret Water Garden, and little ones (ages 4 and under) can experience the magic of Pollywog Pond in a kid-size fishing boat. The museum also hosts traveling exhibits and seasonal special events.

Fort D. 920 Fort St.; (573) 339-6300. Located in Fort D Park, this is the only fort remaining of four Civil War forts created to protect the city of Cape Girardeau from Confederate attack. Built at the beginning of the Civil War in the summer of 1861, it was designed by German-American engineers from St. Louis and constructed by Union soldiers of the 20th Illinois Infantry, Bissell's Engineers of the West, and local militia. The earthwork walls remain intact, and there is interpretive signage located throughout the grounds to help bring the fort's storied past to life. Admission is free, and the park is open to the public from dawn to dusk year-round.

Lazy L Safari Park. 2763 CR 618; (573) 243-7862; www.lazylsafari.com. This 15-acre family-owned-and-operated animal park offers visitors a chance to get up close and personal with a variety of species from A to Z, including alpacas, antelopes, aoudads, birds, camels, cavies, deer, donkeys, emus, goats, ibex, kangaroos, llamas, ostriches, porcupines, reptiles, rheas, tortoises, wallabies, and zebras. Visitors can walk the grounds at their own pace or visit the petting zoo area, where you can feed pygmy goats; visit baby animals in the nursery; check out the reptile aquariums; or see what emu eggs look like in the incubator. There's also a gift shop and picnic shelter on-site. The animals are part of the owners' ranch breeding program and alternative livestock business, which includes supplying animals for movies and commercial work as well as holiday nativity scenes and animal rides at fairs and special events. Open daily from Memorial Day to Labor Day and weekends only in Apr, May, Sept, and Oct. Closed Nov through Mar.

St. Louis Iron Mountain & Southern Railway. Intersection of Highways 61 and 25; (573) 243-1688; www.slimrr.com. Here's a unique way to spend a Saturday afternoon: Take a 2-hour train ride along the rails of southeast Missouri and hear stories about outlaws Jesse James and Bonnie and Clyde, hobo history, and the pioneering spirit of the Iron Mountain Railroad. The St. Louis Iron Mountain & Southern Railway is the only full-size passenger train in the region, so you can ride in a coach car pulled by the Pennsylvania Diesel #5898, built in 1950, and experience the passenger train era of days gone by. The company offers special dinner trains as well as themed excursions like the Spider Express Halloween Train, Rock 'n' Roll Express, Chocoholic—All Things Chocolate, and the Santa Express. Open May thru Dec.

Tower Rock Winery. 10769 Hwy. A, Altenburg; (573) 824-5479; www.towerrockwine .com. Located about a half hour outside of Cape Girardeau is Tower Rock Winery, a small winery tucked into the southeast Missouri countryside. The 3-acre vineyard produces the red wine grape Cynthiana as well as white wine grapes Seyval, Traminette, Vidal, and Vignoles. Tower Rock also sources choice grape varieties from neighboring vineyards to produce its award-winning dry and semidry handcrafted wines. A selection of sausages, cheeses, crackers, and other light snacks are available for purchase, along with beverages like sangria, steamed mulled wine, hot cider, sparkling grape juice, beer, and soft drinks. During their annual October Winestock celebration, the winery features free live music on weekend afternoons as well as expanded indoor seating, a heated veranda, and 2 fire pits. Open Thurs through Sun.

Trail of Tears State Park. 429 Moccasin Springs; (573) 290-5268; www.mostateparks .com/park/trail-tears-state-park. Trail of Tears State Park is a certified site on the Trail of Tears National Historic Trail. The visitor center features exhibits that tell the tale of the forced relocation of Cherokee Indian groups during the winter of 1838–39, as well as details about the recreational opportunities available in the park. There are 4 trails that range in length from the 0.5-mile Nature Trail to the 10-mile Peewah Trail, which is used by both hikers and equestrians. The Peewah is a moderately difficult trail that winds through the 1,300-acre Indian Creek Wild Area and is one of the most remote parts of the park. It features hardwood forests of white oak, black oak, tulip poplar, and hickory. Anglers can fish for catfish, perch, and carp in the Mississippi River or cast a line for bass, bluegill, and catfish in the stocked 20-acre Lake Boutin. Swimming, boating, and canoeing are also permitted. The park also features a number of shaded picnic sites, hiking and horse trails, and the chance to spot migratory waterfowl, white-tailed deer, turkeys, hawks, and foxes. Large trees on the bluffs and cliffs along the river are popular winter roosting sites for bald eagles.

Basic campsites can be found in the heavily wooded area of the park, while campsites with electricity and sewer hookups are available near the river. Campground facilities include modern restrooms, laundry facilities, hot showers, and a dump station. For backpackers, a primitive camping area borders a loop of the Peewah Trail. The Mississippi River Campground, located near an active railroad, is open and reservable year-round, while Lake Boutin's campground is only open May through Oct.

where to shop

Annie Laurie's Antiques. 536 Broadway St.; (573) 339-1301; www.capeantiqueshop .com. Housed in the former Brinkopf-Howell Funeral Home, this vintage clothing store also offers a smattering of unique furniture, collectibles, primitives, and other fun stuff. The friendly, helpful staff knows their inventory, so you don't have to dig too much—unless you want to! Featured as "a definite stop" in *Southern Living* magazine's editors' list of southern antiques shops. Open daily.

Lazy L Gift Shop. 2763 CR 618; (573) 243-7862; www.lazylsafari.com. Located on the grounds of the Lazy L Safari Park, the critter-centric gift shop features souvenir mugs, T-shirts, hats, key chains, stickers, toys, and puzzles as well as handcrafted items, animal jewelry, stuffed animals, and animal-print purses. Some of the shop's more unique—and "homemade"—items include deer antlers, peacock feathers, ostrich eggs, and porcupine quills.

The Painted Wren Art Gallery. 5 N. Main St.; (573) 579-1000. This 2,800-square-foot gallery displays works by various artists, including jewelry, woodworks, paintings, pastels, drawings, photographs, and books. The gallery also features ceramics, digital nature images, children's coloring books, art prints and note cards, and personalized glass-inlaid concrete stepping stones. Open Thurs and Sat 1 to 6 p.m. and Fri 1 to 8 p.m.

Somewhere in Time. 108 N. Main St.; (573) 335-9995; www.shopsomewhereintime antiques.com. Somewhere in Time specializes in 19th- to mid-20th-century vintage and antique items including paper goods; costume jewelry; vintage clothing, hats, and purses; and home decor, china, and dishes. There's also a selection of "mantiques," like the collection of antique fishing lures, bolo ties, and old-school gadgets. The store is laid out with several vignettes that showcase different eras and interests. Open daily.

West Park Mall. 3049 William St.; (573) 339-1333; www.shopwestpark.com. Major shopping mall with big-name retailers like Aeropostale, Macy's, Old Navy, Radio Shack, Victoria's Secret, JCPenney, rue21, Gymboree, and Hollister. Open daily.

where to eat

Della Italia Ristorante. 20 N. Spanish St.; (573) 332-7800; www.bellaitaliacape.com. A casually upscale Italian eatery serving traditional soups, salads, pizzas, and pasta dishes for lunch and dinner. Try the Pasta Leonardo (grilled chicken, Italian sausage, Roma tomatoes, artichokes, and penne pasta topped with marinara and mozzarella), Seafood Cannelloni (cannelloni shells stuffed with shrimp, scallops, and lobster and topped with Alfredo sauce), or Ravioli Formaggi (cheese ravioli with broccoli, zucchini, and Roma tomatoes in a tomato cream sauce). $$.

Buckner Brewing & Ragsdales Pub. 132 N. Main St.; (573) 334-4677; www.buckner brewing.com. Ragsdales Pub is located directly below Buckner Brewing, right on the river. The pub features all of the locally brewed Buckner microbrews along with a full bar and a menu of foods that go great with beer. In addition to seasonal brews, the beer menu highlights a variety of unfiltered selections like Clyde's Ale, River Street Honey Wheat, and Pilot House Porter. Non-liquid specialties include Ozark Mountain Fried Pickles, Beer Cheese Soup (creamy three-cheese soup made with their handcrafted Amber Ale), Chipotle Barbecue Chicken Pizza (hickory-grilled chicken breast, bacon, tangy smoky pepper barbecue sauce, red onion, and green peppers with melted mozzarella, provolone, and Parmesan cheeses), the Hickory Grilled Soy Burger for the vegetarians, and Bourbon Street Chicken (Jamaican jerk and Cajun seasoned chicken served with a chipotle-lime dijonaise). $–$$.

My Daddy's Cheesecake. 265 S. Broadview St.; (573) 335-6660; www.mydaddys cheesecake.com. The regional chain got its start in Cape Girardeau, and the casual eatery serves up an array of breakfast items like fresh-baked biscuit, sourdough, and croissant sandwiches; omelets; biscuits and gravy; and fruit parfaits. For lunch and dinner the menu offers soups, salads, sandwiches, and wraps, and desserts include muffins, cookies, and, of course, cheesecake. Flavors range from the Mississippi Mud (creamy dark chocolate cheesecake smothered with dark chocolate topping and drizzled with white chocolate) to the Scarlet O'Hara (Oreo crust filled with strawberries and raspberries swirled into the cheesecake, finished with white chocolate curls) and the N'Orleans Praline (cheesecake topped with caramel and a layer of pecans). $.

where to stay

Bellevue B&B. 312 Bellevue St.; (573) 335-3302; www.bellevuebandb.net. The restored 1891 Queen Anne Victorian home is located in the heart of historic Old Town Cape. Three of the 4 guest rooms have queen-size beds, with the Girardot room being the only one with a king-size bed. Amenities include Egyptian cotton towels and bed linens, flat-screen LED televisions, DVD players and DVDs, CD players and CDs, and in-room Wi-Fi. Three-course breakfasts are served, featuring delicacies such as fresh spinach quiche with roasted tomato and sage, pumpkin-maple coffee cake, and cheese and cherry turnovers with port cherry preserves. $$.

Neumeyer's Bed & Breakfast. 25 S. Lorimier St.; (573) 335-0449. The B&B is located within a Craftsman-style bungalow that was built in 1910. There is a 2-room suite with 2 baths and another individual room available for guests. Both rooms have queen-size beds and modern private bathrooms. Guests enjoy a hearty breakfast of egg casseroles, waffles, and other dishes, along with fresh-baked breads and coffee each morning. $.

day trip 05

south

throw me something, mister!:
sikeston, mo

sikeston, mo

Geographically situated just north of the Missouri "Bootheel," Sikeston is the halfway point between St. Louis and Memphis, Tennessee. Founded in 1860 and named for the city's founder, John Sikes, the sleepy town is home to a little more than 16,000 residents and is known for its outlet mall and a home-style restaurant that tosses dinner rolls across the dining room.

getting there

Sikeston is located just 149 miles south of St. Louis. Head south on I-55 for 27 miles, then take exit 66B and merge onto US 60 West toward Dexter/Poplar Bluff for a little more than 3 miles. Take the ramp to US 61 North and turn onto US 61 North, following it for 1.6 miles. Make a left on E. Malone Avenue/US 60 Business.

where to go

Beggs Family Farm. 2319 Hwy. U; (573) 471-3879; www.beggsfamilyfarm.com. This family-run farm is a real working farm that's been in business since 1895. The Beggs family offers seasonal events like the Fall Harvest Festival, which takes place every Oct. Activities include exploring The MAZE cornfield maze and the Miner Max maze, wagon rides, feeding the goats and interacting with the other farm animals, and the chance to pick your own

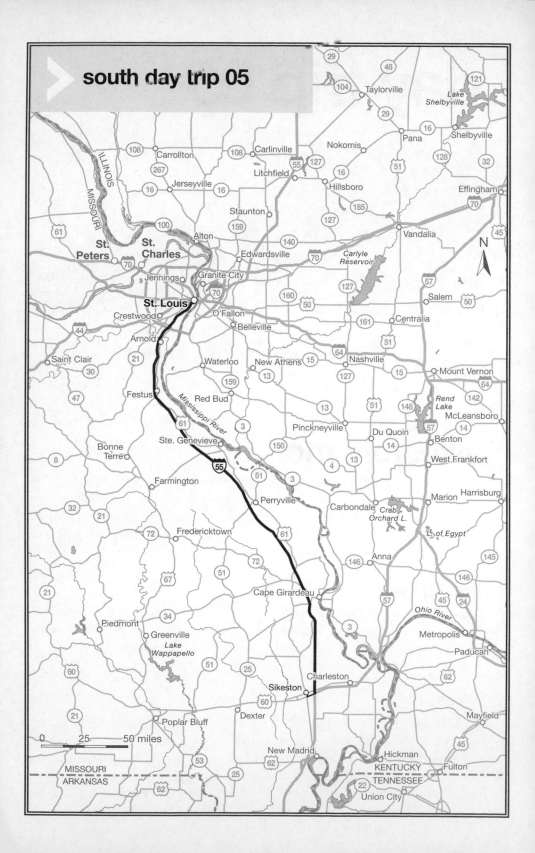

pumpkin. During the summer months, visitors can pick their own watermelons, enjoy a lively puppet show, play some Moonlight Barnyard Golf, and watch pig races.

Blodgett's Paintball & Fun Factory. 3921 Hwy. H; (573) 471-9197; www.blodgettpaint ball.com. This family-friendly factory of fun offers an intense outdoor paintball course as well as laser tag games, indoor kiddie carnival rides, an arcade, and a Softplay area for the small fry. There's also a snack bar on-site that sells pizzas and sodas. No alcohol served or allowed.

The Sikeston Depot–Cultural Center & Museum. 116 W. Malone Ave.; (573) 481-9967; www.sikestondepotmuseum.com. Sikeston's renovated train depot was originally built in 1916 next to the busiest tracks in southeast Missouri. Listed on the National Register of Historic Places, the depot contains a museum that features permanent and rotating exhibits illustrative of the area's culture, as well as a gallery with changing displays by local artists in a variety of mediums. The Upper Gallery houses the museum's permanent exhibit about the Mississippian Indian tribe and displays detailing the area's history in the cotton industry. The Sikeston Room shows the town's growth through artifacts, films, and photos, while the Main Gallery displays include items referencing the history of Parks Air Base and the invention of the mechanical horse. There's also a cultural center that displays traveling exhibits from regional and national museums. Admission is free. Closed Mon.

Southeast Missouri Agricultural Museum. 521 CR 532; (573) 471-3945. The museum features more than 6,000 pieces of antique farm equipment and showcases the region's agricultural heritage. Many of the items are from the 19th century and include tractors, combines, wagons, and other representative tools. The complex also contains historic outer buildings, including 2 Missouri log cabins built in the 1880s, a wooden railroad caboose, post office, schoolhouse, newspaper office, bank, and a reconstructed service station from the 1920s. Open year-round. Closed Sun.

where to shop

Granny's Antiques. 519 CR 532; (573) 471-9241. Located adjacent to the Southeast Missouri Agricultural Museum, Granny's Antiques offers a different take on local history. As the owner says, the 5,000-square-foot store includes "a little bit of a lot of different things." From primitives and classic furniture to mid-20th-century knickknacks and decor, the shop is a great place to hunt for buried treasure. The owner lives "up the hill" from the store, so if you happen to come by and it's not open, just give her a call on the cell phone number listed here and she'll "run down and let you in." Granny's is "almost always" closed on Sun.

Sikeston Factory Outlet Stores. 100 Outlet Dr.; (573) 472-2222; www.sikestonoutlet .com. One of the more popular outlet malls in the region, the mall is conveniently located along I-55 and has such stores as Carter's Childrenswear, Dress Barn, Bass Company

Store, Famous Footwear Outlet, rue21, L'Eggs/Bali/Hanes, Bon Worth, and Kitchen Collection, among others. Open daily except for major holidays.

where to eat

Dexter Bar-B-Que. 124 N. Main St.; (573) 471-6676; www.dexterbbq.com. Dexter's is a small regional restaurant chain that specializes in hickory-smoked pork and beef brisket barbecue for lunch and dinner. In addition to the usual lineup of dry-rubbed barbecue ribs, chicken, and turkey, the menu includes burgers and side dishes like coleslaw, baked beans, potato salad, and fries, with cobbler for dessert. $–$$.

Jay's Krispy Fried Chicken. 218 N. Main St.; (573) 471-8472. Known for their fried chicken and hearty Southern-style breakfasts—the biscuits and gravy receive high marks—Jay's offers quick, friendly service and inexpensive eats. It's a "must-eat" spot if you're a fan of chicken livers or gizzards—both are coated in the same lightly seasoned breading as the chicken and are big hits with fans of those particular parts of the bird. Jay's also offers a lunch buffet on weekdays and on Sun. $.

Lambert's. 2305 E. Malone Ave.; (573) 471-4261; www.throwedrolls.com. Lambert's has been a southeastern Missouri favorite since 1942. You'll see their billboards touting themselves as the "Home of the Throwed Rolls" along your drive through the region. The menu features Southern-style staples like fried shrimp, catfish, pork chops, hog jowls, and chicken gizzards along with chicken and dumplings, meat loaf, ribs, salads, and sandwiches. But no matter what you order, you're eligible for the free "pass arounds," tasty foodstuffs toted around by servers in large pots while you wait for your meal—they range from fried potatoes and onions and black-eyed peas to macaroni and tomatoes and fried okra. The servers are the ones who throw the hot rolls to you as well—oversize yeasty missiles that go great with sorghum and butter. No credit cards accepted, but they will take a check. $–$$.

Patrick's Deli-Que. 1203 E. Malone Ave.; (573) 475-9919. Located at the Sikeston Factory Outlet Mall, Patrick's offers sustenance for the shopper on the go. Choose from an array of deli sandwiches, soups, salads, large stuffed baked potatoes, and barbecue specialties. When it's cool outside, take advantage of the cozy fireplace and the free Wi-Fi to continue your shopping experience online while you eat. Open for lunch and dinner Tues through Sat and for lunch only on Sun. $.

southwest

day trip 01

southwest

historic route 66:
eureka, mo; pacific, mo;
gray summit, mo

route 66

All of these small towns along historic Route 66 are located within a few miles of each other along I-44, the modern-day equivalent of the Mother Road. Each offers a unique experience or attraction along the way, much like it was during the heyday of "The Main Street of America," when families packed the kids in the station wagon and "motored west" in search of adventure.

In 1926 Route 66 was designated as a federal highway, and it spanned some of the most remote country in the US between Chicago and Los Angeles. The road still occupies a special place in American popular culture and history, representing American mobility, independence, and the search for new experiences. Route 66 became one of the greatest migration routes in our country's history and was labeled the "Mother Road" by author John Steinbeck.

Today the route remains lined with miles of mostly rural landscape, but there are still a number of unique attractions and diversions along the way. Driving this stretch of Route 66 is more about the journey than any one destination. From the converted old 1935 roadhouse in Route 66 State Park to the remaining icons and signage throughout the Missouri portion of the famed highway's former course, the area is dotted with entertaining options. As you pass through Pacific, you'll see the old Pacific 66 Liquor sign that has been restored as a Route 66 sign, along with the Red Cedar Inn, built in 1943. Driving through Villa Ridge,

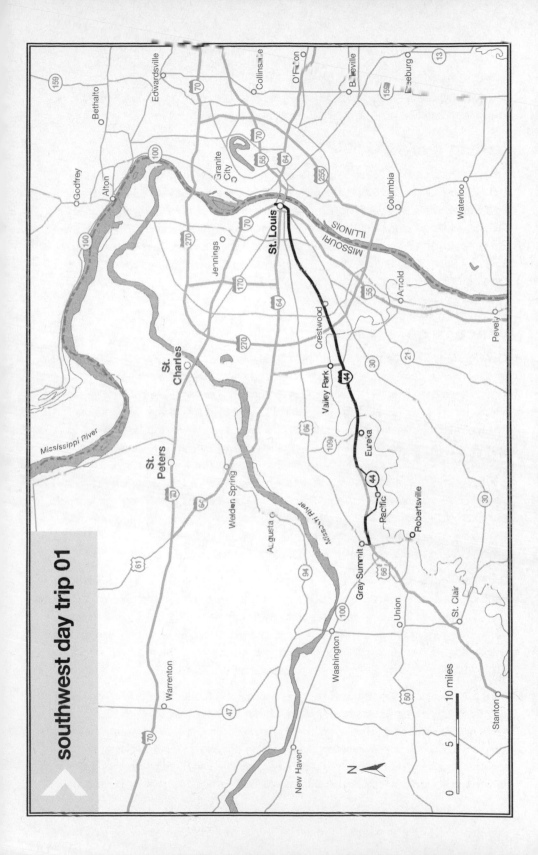

southwest day trip 01

you'll see the Sunset Motel, and Cuba features Mother Road icons such as the Wagon Wheel Motel and the Old Phillips 66 Service Station, both of which were built in the 1930s.

getting there

Eureka is situated about 25 miles from downtown St. Louis via I-44 West. Take exit 264 for MO 109 South, then turn left onto MO 109 South for a little more than 0.5 mile and make a right onto S. Central Avenue. Pacific is less than 10 miles from Eureka. Take I-44 West/US 50 West for 7.5 miles to exit 257 for I-44 Business toward Pacific, then turn left on Viaduct Street. Make the first left onto W. Osage Street and follow it for about a mile, then turn right on N. 1st Street. Gray Summit is only 5 miles away, so travel along I-44 West/US 50 West for about 3.5 miles and take exit 253 for I-44 Business/MO 100 East toward Gray Summit, then make a right onto MO 100 East.

where to go

Endangered Wolf Center. 6750 Tyson Valley Rd., Eureka; (636) 938-5900; www .endangeredwolfcenter.org. Located on 63 wooded acres within Washington University's Tyson Research Center, the Endangered Wolf Center is a temporary home for a variety of wolves and other canids awaiting their opportunity to become candidates for reintroduction into their native habitats. The center, which coordinates efforts with the US Fish & Wildlife Service, has been responsible for successful managed breeding and reintroduction programs for such species as the Mexican gray wolf and the red wolf. Visitors can take a 1-hour guided walking tour of the wolf enclosures for a look at some of the world's most endangered canids, like the maned wolf from South America, the African wild dog from central/south Africa, the Mexican gray wolf, and the swift fox, one of the world's smallest canids. The center encourages you to bring cameras and binoculars for the ultimate up-close and personal view. Reservations are required for tours, so be sure to call ahead.

Greensfelder Park. 4515 Hencken Rd., Eureka; (314) 615-4386. Located just north of Six Flags St. Louis, Greensfelder is a 1,600-acre park filled with shady trails and spectacular views. In addition to 4 regular campsites, 6 family campsites, and 18 equestrian campsites, there are 6 reservable picnic shelters, a nature learning center, a playground, and a TRIM orienteering course. Eight walking and biking trails are waiting to be explored, ranging in length from the Overlook Trail's 0.8 mile to the Green Rock Trail's 14.5.

Purina Farms. 200 Checkerboard Dr., Gray Summit; (314) 982-3232; www.purina.com/purina-farms/purinafarms.aspx. Located on more than 300 acres of rolling hills in Gray Summit, Purina Farms is an animal lover's dream. In addition to a full-size barn containing domestic farm animals, the attraction offers a variety of informative pet displays, hands-on activities, animal demonstrations, and holiday-themed events. There are petting areas, hayloft tunnels, and milking demonstrations, as well as performances by herding dogs demonstrating their expertise at corralling farm animals. At the Visitor's Center kids can play in the hayloft, milk a cow, take a tractor-drawn wagon ride, and watch canine performances of flying disc, diving dog, and agility. Purina Farms features the Incredible Dog Arena, the Pet Center with dogs and cats, an indoor theater, concession and hospitality areas, an informational center, and a gift shop that stocks unique gift and souvenir merchandise as well as items with a specific breed theme. The newly opened Purina Event Center is a state-of-the-art indoor facility that hosts a variety of canine activities from conformation shows to performance events like obedience, agility, rally, and flyball. Open seasonally mid-March through mid-November. Closed all major holidays. Call before you go because reservations are required.

Robertsville State Park. 900 State Park Dr., Robertsville; (636) 257-3788; www.mostate parks.com/park/robertsville-state-park. Fishing and camping are the main activities available at Robertsville State Park. Bounded by the spring-fed Meramec River on the northern and western sides and Calvey Creek on the east, anglers can try their luck catching smallmouth bass, bluegill, and crappie. Boaters, canoeists, and those in search of a good picnic spot are also drawn to the park. There's a boat-launching area with a large, easily accessible parking lot for vehicles and boat trailers, along with plenty of shady picnic sites that offer excellent views of the river and scenic bluffs. Because of its location between the river and the creek, Robertsville attracts an array of waterfowl like great blue herons, green herons, and a variety of ducks. There's only one short trail in the park—less than a mile long—but it meanders through the hardwood forest of black oak, northern red oak, white oak, and shagbark hickory trees. Campers can utilize 12 basic and 15 electric campsites that include a sanitary dump station, modern restrooms, showers, laundry facilities, and water hydrants. Many of the sites are reservable, and fees for first-come, first-served campers are collected at the campsite daily after 3 p.m. Firewood is also available for purchase from the fee collector. The campground is open Mar through Nov, but the showers, laundry, and dump station are only available during the in-season, which is Apr through Oct.

Route 66 State Park. I-44 at Lewis Rd., exit 266, Eureka; (636) 938-7198; www.mostate parks.com/route66.htm. Located along the historic Mother Road, Route 66 State Park showcases the history and mystique of the highway that has been called "The Main Street of America." The fabled highway has come to represent American mobility, independence, and the spirit of adventure. Located along the original Route 66 corridor, the 419-acre park is a boon to visitors who want to enjoy nature and see interesting historical displays showcasing Route 66. Bridgehead Inn, a 1935 roadhouse, serves as the park's visitor center and houses a collection of artifacts from the Mother Road. Displays include examples of the unique architecture of the buildings and towns along Missouri roadways from the 1930s to the 1960s and samples of the souvenirs that were once sold along the route. There's also a modern-day gift shop offering Route 66 items that's open daily from Mar through Nov. The park itself features level walking, bicycling, and equestrian trails and offers road-weary travelers a place to picnic, bird-watch, stretch their legs, or just enjoy nature. It is populated with more than 40 types of birds among the oak, hickory, river birch, cottonwood, and pine trees, along with a diverse array of plants, deer, and wild turkeys.

Six Flags St. Louis. I-44, exit 261, Eureka; (636) 938-4800; www.sixflags.com. Six Flags has plenty of ways to make even the biggest thrill-seekers scream with delight. There are heart-pumping options like Tony Hawk's Big Spin, the Evel Knievel roller coaster, the Boss wooden roller coaster, Mr. Freeze, Batman the Ride looping super coaster, the Screamin' Eagle, Superman Tower of Power, and the Ninja steel coaster. In 2011 Six Flags St. Louis added a real screamer to its long list of thrill rides with SkyScreamer, a tower ride that guarantees to take your breath away. The ride, which holds 32 guests at a time, features 2 open-air swings that climb to the top of the SkyScreamer tower while spinning around and around. Brave souls who ride the new thrill ride will end up more than 230 feet into the air as they are swung around in a 98-foot circle at speeds of more than 40 mph.

Visitors can cool off at Thunder River's 7 acres of whitewater rapids, at Hurricane Harbor water park, or on the Tidal Wave ride as a 20-person boat drops over a 50-foot waterfall into 300,000 gallons of water. The Wahoo Racer is a 6-lane waterslide that propels riders along 262 feet of steep drops and rolls. There's also the Colossus Ferris wheel, the Log Flume, Highland Fling, Rush Street Flyer, River King Mine Train, Tom's Twister, the Joker, Dragon's Wing, the Rock Wall Climb, Speed O'Drome Go-Karts, and Shazam!—to name just a few. The popular Scooby-Doo! Ghostblasters ride takes thrill-seekers through a scary swamp adventure.

During the summer months, this Six Flags location hosts a number of live pop and country music concerts at the Old Glory Amphitheater located on-site. Tickets to the shows are an additional fee to the park admission price. After the sun sets, Six Flags lights up the night with Glow in the Park, a nighttime parade featuring 6 custom-designed floats, mobile units, and 65 light-adorned drummers, puppeteers, singers, dancers, and stilt walkers. In addition to all of the rides and activities, there are plenty of family entertainment options such as Miss Kitty's Saloon Revue, the Palace Theater, the Empire Theater, and "Merlin's Magic Academy" at Sound Stage #2.

World Bird Sanctuary. 125 Bald Eagle Ridge Rd., Valley Park; (636) 225-4390; www .worldbirdsanctuary.org. The World Bird Sanctuary is a bird facility like no other in the world. Visitors are able to view eagles, owls, hawks, falcons, vultures, parrots, and other creatures in a majestic park setting. There's a collection of large outdoor avian exhibits that house a variety of non-releasable birds of various species, along with live raptor exhibits filled with bald eagles, red-tailed hawks, peregrine falcons, and Eurasian eagle owls. Picnic pavilions are surrounded by bird feeders, bird baths, and butterfly gardens designed to attract our feathered friends, and the 0.5-mile-long Hickory Trail is ideal for wildlife watching. The sanctuary has a variety of educational programs, seasonal shows, nature trails, and displays that help visitors understand the relationship between birds, their environment, and humans.

Naturalists are on hand to discuss the birds' role in the world and the problems they face, with many of the "teacher" birds on display for up-close viewing. Free entry and parking. Open daily.

where to shop

Wallach House Home Furnishings, Antiques & Gifts. 510 West Ave., Eureka; (636) 938-6633; www.wallachhouse.com. Wallach House literally has something for everyone among its 3 levels of home furnishings, gifts, apparel, jewelry, accessories, and antiques. There are 9 shops within Wallach House, including the Faded Rosé, offering Missouri wines, gourmet foods, and wine-related accessories; Gerard's Antiques, specializing in wooden German figures and M. I. Hummel figurines; and Wallach House Antiques, which features antique wooden furniture and jewelry. Open daily.

Winding Brook Estate Lavender Shoppe. 3 Winding Brook Estate Dr., Eureka. (636) 575-5672; www.windingbrookestate.com. Housed in a 100-year-old farmhouse, the shop features products such as Winding Brook Estate all-natural lavender bath and body products, wedding and baby gifts, Vietri Italian glass and ceramics, and an assortment of award-winning jams and jellies, mustards, vinegars, tapenades, salad dressings, chocolates, and cheese ball, dip, and soup mixes. You can also pick up some unique home decor items and things for the kitchen ranging from aprons and culinary spices to furniture, lavender pillows, and linens, along with numerous wreaths and floral arrangements made with lavender, dried botanicals, and silks. The shop is closed during Jan.

where to eat

Joe Boccardi's Ristorante. 128 Boccardi Ln., Eureka, (636) 938-6100; www.joeboccardis .com. Hailing from St. Louis's highly esteemed Italian neighborhood known as "The Hill," Joe Boccardi's is known for its St. Louis–style pizza but the menu also includes a variety of other tasty options. Choose from an assortment of salads, sandwiches, pasta dishes, and entrees including seafood, chicken, or steak. Try some of the house favorites like the Spinach Artichoke Toasted Cannelloni or specialty pizzas like the meaty Pizza Alla Raffaele (hamburger, pepperoni, sausage, bacon, and Canadian bacon) and the Joe's Special Original (hamburger, mushrooms, pepperoni, onions, and green peppers). $–$$.

The Original Fried Pie Shop. 1 W. 5th St., Eureka; (636) 587-7743; www.theoriginalfried pieshop.com. Using a recipe dating back to the late 1890s, the shop sells big hot, fresh fried pies with a variety of ingredients. They break the menu into 3 sections—fruit, cream, and meat—although you can mix and match the fruit and cream options to create your own. The breakfast pies include sausage, egg and cheese, or bacon, egg, and cheese, while the lunch/dinner options include homemade pies filled with chicken or beef and vegetables, or spinach and mushrooms, as well as Tex Mex and pizza-style pies. $.

Super Smokers Bar-B-Que. 601 Stockell Dr., Eureka. (636) 938 9742; www.super smokers.com. The menu includes the usual suspects, like ribs, barbecue sandwich plates, and smoked turkey and chicken, as well as the world's heartiest appetizer, barbecue nachos. Super Smokers is a regular top 10 finisher in the annual Memphis in May International Barbecue Festival. $$.

where to stay

Yogi Bear's Jellystone Resort at Six Flags. 5300 Fox Creek Rd., Eureka; (800) 861-3020; www.eurekajellystone.com. Jellystone Resort has premium camping facilities less than 0.5 mile from the Six Flags St. Louis amusement park. The 35-acre facility offers paved roads, full or water/electric hookups, shaded level sites, 50-amp electric, pull-throughs, clean restrooms and hot showers, propane, a dump station, a Laundromat, and fire rings and picnic tables at each site. There are computer modem hookups at the nearby Ranger Station and a fully stocked camp store complete with groceries, camping and RV supplies, firewood, ice, and souvenirs. Jellystone also offers tent/pop-up sites with the aforementioned amenities or deluxe (water/electric) or primitive sites. Plus you can meet Yogi Bear "in person" as well as swim in the pool, play minigolf or arcade games, watch movies, or take a train ride. If you and the kids aren't into roughing it, rent one of the climate-controlled cottages. Each one sleeps 6 and features 2 bedrooms, a private bath, a covered dining porch, an outdoor grill, and a fire pit for everybody's favorite camping activity—roasting marshmallows. The kitchen is fully equipped with dishes and cookware, and bed linens and towels are also provided and the cottages offer free high-speed Internet access and satellite TV. $.

day trip 02

southwest

feeling adventurous:
sullivan, mo

sullivan, mo

Sullivan is a short, 65-mile trek southwest of St. Louis along the old San Francisco Railroad and Route 66 corridor. Nicknamed the "Gateway to the Ozarks," the area was founded in the early 1800s by Stephen Sullivan, a member of Daniel Boone's traveling party, on a return trip from Kentucky. Sullivan and his wife were recruited by the famed frontiersman who told Kentuckians about the abundant land surrounding the Meramec River. The railroad reached the small settlement in 1858, and the town was laid out and named Sullivan by the railroad company. Today the town boasts 6,700 residents who enjoy life in the scenic, quiet, and largely rural community.

getting there

From St. Louis, follow I-44 West signs for I-44 West/Tulsa/12th Street/Gravois Avenue for 64 miles and take exit 226 for MO 185 South toward Sullivan. Turn left onto MO 185 South, then take the second right onto E. Springfield Road and turn left onto N. Church Street. Turn right at the second cross street onto W. Vine Street, then make a slight right onto W. Washington Street.

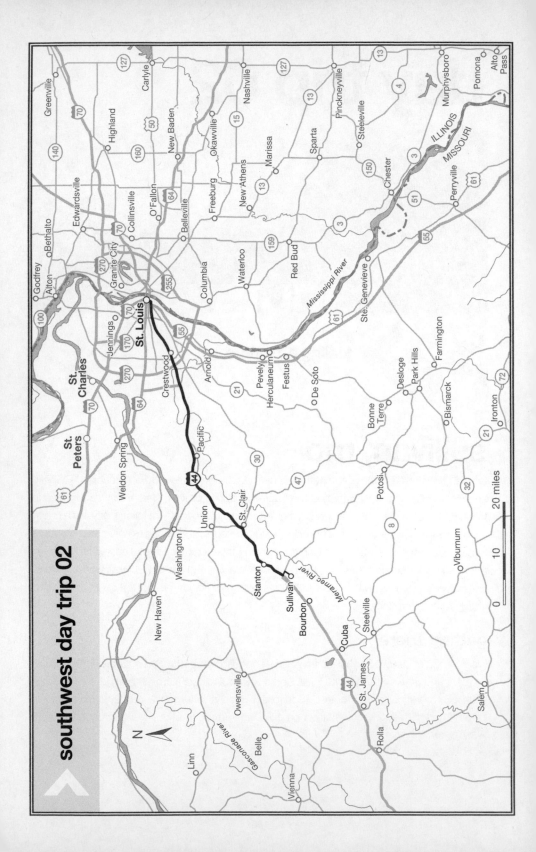

southwest day trip 02

where to go

Caveman Zipline at Meramec Caverns. 1135 Hwy. W, Stanton; (573) 468-3166; www
.cavemanzipline.com. Fly through the air with the greatest of ease at Meramec Caverns in
nearby Stanton—America's Cave has a fun and exciting attraction that adrenaline junkies
will love. The Caveman Zipline offers a chance to "fly" through treetop canopies and the
natural cave bluffs of the Meramec at speeds up to 50 mph. Zips vary from 250 to 1,250
feet during the 90-minute-long guided tours, and you'll be cruising at heights of 54 to 82
feet above the ground. The ride through the trees includes walks on 3 swinging sky-bridges
and 4 zip rides. Available for (almost) all ages, the tours include historical information pertain-
ing to the area, plus all of the necessary safety equipment and information.

Jesse James Wax Museum. I-44, exit 230, Stanton; (573) 927-5233; www.jessejames
waxmuseum.com. Learn the true story about the notorious outlaw Jesse James with a stop
at the Jesse James Wax Museum. The tour includes a look at the world's only live film foot-
age of Jesse James along with photos, displays, lifelike wax figures, paperwork including
witnesses' affidavits, antiques, and a collection of vintage firearms and personal posses-
sions belonging to James and his gang.

Meramec Caverns. I-44, exit 230, Stanton; (800) 676-6105; www.americascave.com.
Nicknamed "America's Cave," Meramec Caverns continues to be a big draw for kids and
adults alike. Nestled beneath the foothills of the Ozarks, the legendary tourist attraction
showcases more than 400 million years of history. Local tribes of Indians once used it as
shelter, and local legend says it was used as a station on the Underground Railroad to hide
escaping slaves. The cave was mined by French colonial miners and Civil War garrisons
who used the cave's natural minerals to manufacture gunpowder. Another selling point that
adds to the cave's mystique is the story that outlaw Jesse James and his gang used it as
a place to stash their horses and loot from train and bank robberies during the 1870s. In
1933 a noted caveologist discovered the 7 upper levels of the caverns, and further exploration revealed more than 25 miles of underground passages. Meramec Caverns opened to
the public in 1935 as a tourist attraction, and its complex and colorful mineral formations
continue to amaze visitors today.

Rangers lead tours through myriad stalagmites and stalactites that took thousands
of years to grow, and explain how Mother Nature built an ancient limestone "Wine Table,"
an entire 7-story mansion, and the rarest and largest cave formations in the world. There's
also an underground river and the "Stage Curtain," which is said to be the largest single
cave formation in the world. Nighttime lantern tours offer a unique spelunking experience,
as guides take visitors through the cave lit only by handheld lanterns. A number of historic
characters make appearances during the 80-minute trek, including an Osage Indian, a Civil
War soldier, and the infamous outlaw Jesse James, who shares tales of folklore and details
about Meramec Caverns' rich history. Reservations are needed for the lantern tours. Other
activities available around these parts include hour-long riverboat rides aboard the *Cavern*

Queen riverboats on the Meramec River (Apr through Sept); 6- to 11-mile-long raft or canoe floats on the Meramec River; and panning for fool's gold, fossils, and gemstones at the Meramec Mining Company (summer months only).

Meramec State Park. 115 Meramec Park Dr.; (573) 468-6072; www.mostateparks.com/park/meramec-state-park. Located along the Meramec River, the park is a favorite with canoeists and anglers, as well as with campers and hikers. Make a stop at the visitor center when you first arrive and pick up additional literature or info about any advisories or notices regarding the park. The center has a number of exhibits and offers a brief slide-show over-view of the park's natural, cultural, and recreational resources. There's a life-size riverbank diorama as well as large aquariums that display up-close and personal examples of the river's aquatic inhabitants. More than 40 caves are located in the park, and naturalist-led tours of Fisher Cave are offered on a seasonal basis. The sights inside Fisher Cave range from low, narrow streamside passages and huge rooms to passageways featuring well-preserved bear claw marks, cave wildlife, and a vast array of calcite deposits ranging from intricate hellectites to massive 30-foot-tall columns. The 461-acre Meramec Upland Forest Natural Area, which is a remote area of the park, features glades, caves, sinkholes, wet meadows, and an assortment of rare plants and animals. Nature discovery programs are provided regularly at the outdoor amphitheater.

Meramec State Park offers well-groomed hiking and backpacking trails, comfortable picnic shelters, and other facilities like a store/grill, cabins, a motel with a conference center, camping, and canoe, kayak, and raft rentals. There are 8 primitive backpacking campsites along the Wilderness Trail, and RV sites with sewer, water, and electric hookups. Hot showers, restrooms, a coin-operated laundry, and a sanitary dump station are available to all campers. Rental cabins are also offered and are outfitted with HVAC, linens, cooking utensils, and dishes.

where to shop

Fanning US 66 Outpost. 5957 Hwy. ZZ, Cuba; (573) 885-1474; www.fanning66outpost .com. In addition to being a full-service archery pro shop, Fanning 66 Outpost in tiny Cuba, MO, has a collection of Route 66 merchandise, cold drinks, snacks, wines, unique Ozark souvenirs, and locally made knives and rustic apparel. You can even try out the archery gear on-site—the shop is home to 4 ranges, including 20-yard and 40-yard indoor ranges, a 60-yard outdoor range, and a TechnoHUNT archery simulator. Open daily.

Fireside Store & Grill. 670 Fisher Cave Dr.; (573) 468-6519; www.meramecpark.com. Here's the place that has everything a good camper needs, including food—bread, soda, beer, ice cream, milk, ice, snacks, etc.—and camping and fishing supplies like tent stakes, sleeping bags, firewood, fold-out chairs, fishing tackle, and line. You can buy your hunt-ing and fishing permits here too. Souvenir hunters will find plenty of prey to bag, including

T-shirts, hats, blankets, jewelry, and toys. There's also a selection of must-have swimming and float gear items like snorkels, water shoes, and inner tubes.

Meramec Caverns Gift Shop. I-44, exit 230, Stanton; (800) 676-6105; www.americas cave.com. You can't leave without getting a little something to help remember your trip to America's Cave, so head over to the gift shop and pick up a Meramec Caverns–emblazoned T-shirt or hat. If your tastes run to the exotic side, splurge a little and browse through the collection of goodies that includes knives, jewelry, books, pictures, toys, and games.

where to eat

Circle Inn Malt Shop. 171 S. Old Hwy 66, Bourbon; (573) 732-4470. One of the mainstays of the Mother Road is the iconic American diner, and the Circle Inn Malt Shop is a prime example. Since opening in the mid-1950s, the roadside eatery has been serving up a slew of standard diner favorites like eggs, pancakes, biscuits and gravy, onion rings, sandwiches, and burgers, along with good old-fashioned milk shakes, malts, and sundaes. Circle Inn still has its original malt machine and soda fountain. $.

Frisco's Grill & Pub. 121 S. Smith St., Cuba; (573) 885-1522; www.friscosgrill.com. Frisco's is a friendly, casual eatery with a large menu and generous portion sizes. Barbecue wings are available by the pound, and the menu includes a selection of starters, soups, salads, and sandwiches like the half-pound hamburger and the Frisco Melt (a quarter-pound burger layered with Swiss cheese, grilled onions, and chipotle sauce on Texas toast), Pasta dishes and chicken and steak entrees are available, along with a kids' menu. Open Tues through Sun for lunch, dinner, and late evening dining. $$.

Meramec Caverns Restaurant. 1135 Hwy. W, Stanton; (573) 468-3166. Located in the main building at Meramec Caverns, the restaurant is more about convenience than stellar cuisine. The family-friendly menu features a respectable amount of home-style cooking, soups, and sandwiches and it's served with a smile (usually). For dessert or a quick snack, choose from the 28 flavors of ice cream. Open for breakfast and lunch daily from Mar through Dec; call for Jan and Feb hours. $.

Missouri Hick BBQ. 913 E. Washington St., Cuba; (573) 885-6791; www.missourihick .com. You may have noticed that if there's one thing Missouri loves, it's barbecue. Missouri Hick's menu includes smoked beef brisket, pulled pork, ribs, bratwurst, and sandwiches, and they serve everything up with down-home style and a casual atmosphere. $–$$.

where to stay

Meramec Caverns Motel. 1135 Hwy. W, Sullivan; (573) 468-4215. The 32-room motel is located in LaJolla Natural Park, overlooking Meramec Caverns Natural Campground. For travelers who don't need anything fancy but don't want to camp, the motel offers quiet, comfortable lodging with rooms that feature 2 double beds, a coffeemaker, cable/satellite TV, a microwave, and the always-welcome indoor plumbing. Meramec Caverns Motel is open Apr through Oct, and reservations are required. Kids stay free. $.

Meramec Caverns Natural Campground. I-44, exit 230, Sullivan; (573) 468-3166. Meramec Caverns' LaJolla Natural Park/Campground is located along the scenic Meramec River among numerous shade trees. Available campsites include 60 tent/RV sites—40 with electric and water and 20 full hookups—and 100 primitive tent sites. There's an on-site camp store, restroom buildings, shower houses, a concession stand, barbeque pits, sheltered pavilions, and a playground. The park is located within walking distance of the activities available at Meramec Caverns. Open Apr through Oct. $.

Meramec State Park Campgrounds. 115 Meramec Park Dr.; (573) 468-6072; www.mo stateparks.com/park/meramec-state-park. The park offers 3 campground areas that provide basic, electric, or sewer/electric/water campsites, as well as group tent areas. From Apr through Oct services include reservable sites, a dump station, showers, water, and laundry. Meramec State Park also offers 11 cabins and 8 duplexes and/or 4-plexes for rent through the park's Fireside Store and Grill (573-468-6519; www.meramecpark.com). $.

day trip 03

southwest

>>> **wine springs eternal:**
st. james, mo; rolla, mo

st. james, mo

St. James is situated in a 1.2-million-acre American Viticultural Area (AVA), which includes Missouri's greatest concentration of vineyards and wineries. The AVA was established in 1987 but it was in the 1800s when Italian immigrants planted the area's first vineyards here, and the tradition—and the grapes—continue to grow. The Italians called the area Rosati, and they thrived as grapes became a big business in the region. Today the area is known colloquially as the "Little Italy of the Ozarks" and officially as the Ozark Highlands AVA.

getting there

You get to St. James, located less than 100 miles from downtown St. Louis, by taking I-44 West. Just follow the signs for I-44 West/Tulsa/12th Street/Gravois Avenue for a little more than 94 miles, then take exit 195 for MO 68/MO 8 toward St James. Stay left at the fork in the road and follow the signs for MO 68/MO 8. Turn left onto MO 68 East/MO 8 East/N. Jefferson Street for about 0.5 mile, then turn right onto W. James Boulevard.

where to go

St. James Tourist Information Center. I-44, exit 195; (573) 265-3899. Stop in for brochures, dining suggestions, special events taking place during your visit, and insider tips for how to get around.

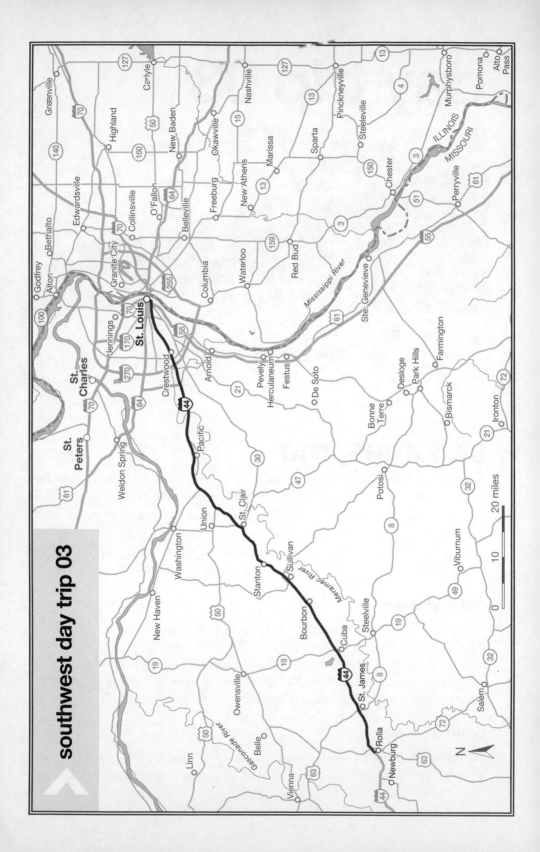

southwest day trip 03

Meramec Vineyards. 600 Rte. B; (573) 265-4404; www.meramecvineyards.com. Founded in 1980 with 15 acres of Concord grape vineyards originally planted by one of the region's first Italian families, Meramec Vineyards produces 9 American-style wines and 5 made in the European style. The on-site restaurant, Bistro d'Vine, offers a handful of entrees and appetizers, and visitors can sample wine in the tasting room or enjoy a glass in the garden area. The gift shop features wine- and food-related items, and the winery highlights artwork for sale by local artists. Open daily.

Rosati Winery Museum. 22050 Rte. KK; (573) 265-3000; www.rosatiwinerymuseum.com. The museum documents the local community and its winery history from 1898 to 1988. It houses a collection of vintage wine-making equipment, old photographs, documents, and ledgers from the 1930s–40s winery era. There's also a short film that documents life in Rosati as told by area residents, as well as a gift shop and wine-tasting room that highlights selected wines from the 8 different regions of Missouri. Pick up some cheese and crackers to snack on, or browse through the assortment of wine accessories and Route 66 merchandise.

St. James Winery. 540 Sidney St.; (800) 280-9463; www.stjameswinery.com. St. James is the largest winery in the state, producing more than 200,000 cases of wine each year. Their 120 acres of vineyards are planted with Catawba, Chardonel, Norton, Concord, Seyval, Vignoles, Chambourcin, and Rougeon grapes, and the winery produces more than 20 award-winning fruit, sweet, dry, dessert, and sparkling wines. They also sell Concord grape juice and 5 nonalcoholic sparkling fruit juice varieties. Visitors can enjoy free samples of wines and juices and take guided tours of the state-of-the-art wine cellar. In 2009 the Critics Challenge wine competition named St. James "Winery of the Year—Eastern US." Open Mon through Sat year-round.

Tacony Manufacturing—Vacuum Cleaner Museum. 3 Industrial Dr.; (573) 265-0500, ext. 4310. This museum sucks. . . . It needs to because it's the world's first vacuum cleaner museum (and factory outlet). Located at Tacony Manufacturing, producer of Riccar and Simplicity vacuums, the collection includes a century's worth of vacuum cleaner history. There are more than 500 examples on display, and they range from early 1910s models to those of more modern times. The vacuum cleaners are displayed in decade-themed vignettes complete with period furniture and memorabilia from each era, including newspaper and magazine ads for the different models.

Three Squirrels Winery. 17301 Rte. B; (573) 265-7742; www.threesquirrelswinery.com. Located at the northern edge of the scenic Ozarks, the Three Squirrels have holed up inside a former dairy barn at the edge of the vineyards. They offer 7 vintages with names like Acorn Red, White Squirrel, and Nutty Red, as well as a selection of cheeses, salami, crackers, snacks, sodas, and bottled beer. Sit and sip on the covered deck overlooking the vineyards or stroll through the on-site art gallery featuring photography, paintings, and ceramics by local and regional artists. The tasting room is open Fri through Sun.

where to shop

Morning Sun Gallery. 107 W. Springfield St.; (573) 263-2830. In addition to showcasing and selling artwork by area artists, the gallery carries antiques, gifts, collectibles, furniture, decor, Tessa Long jewelry, and Kris Ash Karma Naturals organic body products. Open Mon through Sat.

Sybill's Saint James Restaurant & Gift Shop. 1100 N. Jefferson St.; (573) 265-4224; www.sybills.com. Located inside the house that's also home to Sybill's restaurant is an upscale gift shop that offers "big city selections and small town service." The shop features silver, monogrammed, and fashion jewelry along with watches, fashionable handbags, scarves, and accent pieces. There's also an assortment of lotions and soaps, candles, wall art, home decor, florals, and seasonal items.

where to eat

Diana's Diner. 103 N. Jefferson St.; (866) 488-9078. Located in the heart of downtown St. James, Diana's serves home-style country cooking for breakfast, lunch, and dinner. The diner receives high marks for its fried chicken, catfish, chicken and dumplings, and homemade pies. $.

Sybill's Saint James Restaurant. 1100 N. Jefferson St.; (573) 265-4224; www.sybills .com. For lunch Sybill's offers a delightful selection of salads and sandwiches as well as entrees like tilapia, homemade lasagna, and grilled chicken pizza. The dinner menu expands to feature such signature entrees as filet mignon, prime rib, salmon, Maryland crab cakes, and smoked-almond-and-pretzel-crusted chicken topped with a cheddar Mornay sauce. There's an extensive wine list as well as a seasonal specialty drinks menu. Sybill's also offers a gluten-free pasta option and a Sunday brunch. Reservations are recommended. Open Tues through Sun. $$$.

where to stay

Lost Creek Ranch & Lodge. Phelps CR 3600; (573) 265-7407; www.lostcreekmo.com. Lost Creek offers private cabin rentals of various sizes near Maramec Spring Park. The Dogwood is a 1-bedroom cabin with a small sleeping loft, and the Valley View Cabin has 3 bedrooms and a large, 14-by-16-foot sleeping loft. For families or groups, the Farmhouse can accommodate up to 9 adults comfortably. It has 2 queen-size bedrooms and a "bunk-house" kind of room with 3 twin-size beds and a set of bunk beds all in one large room on the upper floor. $–$$.

Painted Lady Bed & Breakfast and Guest House. 1127 S. Jefferson St.; (573) 265-5008; www.paintedladybandb.com. Decorated in "country Victorian" style, the Painted Lady features 5 different lodging options including guest rooms/suites and separate guest houses. The Little Tara is a private cottage separate from the main house, and the

2-bedroom Guest House sleeps 6. There are in-room Jacuzzis and hot tubs, and the property offers nightly turndowns, chocolates, and a full country breakfast. $–$$.

rolla, mo

Perched in the middle of the south-central Ozarks Highland region midway between St. Louis and Springfield, MO, Rolla is a city of less than 20,000 that serves as the county seat of Phelps County. It is home to the Missouri University of Science and Technology—formerly known as the University of Missouri–Rolla—a premier technological research college. Most of the 7,200 members of Missouri S&T's student body come here to study engineering, computing, mathematics, and science, although the school also offers majors in humanities, social sciences, arts, and business.

The area's first settlers arrived in the early 19th century, working as farmers and iron workers along the local rivers, which include the Meramec, the Gasconade, and the Little Piney. The state officially established Rolla as a town in 1858, and it has served as a transportation and trading center throughout its history. It was the original terminus of the St. Louis & San Francisco Railroad, and the BNSF Railway still literally runs directly through town.

getting there

From St. James, Rolla is a quick 17-minute drive along I-44 West. Follow I-44 toward Rolla/ St. James/Salem for about 10 miles and take exit 185. At the traffic circle, take the fourth exit onto Nagogami Road/ Route E and continue straight onto W. 14th Street. Turn right on N. Bishop Avenue, then make a left onto W. 10th Street.

where to go

Rolla Area Chamber of Commerce & Visitor Center. 1311 Kingshighway; (573) 364-3577; www.visitrolla.com. Stop in to get information on local attractions, restaurants, hotels, and B&Bs or just grab a free cup of coffee and stretch your legs on the walking trail. Complimentary Wi-Fi is available as well. Closed Sun.

Blue Bonnet Special Steam Train. Schuman Park at 16th and Walnut Streets; (573) 364-4278. Thomas the Tank Engine hasn't got anything on this behemoth. The Blue Bonnet Special is one of thirty 1500 series engines built in 1923 for the Frisco Railroad. It has a 4,500-gallon oil-burning boiler, weighs 350,000 pounds, and was deeded to the city of Rolla on June 13, 1955. Free.

Kokomo Joe's Family Fun Center. 10450 Rte. V; (573) 341-5656; www.rollaskatezone .com/kokomo_joes. Good old-fashioned family fun that includes go-karts for adults and kids, an 18-hole miniature golf course, a driving range with enclosed and open tee boxes and grass tee area, softball and baseball batting cages, an arcade, and a bounce area with an inflatable double waterslide and an inflatable obstacle course.

Maramec Spring Park. 21880 Maramec Spring Dr.; (573) 265-7387; www.maramec springpark.com. Located approximately 6 miles east of St. James, Maramec Spring Park contains 1,860 acres of forest and fields for camping, hiking, picnicking, and fishing for trout in the stocked spring. The park is home to 2 free museums: the Maramec Museum, which houses cultural and natural history exhibits, including a 21-foot bluff, waterfall, and 500-gallon aquarium; and the Agriculture Museum, which has a collection of antique farm machinery from the 1800s and exhibits like Granny's Kitchen and the Blacksmith Shop. The 1.5-mile Spring Branch Trail takes you around Maramec Spring and the Spring Branch, then leads you to the Spring Pool, where you can feed the enormous trout that live in the pool. Feed machines are located on-site (which explains how the trout got so enormous). There are 58 campsites near the Meramec River, each with a fire pit and a picnic table. The Company Store sells refreshments, fishing supplies, ice, camping amenities, fishing licenses, and assorted souvenirs. By the way, the Meramec River and Maramec Spring have the same name but are spelled differently—this is due to the fact that many Ozarkers lacked a formal education and were somewhat illiterate at the time the spring was named. The James Foundation, which oversees the park, opted to keep the name spelled Maramec.

Missouri S&T Mineral Display. 125 McNutt Hall, Missouri University of Science and Technology campus; (573) 341-4616; www.mst.edu. Housed in McNutt Hall, the minerals museum has 3,500 specimens from all over the world, including gold, diamonds, and meteorites. The collection is an extension of an exhibit from the 1904 World's Fair held in St. Louis's Forest Park. Free admission. Open Mon through Fri.

Newburg Children's Museum. 120-B Water St., Newburg; (573) 762-3077; www.newburg childrensmuseum.org. Located a little less than 10 miles from downtown Rolla, the natural history museum is housed in the 2-story annex of the Historic Houston House. The exhibits and hands-on activities are themed around earth, water, sky, and man. There are 8 rooms to explore, including the Rock and Fossil Room, Sea Room, Ethnic Room, and the Science Hands-On Activities area. The Sea Room simulates an underwater habitat and contains seaweed, sponges, and corals and shells from the Caribbean, South Africa, and the Atlantic and Pacific coasts. In the Ethnic Room there are exhibits highlighting different cultures from around the world, including Africa, Cambodia, China, Japan, and South America. Kids of all ages will enjoy the Science Hands-On Activities area, which includes a kaleidoscope, an oscilloscope, and a magnifying glass that allows you to see your blood vessels and other "invisible" things on a television screen. Open Tues and Sat from 10 a.m. to 1 p.m. and by appointment.

Onondaga Cave State Park. 7556 Hwy. H; (573) 245-6576; www.mostateparks.com/park/onondaga-cave-state-park. The highlight of the park is the chance to tour the Onondaga and Cathedral Caves. Onondaga Cave is a National Natural Landmark filled with towering stalagmites, stalactites, active flowstones, and a river that flows through it. The 75-minute-long guided tours feature lighted paved walkways, and the knowledgeable guides provide information about such geologic wonders as the King's Canopy, the Twins, and other unusual secondary mineral formations. Tours of Onondaga Cave depart from the park's visitor center. Tours of the Cathedral Cave are for more adventurous amateur spelunkers. The lantern tours, which begin at the campground shower house, last about 2 hours and are more strenuous than the Onondaga Cave excursion, covering 1.6 miles round-trip. Cave temperatures are about 57°F (13°C) year-round so you'll probably need a jacket, but you'll definitely need comfortable shoes no matter what tour you take. The park also offers a number of aboveground diversions, including canoeing and fishing in the Meramec River, and beautiful views from the Vilander Bluff Natural Area. Call for tour times and dates.

The Zone. 555 Blues Lake Pkwy.; (573) 341-5700; www.rollaskatezone.com. The area's only roller-skating complex is also home to laser tag, a laser maze, an arcade with more than 40 video games, a bounce area, a soft-play jungle gym, and an area designed for kids ages 7 and under. The Zone offers skating lessons and has an on-site skate shop featuring quad and inline skates, and a full-service concession stand.

where to shop

Mule Trading Post. 11100 Dillon Outer Rd.; (573) 364-4711. Located along historic Route 66, the Mule stocks a little bit of everything, like Route 66 and Missouri souvenirs, antiques, Amish products, gifts, knives, swords, and other fun stuff. Look for the iconic neon mule sign. They profess to be open daily, but you'd better call ahead to see what the hours are for that day.

Orval Reeves Art Gallery. 606 Cedar St.; (573) 364-7446; www.orvalreeves.com. The gallery features works by local artists, including ceramics, bronze pieces, unique jewelry designs, and beautiful paintings of outdoor scenes by the gallery's namesake.

where to eat

A Slice of Pie. 601 Kingshighway; (573) 364-6023; www.asliceofpie.com. They serve lunch at A Slice of Pie—you can choose a salad, some quiche, a potpie, or soup with fresh homemade bread—but what sets this place apart is dessert. There are always 30 different pies available, such as apple (both American and Dutch), blackberry crumb, Boston cream, coconut buttermilk custard, Tahitian cream, Toll House, and many, many more. They also sell whole quiches, potpies, cakes, cheesecakes, and no-sugar-added mini pies. $.

Alex's Pizza Palace. 122 W. 8th St.; (573) 364-2669; www.alexspizza.com. Alex's has been a Rolla favorite since 1964. The menu includes sandwiches, salads, calzones, and appetizers, but the homemade pizza sauce and fresh pizza dough are what makes the eatery special. Try the gyros pizza (gyros meat, tomatoes, and onions), the chicken Florentine (chicken, fresh spinach, basil, artichoke hearts, and tomatoes), the Mediterranean (tomatoes, black olives, fresh spinach, basil, feta cheese, and banana peppers), or the house special (beef, pepperoni, mushrooms, green peppers, and onions). $–$$.

Bandana's BBQ. 1705 Martin Spring Dr.; (573) 426-3331; www.bandanasbbq.com. One of the St. Louis region's most popular barbecue joints, Bandana's offers Southern-style BBQ that's seasoned with a dry rub and slow-cooked without sauce over a pit of select hardwoods. The meat is then hand-cut to order right from the smoker. Bandana's menu features pork, beef, chicken, and ribs. $–$$.

Matt's Steakhouse. 12200 Dillon Outer Rd.; (573) 364-1220; www.mattssteakhouse .com. Enjoy casual dining in a slightly more refined atmosphere at Matt's Steakhouse. The menu features steaks, chops, and a few seafood and pasta dishes. There's also a full-service lounge. Open for lunch and dinner Tues through Sat. $$.

Public House Brewing Company. 600 North Rolla St., Ste. B; (573) 426-2337; www .publichousebrewery.com. The brewpub is the first brewery in the history of Rolla, and they serve up an array of beers that are brewed right on the premises. The beverage menu changes with new additions to the hops-infused lineup, but some of the standard offerings are Cream Ale, Bird and Baby Mild, Revelations Stout, Belgian Single, Tire Swing IPA, and Wanker's ESB. There are also about 20 wine options available, along with a very limited food menu that includes cheese and sausage, chips, and some desserts. However, since they don't offer a lot of non-liquid sustenance, the brewpub's food policy allows guests to bring their own food, saying, "If we don't make it and serve it here, you are welcome to bring it with you to enjoy with our tasty beers." You can even have food delivered to the pub! $.

Randy's Roadkill Barbecue Grill. 12670 Rte. E; (573) 368-3705; www.randysroadkillbbq .com. Located about 4 miles north of downtown Rolla on the edge of the family farm, Randy's is a family-owned restaurant that's kid-friendly. If you're a vegetarian, well, you're out of luck—the eatery specializes in ribs, barbecue sandwiches, shredded beef, pulled pork, sausage, brisket, smoked chicken, and turkey. $$.

where to stay

A Miner Indulgence Bed & Breakfast. 13750 Martin Spring Dr.; (573) 364-0680; www .minerinn.com. The charming brick colonial is situated on a small wooded bluff that was once a Civil War encampment. There are 2 spacious guest rooms available in the home, which is decorated with a number of unusual antiques like a corn shucker, newspaper delivery wagon, and yarn weasel. Both of the guest rooms includes a private bath and sitting room. There's also a hot tub and in-ground pool for guests' use, and a full country breakfast is offered daily. The inn will also accommodate special dietary requirements if notified when the reservation is made. $.

west

>>>

day trip 01

west

>>> **wild times:**
wildwood, mo

wildwood, mo

Wildwood is a far-flung, third-ring suburb of western St. Louis County created in 1995 when residents of this previously unincorporated portion of the region overwhelmingly approved the decision to incorporate. Families have flocked to the 68-square-mile city, and it's now home to more than 35,000 residents. In addition to a plethora of new homes and subdivisions, Wildwood still has an abundance of native woodland areas, rural roadways, and lots of wide open spaces, including trails, parks, and reserves such as Rockwood and Babler State Parks.

getting there

From downtown St. Louis, take I-64 West/US 40 West for approximately 20 miles, then take exit 19B toward Clarkson Road. Make a left onto MO 340 West/Clarkson Road and follow it for about 4.5 miles, then turn right onto MO 100 West/Manchester Road. Continue on MO 100 West for 3 miles and take the MO 109 ramp to Eatherton Road. Turn left onto MO 109 South and continue for about 0.5 mile, then turn right onto Manchester Road.

where to go

Dr. Edmund A. Babler Memorial State Park. 800 Guy Park Dr.; (636) 458-3813; www .mostateparks.com/park/dr-edmund-babler-memorial-state-park. Named for physician

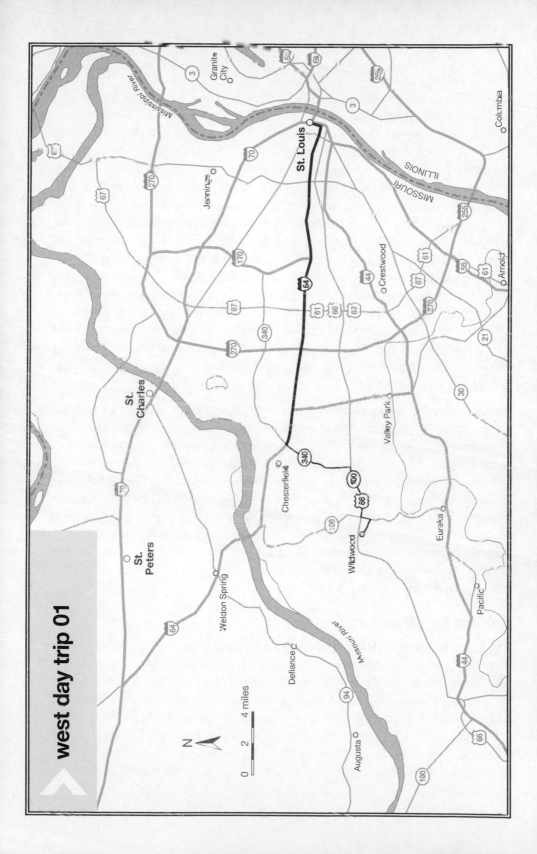

and surgeon Dr. Edmund Babler, the park features picnic sites, a 1.75-mile paved bicycle trail, hiking and equestrian trails, and camping, including an ADA-accessible group camp. There's also a multipurpose court for tennis, volleyball, basketball, and other sports. Trails range from the 1.25-mile-long Hawthorn and Virginia Day Memorial hiking trails to the 6-mile-long equestrian trail. Anglers can fish for orange-throated darters, bleeding shiners, and logperch in Bonhomme and Wild Horse Creeks along the park's western boundary. Many of the structures at Babler were built in the 1930s by Civilian Conservation Corps (CCC) workers, including the covered shelters, buildings, bridges, and the massive stone gateway made with rocks quarried from the area. Twenty-two of the CCC structures are listed on the National Register of Historic Places. The River Hills Visitor Center houses exhibits about the park's plant and animal life. A walk-through diorama explores the old-growth forest ecosystem, and naturalist staff members offer a variety of interpretive programs. Babler is full of maturing old-growth forests, such as Cochran Woods' century-old white oak, northern red oak, sugar maple, and walnut trees, and the Southwoods Hollow Natural Area's towering oaks and sugar maples have remained undisturbed since presettlement times. The park offers basic and electric campsites, along with special-use and group camping areas. Open year-round.

Hidden Valley Ski Resort. 17409 Hidden Valley Dr.; (636) 938-5373; www.hiddenvalleyski .com. Hidden Valley offers a quick fix for Midwestern skiers on a budget. Utilizing an intricate man-made snow system when Mother Nature doesn't cooperate, the 30-acre resort features 6 beginner and 5 intermediate slopes, an advanced trail, and an expert glades area. There are 2 terrain parks for snowboarders: Outlaw, which has rails, jumps, and plenty of jibs; and Badlands for those who prefer the challenge of the half-pipe. All of the trails are lighted for night skiing nightly, and Hidden Valley offers midnight skiing on Fri and Sat starting in late Dec, weather permitting. There are 6 chairlifts, including a quad chair, and skiing lessons are offered for ages 3 and up. Rental skis and snowboards are available on-site, and the 10,000-square-foot lodge is equipped with a bar, cafeteria, Ski Patrol first-aid station, and retail store. Open seasonally.

where to stay

Dr. Edmund A. Babler Memorial State Park Campground. 800 Guy Park Dr.; (636) 458-3813; www.mostateparks.com/campgrounds/dr-edmund-babler-memorial-state-park. Camp in one of Babler's reservable basic or electric campsites and take advantage of the showers, playground, grills, fire pits, and dump station. Reservations are accepted for stays year-round, and there's a 2-night minimum stay on weekends. The park also has an ADA-accessible group camp with the Jacob L. Babler Outdoor Education Center, a barrier-free resident camp for those with special needs. It offers a full-service, outdoor education environment for organized groups with members that have specific physical or emotional requirements. $.

day trip 02

west

>>> **daniel boone slept here:**
defiance, mo

defiance, mo

In a deep valley just west of St. Louis lies the tiny town of Defiance, MO, an unincorporated community in St. Charles County. Bicyclists roll in via the Katy Trail, which runs through the town near the Missouri River. Its biggest claim to fame is that it was the final home of frontiersman Daniel Boone, who settled in the Femme Osage Valley in 1799 after receiving a Spanish land grant. The settlement didn't have a name while Boone resided here—that came in the late 1800s when the Katy Railroad arrived. The town got its name after defying the efforts of the people of Matson, a small town that also coveted the Katy Railroad's depot and sidetracks planned for the area.

getting there

From St. Louis, follow I-64 West/US 40 West for about 29 miles, then take exit 10 for MO 94 South. Make a left onto MO 94 West and continue for a little more than 7 miles. Turn left to stay on MO 94 West and continue for 1.5 miles.

where to go

Chandler Hill Vineyards. 596 Defiance Rd.; (636) 798-2675; www.chandlerhillvineyards .com. Set among rolling hills of Chambourcin, Vignoles, and Pinot Gris grapes, Chandler Hill features an elegant 5,000-square-foot tasting room, winery, marketplace, and restaurant.

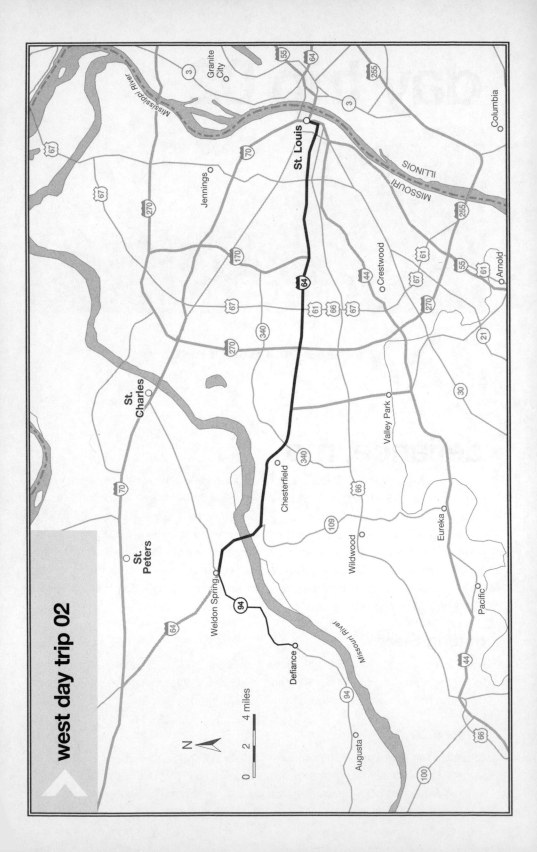

west day trip 02

Take a tour of the wine-making facility to see how they harvest, produce, and age their wines, then head for the tasting room and pull up a chair. If it's warm, venture out onto the 4,500-square-foot wine deck and enjoy the view of the lake and the Missouri Valley, or curl up on the couch and enjoy the large fireplace during cooler weather. The tasting room offers 10 wines from California, Oregon, and Washington State as well 6 from Missouri, including their own estate-grown Old Bridge Chambourcin. Closed Mon.

Historic Daniel Boone Home & Boonesfield Village. 1868 Rte. F; (314) 798-2005; www .lindenwood.edu/boone. The village includes the 4-story home built by Daniel Boone and his sons in 1810, where Boone lived until his death in 1820. The house has 7 fireplaces, a ballroom, and a variety of everyday items such as a collection of flintlock long rifles, Mrs. Boone's butter churn and sewing basket, Daniel's writing desk, and the family dishes. There's also a Missouri frontier village that includes a one-room schoolhouse; church; general store; gristmill; pottery; printer's, carpenter's, and dressmaker's shops; and other homes.

Sugar Creek Winery. 125 Boone Country Ln.; (636) 987-2400; www.sugarcreekwines .com. Located just off the scenic Lewis and Clark Trail, Sugar Creek is on a hillside over-looking the Katy Trail and the Missouri River Valley. The winery produces more than a dozen vintages, including 5 estate wines. The Vidal Blanc, Chardonel, Chambourcin, Norton Cyn-thiana, and Michael's Signature Red are all grown and bottled on-site, and they produce 9 additional wines: a port, a blush, 2 reds, 2 whites, and 3 fruit wines. Enjoy a glass or share a bottle on the wine terrace among fields of French and American hybrid grapes, or visit the parlor and tasting room inside the visitor center. There's live music in the gazebo on week-ends Apr through Nov, and you can snack on cheese, sausage, and crackers purchased on-site. Open daily.

Yellow Farmhouse Winery. 100 Defiance Rd. at MO 94; (314) 409-6139; www.yellow farmhousewines.com. Perched atop the hills overlooking the nearby Missouri River Valley, the Yellow Farmhouse Winery is a charming spot to spend an afternoon. They offer 10 varie-ties of vino: Norton Biker Bar Red, Compass Rose, Rosso Dolce, Chardonnay, River Valley White, Traminette, Vignoles, Edelweiss, an estate-bottled Chambourcin, and Drop Dead Red—so named because "it's drop dead good." Bring a blanket and stop by the tasting room for some of Yellow Farmhouse's handcrafted wines and locally made confections, cheeses, dipping mustards, and sausages, and then head for Picnic Hill. The wine-tasting room and Winegarden are open Sat and Sun afternoons during the spring, summer, and fall months, and they frequently offer live entertainment.

where to eat

Chandler Hill Vineyards Restaurant. 596 Defiance Rd.; (636) 798-2675; www.chandler hillvineyards.com/restaurant. Select from a menu of sandwiches, salads, and small plates like penne with chicken, spinach, and tomato cream; crab cakes with mustard-lemon mayonnaise; and pork tenderloin medallion with locally grown squash and eggplant. Sandwich options include the Vineyard Chicken Salad Sandwich (white meat chicken, grapes, apples, and roasted pecans served on a croissant), Roasted Portobello Melt (portobello mushroom, herb goat cheese, roasted red pepper, and caramelized red onion on toasted wheat-berry bread), and Chicken and Brie Panini (roasted chicken breast, brie, Granny Smith apple, and raspberry hot pepper jam on multigrain bread). Save room for dessert—order the assortment of artisan chocolates paired with a flight of 3 Chandler Hill wines. Closed Mon. $$.

Wine Country Gardens Restaurant & Wine Garden. 2711 MO 94; (636) 798-2288; www.winecountrygardens.net. Set in the hills overlooking the Missouri River Valley, the restaurant is located on the grounds of a 42-acre nursery filled with perennials, flowering shrubs, annuals, and tropicals. At the center of it all is a 110-year-old farmhouse with a 12-foot-wide wraparound porch and 3 outdoor patios available for lunchtime dining from a menu of hot and cold sandwiches, salads, and appetizers. Try the hand-cut coconut tempura chicken with island mango dipping sauce, or share a basket of homemade chips served with remoulade or Welsh cheese dipping sauce. For dessert have some warm battered apple crescents with caramel sauce or a slice of Bailey's cheesecake. The wine list includes domestic and imported vintages, and indoor dining is available in the Cafe and Wine Bar. Open Apr through Nov. $.

day trip 03

west

missouri wine country:
augusta, mo; washington, mo;
hermann, mo

America's first wine district was created in the hills of Missouri in the 1800s when immigrants from Germany's Rhine River Valley moved to the area. After Missouri achieved statehood in 1821, thousands of immigrants relocated to the region from Europe in an effort to escape political, religious, and economic oppression. The Germans found that the ground was too rocky to be suitable for many crops, but it proved to be ideal for growing the grapes used to make wine, so they planted vineyards and constructed wine cellars in and around the small towns of Augusta and Hermann. The grape-growing and wine-making business continued to flourish in the area, and by the turn of the 20th century, there were 60 wineries and an annual production of more than two million gallons of wine.

Today there are more than two dozen wineries in Missouri, and many have tasting bars and picnic areas that are great places to spend an afternoon. During September and October many of the wineries have special events and live entertainment on weekends, and if you time your visit right, you can enjoy some spectacular fall foliage as well. Admission is free to all of the wineries, except during special events like Labor Day weekend and during the month-long Oktoberfest.

augusta, mo

Augusta was founded in 1836 by Leonard Harold, one of the settlers who followed Daniel Boone to Saint Charles County, and named after Harold's wife. Located along the bluffs

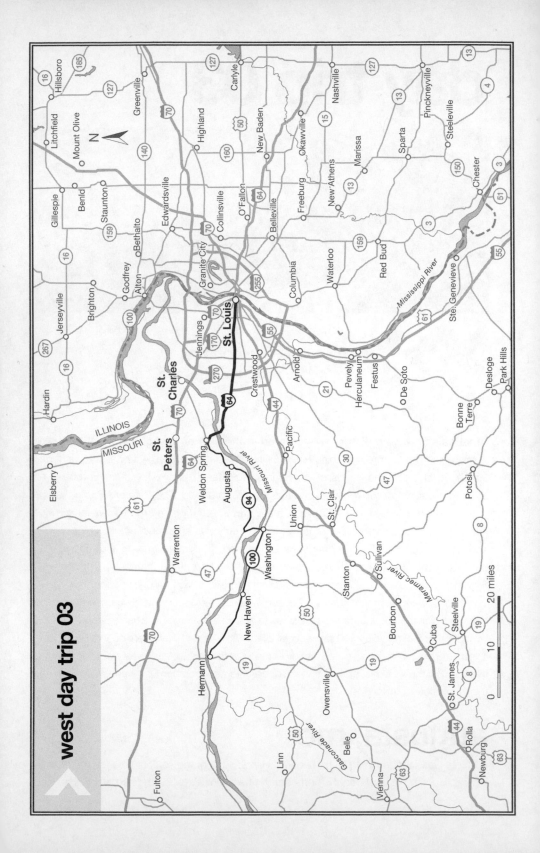

above the Missouri River Valley, the town of approximately 300 is home to several Missouri wineries that offer visitors a chance to enjoy the fruits of the vintners' labors and have a picnic with spectacular views of the rolling hillsides. In 1980 Augusta was recognized as the first US Wine District, or Viticultural Area #1, because of its unique soil, climate, historical significance, and the quality of wines produced from grapes grown in its vineyards dating back to the 1800s.The concentration of wineries along MO 94 has led to the road's being called the Missouri Weinstrasse, or Wine Road.

getting there

From St. Louis, take I-64 West/US 40 West for approximately 29 miles, then take exit 10 for MO 94 South. Make a left onto MO 94 West and continue for a little more than 7 miles. Turn left to stay on MO 94 West for a little less than 2 miles and make a left on MO 94 West/Defiance Road. Take the first right onto MO 94 West and follow it for about 8 miles, then turn left on Jackson Road. Continue on Jackson Road for about 0.5 mile, then take the third left onto Chestnut Street.

where to go

Augusta Winery. 5601 High St.; (888) 667-9463; www.augustawinery.com. Sit and sip some vino on the terrace and enjoy the scenery at the award-winning Augusta Winery, which was founded in 1980. The winery is a 3-time winner of the Governor's Cup for Best Missouri Wine, and they produce 5 reds, 8 whites and rosés, 2 fruit wines, and a port. Their 2008 Norton received gold medals at the 2011 Florida State Fair International and the 2011 Missouri Wine Competition. Wine classes are offered in the Owl's Nest, which also offers indoor seating during cold-weather months. During the spring, summer, and fall, the Wine & Beer Garden is the spot for free live entertainment on weekends, and it offers a relaxing place to enjoy some locally made cheese and sausage. The tasting room features a gift shop, custom-labeled wine, and made-to-order gift baskets.

Blumenhof Vineyards & Winery. 13699 MO 94; (800) 419-2245; www.blumenhof.com. Blumenhof is located in Dutzow, MO's oldest German settlement, founded in 1832. The winery grows 8 varieties of grapes and produces a number of vintages, including a sweet white, 4 semisweet wines, a dry red, and 3 semidry award-winning whites including Missouri Weinland, a bronze medal winner at the Mid-American Wine Competition, and the floral, spicy Femme Osage, awarded Best of Class at the Missouri Wine Competition. In 2011 Blumenhof claimed the coveted Governor's Cup for its 2010 Valvin Muscat, a semisweet white wine. They offer a happy hour in the tasting room every Fri, and there's live entertainment on Sat from Mar through Nov.

Louis P. Balducci Vineyards. 6601 MO 94 South; (636) 482-VINO (8466); www.balducci vineyards.com. Family-owned and -operated since 1987, the picturesque farm and vineyard surrounded by thickly wooded hills produces 8 wine varieties. Visit the tasting room and find a favorite vintage, or bring your own blanket and have a picnic on the spacious grounds. The make 2 dry whites, 2 dry reds, and 2 semidry wines as well as a sweet white and a port. Open daily.

Montelle Winery. 201 Montelle Dr.; (888) 595-9463; www.montelle.com. Perched high atop Osage Ridge, Montelle offers views of the Missouri River, the village of Augusta, and the surrounding wine-growing region. Special events include live music and Sunset Dinners held on the large outdoor terrace. In addition to 4 fruit wines, 6 whites, 2 port/icewines, and 5 reds, Montelle has a distillery and produces 5 spirits: Golden Delicious, Grappa, Grappa de Traiminette, Pear "Eau de Vie," and Peach "Eau de Vie." Their 2010 Dry Vignoles was awarded a silver medal at the Mid-American Wine Competition, and the 2010 Seyval Blanc brought home gold.

Mount Pleasant Estates. 5634 High St.; (636) 482-9463; www.mountpleasant.com. Mount Pleasant offers stunning views of the rolling hills and lush green flatland that connect the hill country to the Missouri River. Founded in 1859, the winery is located in the Augusta Appellation, the first government-appointed wine-growing district in the US. The original hand-dug cellars were completed in 1881. On weekends visitors can take a free guided tour of the grounds and the winery's historic buildings to learn about early wine-making techniques and how the wines are made today. Mount Pleasant grows 12 grape varieties on 78 acres, and there's a 4,000-square-foot tasting room and an outdoor terrace that offers great bluff-top views of the Missouri River Valley. They also offer wine classes, winemaker dinners, and holiday-themed events throughout the year. Open daily.

Noboleis Vineyards. 100 Hemsath Rd.; (636) 482-4500; www.noboleisvineyards.com. The newest vintners on the Augusta block, the boutique winery offers wines made from grapes in their own vineyards and produced on-site. Noboleis produced their first wines in 2009, and in 2010 they started picking up awards at the Missouri Governors Cup. There's a cafe menu of sandwiches, pizzas, and salads that can be enjoyed indoors in the tasting room or outdoors on the patio overlooking the vineyards. The winery produces 4 reds, 5 whites, and a blush wine. Open daily.

where to eat

Appellation Cafe. 5634 High St.; (636) 482-9463; www.mountpleasant.com. The cafe offers a casual-dining menu of made-to-order burgers, wraps, salads, and sandwiches as well as Mount Pleasant Estate's wines by the glass or bottle. Lunch is available daily Apr through Oct. The winery's Express Corner offers "grab and go" convenience for those in search of wine country picnic fare like fresh-baked bread, sliced cheeses, sausages, crackers, chips, and spreads. $$.

Augusta Brewing Company. 5521 Water St.; (636) 482-2337; www.augustabrewing .com. Located on the Katy Trail, the casual eatery offers a simple lunch menu of salads and appetizers like baked brie topped with raspberry-chipotle sauce and served with crackers and bread, along with an assortment of sandwiches and wraps. The dinner menu includes entrees such as barbecue ribs, Pasta Pignoli (sausage, tomatoes, pine nuts, and mozzarella over fresh spaghetti), Chicken Curry Stew (chicken, potatoes, carrots, and spinach served in a creamy curry sauce over rice), and lemon-ginger mahi mahi. The beer menu includes the brewery's flagship Tannhauser, a copper-colored ale made primarily from American hops, along with a Kölsch-style Augusta Blonde, an unfiltered fruity Hefeweizen, Hyde Park Stout, 1856 IPA, and Augustiner Maibock. They also serve the fresh-brewed Rocket Root Beer. Open for lunch daily and dinner on Fri and Sat only. Pet friendly. $$.

Klondike Cafe at Montelle Winery. 201 Montelle Dr.; (888) 595-9463; www.montelle .com. Open for lunch year-round, the cafe serves up salads, wraps, and specialty sandwiches such as the Klondike (pesto Parmesan ham, mesquite-smoked turkey, Genoa salami, Swiss cheese, sliced tomato, red onion, romaine lettuce, and Dijon mustard on rosemary focaccia). On weekends the menu expands to include 12-inch gourmet pizzas like the Jack Daniels BBQ Chicken (house-made Jack Daniel's sauce, shredded mozzarella, grilled chicken breast, caramelized onions, roasted red peppers, bacon, and green onions) and the Tuscan (roasted garlic butter, mozzarella and Asiago cheese, asparagus, roasted red peppers, shaved prosciutto, and caramelized onions). You can also preorder gourmet picnic platters of varying sizes and set off on your own to enjoy the wine and the scenery. The Klondike Cafe Platter has quartered versions of the Klondike, Londonport Roast Beef, Mesquite Smoked Turkey, Muffaletta, and Cuban sandwiches, while the Presidential Cheese Platter has Roquefort blue, La Petite Crème brie-style, Gouda, hummus, tapenade, and fruit compote. $–$$.

where to stay

Apple Gate Inn Bed & Breakfast. 5549 Main St.; (636) 228-4248; www.applegate-inn .com. Located just a block from the Katy Trail and decorated in Early American style, the B&B features 3 guest suites, each with a private bath and private entrance. The Jacuzzi Suite has a queen-size mansion bed, walk-in closet, sitting area, and satellite TV, and a private upper-level balcony. The Sauna Suite was once used as the summer kitchen of the house, and it includes a private full-size cedar sauna. Suite 3 features a sitting room with a gas fireplace and satellite TV, and a kitchenette with dishes and appliances. A full hot breakfast is served each morning. $$.

Augusta Wine Country Inn. 5619 5th St.; (636) 482-4307; www.augustawinecountry .com. Located just a short walk from Mount Pleasant Estates and Augusta Winery, the inn has 3 guest rooms, each with a private bathroom and wireless Internet access. The Turnbull Suite is furnished with a wrought-iron king-size Victorian bed and has a private seating area.

The Powers Suite features a queen-size Victorian mansion bed, private seating area, and wireless Internet access, while the Mary Frazier Suite has a queen-size bed, a private seating area, and a large marble shower. Breakfast includes coffee, juice, fruit, sweet breads, and signature dishes like stuffed French toast, eggs Benedict, and sausage and potato pancakes. $$.

Edelweiss Guest House. 5567 Walnut St.; (636) 482-4307; www.augustawinecountry .com/locations/edelweissguesthouse.htm. Owned and operated by the same friendly folks who run the Augusta Wine Country Inn, the Edelweiss Guest House is located directly across from the Augusta town square. There are 6 guest rooms featuring king- or queen-size beds, private bathrooms, Jacuzzi tubs, and modern conveniences. Hors d'oeuvres and wine are served at check-in, and the daily gourmet breakfast includes coffee, juice, fruit, sweet breads, and signature dishes like stuffed French toast, eggs Benedict, and sausage and potato pancakes. $$.

H. S. Clay House & Guest Cottage. 219 Public St.; (314) 504-4203; www.hsclayhouse .com. Centrally located in the heart of the action, the H. S. Clay House offers several unique options for overnight accommodations. The Turret Suite takes up about half of the second floor and features vaulted ceiling skylights, a private bath, sitting area, fireplace, and queen-size four-poster bed. On the third floor, the Tree Top Suite has a queen-size sleigh bed, private bath, sitting room, skylight, and small library. There are 3 additional bedrooms—Marie's Room, Robert's Room, and Courtney's Room—that feature a queen-size bed, sitting area, and private bath. Outside there's a covered patio, hot tub, pool, double-tiered deck with lounge chairs and umbrella tables, a fish pond, and woodland and perennial gardens. Across the street from the Clay House, the Guest Cottage has 2 sitting rooms, a fireplace, leather chairs, a small kitchen, a bedroom with a vaulted ceiling, and satellite television. The bathroom features a Jacuzzi tub and shower. Guests can choose from a feast of breakfast options, including freshly ground coffees, teas, juices, beignets or muffins, and main courses like eggs Benedict, shirred eggs, custard French toast, quiches, country-style potatoes, maple-glazed peppered bacon, and sage sausage. $$–$$$.

The Lindenhof Bed & Breakfast. 5596 Walnut St.; (636) 228-4617; www.lindenhof-augusta .com. There are 4 guest suites, all with queen-size beds and private bathrooms. The Harmonie Room and the Rose Room feature 6-foot-long, 3½-foot-wide claw-foot "Champagne Massage" tubs with heated air jets that were custom-made for the Lindenhof. The 2 smaller rooms are Clara's Cottage Room, with a queen-size bed and a bathroom with a walk-in shower, and the Bright Star Room, which has a built-in bed and a small bathroom with a shower. Outside there's a patio with a stone fireplace and a hot tub. The breakfast menu varies, but the specialty of the house is French toast stuffed with cream cheese and white chocolate cream and topped with fresh berries and berry syrup. $$.

washington, mo

Washington is a quaint small town founded in 1799 by followers of Daniel Boone who blazed a trail westward from the hills of Kentucky to the wilderness of east-central Missouri. In the 1830s a dozen Catholic families from Hanover, Germany, settled in the area and created a German influence that still remains today. Entrepreneurs have played a key role in Washington's history, as John B. Busch, older brother of brewing magnate Adolphus Busch, established a brewery in town and bottled the very first Busch Beer in the 1850s, and Austrian immigrant Franz Schwarzer began manufacturing his world-famous zithers at a local factory in 1866. In 1869 another local family made its mark on the world when Henry Tibbe and his son Anton started producing corncob pipes in Washington, and the town is now officially on the map as the Corncob Pipe Capital of the World.

Today Washington is home to more than 14,000 residents, and the downtown historic district has a unique collection of small galleries, specialty shops, antiques stores, and restaurants.

getting there

From Augusta, follow the twists and turns of Augusta Bottom Road about 0 miles to MO 47 South and make a left. Continue along MO 47 for about a mile, then take the third right onto E. 3rd Street and follow it for a little less than a mile to Washington.

If you prefer an even more scenic route, follow the Missouri Weinstrasse— it doesn't take much longer and the scenery is really nice. Take MO 94 West for about 7.5 miles and turn left to stay on MO 94 West. Follow it for a little under a mile, then make a left onto MO 47 South and continue for about 3.5 miles. Turn right onto E. 3rd Street.

where to go

The Art Center. 120 W. Main St.; (636) 239-5544; www.theartcentergallery.com. The Art Center showcases more than 20 artists' works, including abstracts and oil paintings, blown glass, sculptures, home decor, jewelry, porcelain, limited-edition prints, functional art, and wood pieces. They also do custom framing.

Corn Cob Pipe Museum. 400 W. Front St.; (636) 239-2109; www.corncobpipe.com. Located in the Missouri Meerschaum Company's nostalgia room, the museum offers insight into the history and manufacturing of corncob pipes and provides information about such famous and fictional corncob pipe smokers as General Douglas MacArthur, Mark Twain, and cartoon sailor man Popeye. Corncob pipes and related souvenirs are available for purchase. The still-operating Missouri Meerschaum Company is the world's oldest and largest manufacturer of corncob smoking pipes. The factory is housed in a 3-story brick structure that was built during the 1880s, and the crew of 40 employees produces more than 3,000 pipes each day. Free admission. Open Mon through Fri.

Röbller Vineyard Winery. 275 Röbller Vineyard Rd., New Haven; (573) 237-3986; www .robllerwines.com. Located in nearby New Haven, Röbller has 16 acres of vineyards that produce their Vidal, Vignoles, Seyval, Traminette, Steuben, Villard Noir, St. Vincent, Chambourcin, and Norton grape varieties. The winery offers an entire line of wines from dry to sweet in both red and white, and their wines focus on French hybrid varieties and European styling in blends. Their limited-edition Hillside Series wines are vintage-specific representations of their vineyard and include the Hillside Blanc 2010, Hillside Cuvee 2009, and Hillside Rose 2010. It is a very family-friendly place, and visitors are encouraged pack up the kids and bring a picnic basket. Röbller holds a number of special events throughout the year, like Bar-B-Que & Blues, Jamaican Sunsplash, and other events featuring live music. Open daily.

Washington Historical Society Museum. 4th and Market Streets; (636) 239-0280; www .washmohistorical.org. The museum features 2 floors of exhibits that illustrate the town's history, including photos and artifacts about the river, steamboats, and area floods. There are also artifacts and displays about John B. Busch's Washington brewery, the corncob pipe industry, and the success enjoyed by local "Zither King" Franz Schwarzer and his zither factory. The museum is open Tues through Sat, Mar 1 through Dec 23.

where to shop

Country Living Real Estate, Antiques & More. #5 W. 2nd St.; (636) 239-1115; www .lausecountryliving.com. The husband-and-wife team stocks their store after searching for treasures and antiques at auctions, garage sales, and flea markets. They then bring all of the good stuff together and put it in one place—their shop—where it's easier for visitors to find. The items in stock are always changing, but they usually include an array of items like quilts, artwork and posters, fishing lures, decoys, glassware, primitives, milk cans, trains, marbles, signs, and books. Call first—store hours are by appointment or chance.

Dusty Attic Antiques. 7458 MO 100; (636) 390-8484; www.dustyatticantiques.net. The shop features classic American and primitive furniture, along with select European armoires, sideboards, and other upscale traditional furniture pieces. They also deal in vintage jewelry and glassware. Open Fri through Sun, but call first to make sure they're open.

Gary Lucy Gallery. 231 W. Main St.; (636) 239-6337; www.garylucy.com. The gallery features local artist Gary Lucy's historic and wildlife prints and originals, with subjects including Lewis and Clark, river life, and animals. Closed Sun.

I.B. Nuts & Fruit Too. 100 W. Front St.; (636) 390-4438; www.ibnuts.com. Offerings include gourmet nuts, candies, and snacks like chocolate amaretto pecans, chocolate peanut brittle, Columbia Crunch (roasted and salted Oriental rice crackers, redskin peanuts, toasted corn, sesame sticks, soya, sunflower meats, and cashew pieces), and Praline Pecans (jumbo pecan halves with a butter-toffee coating). Gift baskets and tins are available as well.

Willow Creek Antiques. 100 Willow Creek Rd.; (636) 583-5247. Housed in a barn 4 miles south of Washington, this shop offers 6,000 square feet of furniture, farm implements, quilts, graniteware, crocks, Depression glass, kitchen items, brass pieces, and collectibles. There's also an assortment of antique toys, wooden trunks, prints, and framed artwork. Open Wed through Sun.

where to eat

The American Bounty Restaurant. 430 W. Front St.; (636) 390-2150; www.bountyres taurantandwinebar.com. A restaurant, wine bar, and gathering spot that offers good food and a great view of the Missouri River, American Bounty is located in downtown Washington's historic Tibbe district in an old wine and tobacco shop that dates back to 1858. The lunch menu includes salads, pizzas, and entrees such as a grilled salmon salad sandwich and the Cancun Wrap (pulled pork, lettuce, pico de gallo, cheese, and Caesar dressing). Dinner entrees include the Nine Way Gourmet Pasta (pasta with blackened chicken, Roma tomatoes, black olives, and scallions in a pesto cream sauce) and beef tenderloin medallions with port reduction and blue cheese crumbles. A wine list offers local products as well as vintages from several West Coast wineries. Upstairs on the second floor is a cozy wine bar that features a full selection of cocktails, beers, and martinis, and the shady patio offers a view of the Missouri River. Both the wine bar and the patio offer a casual dining menu of burgers, sandwiches, and stone-hearth oven-baked pizzas. Specialty pizzas include the Baked Alaska (crabmeat, lemon, green onion, tomato, and sour cream) and the Mardi Gras (crawfish, andouille sausage, peppers, and onions). The restaurant is open Tues and Wed for dinner only, and Thurs through Sun for lunch and dinner. The wine bar is open Wed through Sat only. Reservations recommended for dinner. $$.

Bugsy's on Main. 201 E. Main St., Union; (636) 584-7832; www.bugsysrestaurant.com. This casual eatery in nearby Union has a menu of hearty entrees like breaded pork cutlets, steaks, linguine and meatballs, and Yankee pot roast. Daily specials include plates of beef Stroganoff, sausage and sauerkraut, fried chicken, and chicken and dumplings. The bar menu offers a number of appetizers like Tommy Gun Chicken Bites, homemade potato chips, toasted ravioli, and potato skins, as well as salads, burgers, thin-crust pizzas, and specialty sandwiches like the Gangster (pastrami, salami, ham, turkey, cheese, lettuce, tomatoes, onions, and whole-grain Dijon mustard on ciabatta bread). Open Mon through Sat, and Sun for brunch only. $$.

Cafe Mosaic. 901 Patients First Dr., next to the Patients First Health Care Center; (636) 390-1722; www.cafe-mosaic.com. Open for breakfast and lunch, Cafe Mosaic serves up a menu of sandwiches, burgers, and lighter fare including breakfast wraps, soups, and salads. Try one of the signature wraps like the Yucatan Grilled Chicken Caesar Wrap (with spring mix, Parmesan cheese, and chipotle-lime-infused Caesar dressing) or a turkey and asparagus bagel sandwich. They also offer a number of specialty espresso drinks like the

Mosaic Dreams (white chocolate and amaretto syrups, steamed milk, and fresh whipped cream, garnished with candied orange zest). Open Mon through Fri. $.

Cowan's Restaurant. 114 Elm St.; (636) 239-3213; www.cowansrestaurant.com. This is Washington's oldest restaurant, est. 1930. With its down-home country atmosphere and home-style cooking, Cowan's is famous for its delicious fruit pies and "Mile High Pies" like butterscotch meringue, chocolate peanut butter, chocolate chip pecan, rhubarb custard, and blueberry crumb. Hearty breakfasts are served all day, including Pecan Cakes (buttermilk pancakes loaded with choice pecan pieces) and the Cowan's Scramble (buttermilk biscuit, scrambled eggs, and melted cheese, topped with sausage milk gravy). In addition to daily specials, the lunch and dinner menu includes sandwiches, burgers, and good old-fashioned American favorites like homemade meat loaf, fried chicken, BBQ pork steaks, fried catfish, and chicken Parmesan. Open Wed through Sat from 6 a.m. to 8 p.m. and Sun from 6 a.m. to 7 p.m. Closed Mon and Tues. $–$$.

where to stay

Brick Inn Bed & Breakfast. 516 W. 3rd St.; (636) 390-3264; www.brickinnbedandbreakfast
.com. Located just 3 blocks from restaurants, shops, and the Missouri riverfront, the Brick Inn has 4 guest rooms, each with a private bathroom. The 2-room Duke and Duchess suite features a king-size bed and a living room with a leather sofa, 2 televisions, and a DVD player, while the remaining 3 rooms also offer king-size beds and 32-inch flat-screen TVs. The public areas include a hot tub and fire pit. Guests can enjoy off-street parking, and there's a free shuttle from the Amtrak station and the Katy Trail. A full hot breakfast is served every day, and guests can dine in the sunroom or on the spacious outdoor patio. $$.

New Haven Levee House. 105 Main St., New Haven; (636) 239-6190; www.leveehouse
.com. Get away from it all and spend the night in a cozy 1876 cottage overlooking the Missouri River in New Haven. Named by the *St. Louis Post-Dispatch* as one of the 6 most romantic spots in Missouri, the house has 2 porches and a fully equipped kitchen and is furnished with locally found antiques and treasures. You'll have the whole house to yourself. The bedroom is located upstairs, and it features a queen-size canopy bed. $$.

hermann, mo

The city of Hermann was established in 1837 as a German Society settlement. The story is that the Hermann area's resemblance to the Rhine Valley prompted scouts from the German Settlement Society of Philadelphia to choose the site for a new colony on the American frontier. Apparently they were disheartened at how quickly their countrymen were assimilating into American society, so they decided to build a new city in the new western territory that would be "German in every particular way." Today Hermann's old-world charm remains, as much of its downtown historic district features more than 150 buildings that are on the National Register of Historic Places. Visitors are attracted to the town's rich history and the slower-paced lifestyle embraced by its 2,700 residents. In 2011 Hermann was named one of "America's Prettiest Towns" by *Forbes* magazine.

getting there

Herman is located only about 28 miles from Washington, MO. Take MO 100 West for about 25 miles and turn left onto Gutenberg Street, then take the third right onto E. 4th Street.

However, if you want to follow the Wine Road, also known as MO 94, take MO 47 North/Franklin Street and follow MO 47 North. Turn left onto MO 94 West and continue for about 7 miles. Turn right to stay on MO 94 West and follow it for a little less than a mile. Take the second left to stay on MO 94 West and continue for another 19 miles. Turn left onto MO 19 South and follow it for about 2 miles, then make a left onto E. 4th Street.

where to go

Adam Puchta Winery. 1947 CR 209; (573) 486-5596; www.adampuchtawine.com. Situated in the Frene Creek Valley, less than 3 miles southwest of Hermann, the Adam Puchta Winery is the oldest continuously owned family-farm winery in Missouri, and it's one of very few in the country that date back to pre-Prohibition days. The winery produces a dozen vintages, and their wines have earned numerous medals in state, national, and international competitions. The tasting room and gift shop are located in the original Puchta family homestead. Open daily.

Hermannhof Winery. 330 E. 1st St.; (573) 486-5959; www.hermannhof.com. Hermannhof originally opened as a brewery in 1852, and today the century-old stone and brick building and wine cellars are listed as a National Historic Site. The winery is situated in Hermann, but the vineyards are located just outside of town. Hermannhof is a small winery producing 15 varieties, including champagne made in the original French *méthode champenoise* process. Hermannhof is a two-time winner of the Brown-Foreman Trophy for "Best New World White Wine." Visitors can tour the historic stone and brick wine cellars and building and sample a variety of wines in the Three California Vineyards Tasting Room, which is located next door. The Hermannhof store also sells authentic German-recipe sausages and a variety of cheeses, which guests can enjoy inside by the fireplace or outdoors under the grape arbor. Open daily.

OakGlenn Winery. 1104 Oak Glenn Pl.; (573) 486-5057; www.oakglenn.com. Situated high on a Missouri River bluff, the winery is located 2.5 miles east of Hermann and offers beautiful views of the vineyards and surrounding countryside. OakGlenn produces more than a dozen wines, including a red port, a white port, and its multiple award-winning Norton. Live entertainment is featured on the outdoor patio most Saturdays from June through

Sept, and an Oktoberfest celebration takes place on weekends during Oct. There's even a wine museum of sorts on the property. In 1859 the land was owned by an internationally known horticulturist and vintner named George Husmann. The George Husmann Wine Pavilion features a 16-panel exhibit about the life of Husmann, considered to be a founding father of the American wine industry. Open daily.

Ride, Rest & Go Bicycle Shop. 215 Schiller St.; (573) 486-9170. Stop in to rent a bike for a ride around town or along the Katy Trail. Featuring Schwinn, GT, and Mongoose bikes and all the necessary accessories, they are open every day but are in the shop for only a few hours on Sun.

Stone Hill Winery. 1110 Stone Hill Hwy.; (800) 909-WINE; www.stonehillwinery.com. Stone Hill has received more than 3,400 medals since 1993, and the winery produces over two dozen red, white, rosé, sparkling, and dessert wines. They also make 3 types of nonalcoholic juices. There are 3 Stone Hill winery locations in the state—as well as 7 vineyards—and the Hermann location offers tours, wine tastings, live music, and special events such as the occasional "grape stomping." Take a guided tour of the cavernous wine cellars and visit one of the 3 tasting rooms, or settle in and enjoy the view overlooking Hermann. The 3,000-square-foot gift shop includes Stone Hill vintages and wine-related accessories and souvenirs. The Vintage Restaurant, located in the winery's restored carriage house and horse barn, offers a menu of steaks, American dishes, and a variety of hearty German cuisine.

Tin Mill Brewing Company. 1st and Gutenberg Streets; (573) 486-2275; www.tinmill brewery.com. Located in a historic century-old tin mill in downtown Hermann, Tin Mill Brewing Company is one of the few German-style microbreweries in the country. Their beers are brewed in accordance with the German Purity Law of 1516, also known as *Reinheitsgebot,* which was a regulation stating that the only ingredients that could be used in the production of beer were water, barley, and hops. Tin Mill also uses the old-world tradition of *kräusening* where newly fermented beer is added to a batch of beer that is almost finished fermenting. The process recharges the fermentation activity and naturally carbonates the beer. The brewery's barley and hops are imported from the noted Hallertau region of Germany, and they brew and bottle all of their beers on-site. Choose from the Skyscraper, Pilsner, Red Caboose, First Street Wheat, Oktoberfest, and Midnight Whistle. Self-guided brewery tours and sampling are offered daily.

where to shop

Antiques Unlimited I. 117 E. 2nd St.; (573) 486-2148; www.antsunltd.com. This store carries an assortment of primitives, glassware, framed artwork, and an inventory of American and European antique furniture and decorator furniture pieces. But what makes it special is the museum/shop-within-a-shop called the Ye Olde Fire Company. One part museum, one part retail outlet, the shop carries firefighting-themed items like toys, knick-knacks, figurines, and gift items as well as a display of firefighter badges, helmets, lanterns, nozzles, and small pieces of modern-era equipment. They're usually open every day, but it's a good idea to call first to make sure.

Antiques Unlimited II. 205 E. 1st St.; (573) 486-8860. Owned by the same couple who owns Antiques Unlimited I, this location serves as a dealers' co-op filled with early country vintage items like glassware, collectibles, stoneware, and other assorted stuff. Open daily.

Bargain Basement Antiques & Collectibles. 205 E. 1st St.; (573) 237-2106. The 13-room store features something for everyone, as each room is chock-full of "stuff" ranging from primitive furniture and quilts to stained glass and garden items. There's one room that has nothing but kids' stuff and several rooms filled with kitchen items. Open Mon through Sat year-round and occasionally on Sun.

Find in Time Antique Mall. 220 E. 1st St.; (573) 486-9121. The 4,000-square-foot antiques mall features 15 vendors offering an eclectic array of furniture, glassware, china, and collectibles. The mall's owner also buys and sells estates, so he has first access to lots of unique items located throughout the area. Closed Tues.

Kunstlerhaus Art Gallery & Pottery Shop. 207 E. 1st St.; (573) 486-2303; www.hermann artists.com. Kunstlerhaus carries fine art, ceramics, metal works, fiber, sketches, wood-work, and folk art by local artists. See artists at work and browse Native American artifacts; beautiful coral, jade, and sterling silver jewelry; handbags; furniture; and handmade pottery. Open daily.

Red Barn Antiques. 523 W. 9th St.; (573) 486-5544. Red Barn features a variety of country antiques and small furniture, architectural antiques, farm- and kitchen-related items, and tools from as far back as the 1700s. They also have an assortment of items from old general-merchandise stores like boxes, barrels, flour tins, and bushel baskets, along with a large selection of lamp components and chimneys. The shop itself was constructed from pieces of a dismantled 100-year-old barn and rebuilt next door to the Red Barn Craft Shop. Open year-round, Mon through Sat.

where to eat

Vintage Restaurant at Stone Hill Winery. 1110 Stone Hill Hwy.; (573) 486-2221; www .stonehillwinery.com/locations/hermann/restaurant. Soups made with Stone Hill wines, salads, and light entrees like breaded deep-fried pickles with creamy horseradish sauce, a German onion tart (caramelized onion and sour cream custard baked in yeast dough), sauerbraten, schnitzel, and other German favorites are offered, as well as sandwiches like the Jaeger's Special (open-faced ground beef topped with roasted garlic mashed potatoes; smothered in a bacon, mushroom, and red wine sauce; and garnished with french-fried onions) and entrees such as pan-sautéed tilapia with remoulade and a smoked pork chop with brandied apples. At dinner the menu expands to include an assortment of steaks, grilled seafood, and chicken dishes. $$.

where to stay

Hermann Hill Vineyard Inn. 711 Wein St.; (573) 486-4455; www.hermannhill.com. Containing 8 upscale guest rooms with great views, fireplaces, Jacuzzi tubs, and king-size sleigh beds, Hermann Hill offers all of the amenities of a hotel stay. Choose from 6 full breakfast options like French toast, waffles, an omelet, or mushroom-crusted quiche, and enjoy nightly deliveries of warm cookies and ice cream topped with port-chocolate-raspberry sauce in your room. $$–$$$.

The Inn at Hermannhof. 237 E. 1st St.; (573) 486-5199; www.hermannhof.com. The inn features 8 modern, king-size, historically decorated suites with such amenities as marble bathrooms with jetted tubs for two, steam showers, and fireplaces. Each suite is named after a historic Missouri steamer and is furnished with restored period pieces that have been collected from the Hermann area. Enjoy a full breakfast of hearty American and German favorites each morning. Diners who prefer lighter fare will be accommodated by request. $$–$$$.

day trip 04

west

>>> **mizzou!:**
columbia, mo

columbia, mo

First and foremost, Columbia is a college town, home to the University of Missouri—more commonly referred to as Mizzou. The university was founded in 1839 and has a 21st-century student population of more than 30,000. Inhabited by more than 100,000 full-time residents, the city was originally incorporated in 1821. Nicknamed "The Athens of Missouri" but more frequently called simply "CoMO," Columbia is located roughly halfway between St. Louis and Kansas City. The regular influx of students and their ever-changing interests and passions help drive Columbia, as the city practically pulsates with live entertainment, sporting events, and arts and cultural offerings throughout the year.

getting there

From downtown St. Louis, find your way onto I-64 West/US 40 West and follow it for about 39 miles, continuing onto US 40 West/US 61 North. Take the exit onto I-70 West/US 40 West toward Kansas City and continue along I-70 for approximately 82 miles. Take exit 128—the exit is on the left—for I-70 Business West toward Columbia, then make a slight right onto Business Loop 70 East and follow it for about a mile. Turn left onto N. College Avenue, then make a right onto E. Broadway.

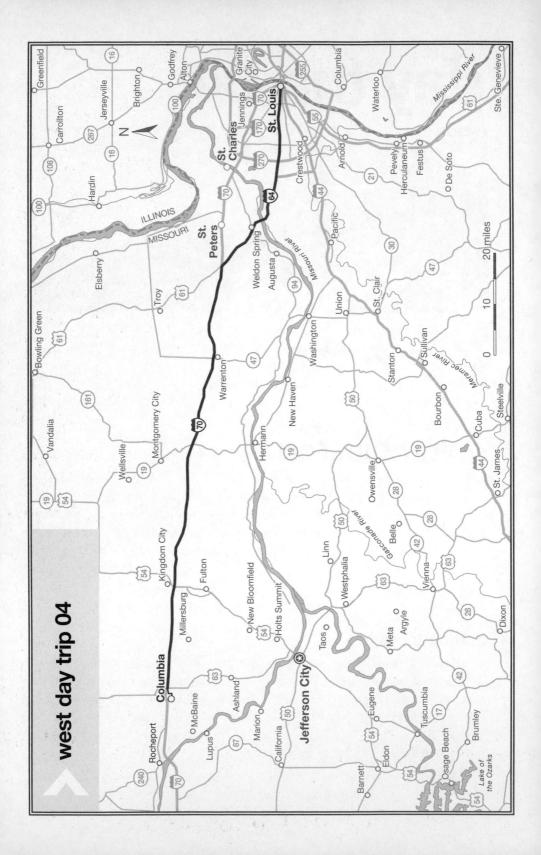

where to go

The Blue Note. 17 N. 9th St.; (573) 874-1944; www.thebluenote.com. This legendary bar and music hall in the heart of downtown Columbia welcomes well-known and up-and-coming bands from the world of rock 'n' roll, blues, alternative country, jazz, reggae—you name it, they've played here. During the summer the Note shuts down the street and hosts monthly outdoor concerts.

Finger Lakes State Park. 1505 E. Peabody Rd.; (573) 443-5315; www.mostateparks .com/park/finger-lakes-state-park. The 1,128-acre park offers a variety of recreational activities like hiking, swimming, fishing, canoeing, scuba diving, camping, picnicking, and off-roading. Finger Lakes State Park was once the site of a coal strip-mining operation, and the many small, isolated lakes left by the mining company were joined by a series of dams and canals, resulting in a 1.5-mile-long strand of water running along the eastern edge of the park that's ideal for canoeing and kayaking. Anglers can fish for black bass; channel, blue, and flathead catfish; striped bass; and crappie at the many fishing holes located throughout the park, and there's a sand beach and changing house for those who just want to cool off in the water. The challenging 2.25-mile Kelley Branch Trail is a hiking and mountain bike path through the wooded hills of the 90-acre Kelley Branch Restoration Area and features steep mounds 20 to 30 feet high. Finger Lakes is also home to more than 70 miles of off-road motorcycle and all-terrain vehicle trails and is one of only two ATV parks in the Missouri parks system. Campers can choose one of 19 basic and 16 electric campsites, with on-season services including a dump station, modern restrooms, and hot showers. The campground is open and reservable year-round. In the center of the park, there's a shaded picnic area, complete with picnic tables and grills.

L. A. Nickell Golf Course. 1800 Parkside Dr.; (573) 445-4213; www.gocolumbia.com. Owned and operated by the City of Columbia's Parks & Recreation Department, the 18-hole golf course and driving range are situated on a 533-acre park called Columbia Cosmopolitan Recreation Area, or Cosmo Park. The course features 3 sets of tees, irrigated zoysia fairways, sand traps, mature trees, bent grass greens, lakes, riding carts, and continuous golf cart paths. Yardage is 5,869 from the white tees, 4,771 from the red tees, and 6,314 from the blue tees. The course offers an adequate challenge for the lower handicappers and a fun and more difficult layout with generous ball-landing areas for higher handicappers and beginners. Call (573) 447-4166 to reserve a tee time. Reservations are available 4 days in advance for non–tee time card holders.

Lake of the Woods Golf Course. 6700 St. Charles Rd.; (573) 474-7011; www.gocolumbia .com. The city-owned-and-operated golf course, located east of Columbia on 145 acres, is open year-round. It features 3 sets of tees, sand traps, mature trees, large zoysia fairways, bent grass greens, lakes, riding carts, continuous cart paths, a tee-to-green watering system, and a clubhouse with concessions. In addition to the 18-hole golf course, the Lake of the Woods Recreation Area features a swimming pool, a fishing lake, and picnic sites. Call (573) 447-4166 to reserve a tee time. Reservations are available 4 days in advance for non–tee time card holders.

Les Bourgeois Vineyards. 14020 W. Hwy. BB, Rocheport; (800) 690-1830; www.missouri wine.com. Situated about 15 miles from Columbia in nearby Rocheport, Les Bourgeois Vineyards offer spectacular bluff-top views of the Missouri River Valley and a variety of award-winning wines. The family-owned-and-operated winery has 27 acres of Chambourcin, Chardonel, Norton, Vidal, and Vignoles grapes, and it's the third-largest winery in the state, producing more than 90,000 gallons a year. In 2010 they were the Jerry D. Mead's New World International Wine Competition Best of Varietal, Best of Class gold medal winner for their Concord, and were the silver medal winner for their Jeunette Rouge. They also won a 2010 Taster Guild International Wine Judging silver medal for their Pink Fox, Concord, and Norton 2008. Sample some vino and hang out with the gift shop cats—appropriately named Syrah and Jeunette Rouge—or enjoy a snack and a beverage at the A-frame picnic area overlooking the Missouri River. Open daily year-round.

Missouri Theatre Center for the Arts. 203 S. 9th St.; (573) 875-0600; www.motheatre .org. Listed on the National Register of Historic Places, the Missouri Theatre is the area's only pre-Depression-era movie palace and vaudeville stage. Modeled after the design of the Paris Opera House, it was built by Boller Brothers Architects of Kansas City in 1928. The interior is an ornate baroque and rococo style of the Louis XIV and XV periods. Performing arts groups that call the venue home include the Missouri Symphony Orchestra, Show-Me Opera, Columbia Civic Orchestra, Missouri Contemporary Ballet, and the Boonslick Chordbusters, who sing unaccompanied four-part harmony. The theater also hosts occasional concerts and performances by stand-up comedians.

Museum of Anthropology. 100 Swallow Hall, University of Missouri campus; (573) 882-3573; http://anthromuseum.missouri.edu. The museum features the largest holding of prehistoric Missouri artifacts in the world, including millions of items dating back as far as 9000 BC. Exhibits focus on Missouri archaeology and Native American ethnographic materials, including the Arctic, Northwest, Southwest, Plains, and Great Basin. The collection of 19th- and 20th-century materials features American carpentry, household items, and agricultural tools, as well as Depression glass, pottery, children's toys and games, books, photographs, sheet music, and gun parts, accessories, and gunsmithing tools. The Museum of Anthropology is home to the largest archery assemblage in the world, including the extensive Grayson Archery Collection. Open Mon through Fri.

Museum of Art & Archaeology. Pickard Hall on the Francis Quadrangle, University of Missouri campus; (573) 882-3591; http://maa.missouri.edu. The museum houses the third-largest art collection in the state and includes artworks from the ancient world along with European and American works from the early Middle Ages to the present. In addition to the Samuel H. Kress Study Collection of important paintings from the Renaissance and baroque periods, exhibits are devoted to Asian, African, pre-Columbian, and Oceanic art. The museum hosts a number of changing exhibitions each year, and there's a special installation focused on the art of Missouri with works by such artists as John Sites Ankeney, Thomas Hart Benton, Keith Crown, Frederick E. Shane, Frank Stack, and Frederick Oakes Sylvester. Closed Mon.

PS:Gallery. 1025 E. Walnut St.; (573) 442-4831; www.perlow-stevensgallery.com. PS:Gallery features rotating exhibits of works by local, regional, and national artists in a variety of mediums, including jewelry, wood, glass, ceramic, paintings, photography, sculptures, and fiber. The gallery's welcoming atmosphere provides visitors with an enjoyable art experience.

Ragtag Cinema & Cafe. 10 Hitt St.; (573) 443-4359; www.ragtagfilm.com. Ragtime is a nonprofit theater that screens independent, international, and art films and other media arts. Activities include a monthly film education series hosted by a MU Film Studies professor, kids' matinees, documentaries, an eclectic array of film festivals, directors and critics programs, and other interactive ways to experience and enjoy the cinema.

Rock Bridge Memorial State Park. 5901 S. Hwy. 163; (573) 449-7402; www.mostate parks.com/park/rock-bridge-memorial-state-park. Located just a short drive outside of Columbia, Rock Bridge Memorial State Park gives outdoorsy types a chance to hike, bike, and peek into Missouri's underworld. The park has a large cave system with a rock bridge, sinkholes, a spring, and the Devil's Icebox, a double sinkhole that offers a view of the underground stream and the feel of cool, refreshing air, which is how it got its name. In addition to an orienteering course, there are 8 hiking and biking trails available, ranging in length from the 0.5-mile Devil's Icebox Trail to the 8.5-mile Gans Creek Wild Area Trail, which can be explored on foot or on horseback. The 2-mile Grassland Trail and 1.75-mile Karst Trail both wind through restored native grasslands and past wooded sinkholes, which provide habitat for wildlife and wetland plants. Picnic sites are located throughout the park, including a reservable picnic shelter, and playground equipment suitable for kids ages 5 to 12 is also available.

State Historical Society of Missouri Main Art Gallery. 1020 Lowry St.; (800) 747-6366; http://shs.umsystem.edu. In addition to an assemblage of past and present Missouri artists, the society's art collection includes one of the largest groups of paintings by George Caleb Bingham, including *Order No. 11,* and a collection of Thomas Hart Benton paintings that contains the *Year of Peril* series, lithographs, and other works. The Main Gallery and Corridor Galleries feature rotating exhibits, and the society frequently hosts traveling exhibitions with ties to Missouri like those detailing elements of the Lewis and Clark expedition.

where to shop

Alleyway Arts. 1107 E. Broadway; (573) 489-0469; www.alleywayarts.com. Alleyway Arts features prints and paintings by local artist David Spear, who offers his urban Americana take on everything from Columbia landmarks and daily life in a college town to broader, classic themes like interpersonal relationships.

Bluestem Missouri Crafts. 13 S. 9th St.; (573) 442-0211; www.bluestemcrafts.com. As a partnership of artists, Bluestem's 3-room gallery features the work of 325 artists and craftspeople from Missouri and its 8 neighboring states. The dynamic and evolving collection includes clay, art glass, wooden baby and kids' toys, metal, stoneware, garden artwork, home decor, and fiber. From traditional to contemporary works, Bluestem's nationally recognized artists set the standard for regional excellence. Free gift wrapping. Open daily.

Columbia Mall. 2300 Bernadette Dr.; (573) 445-8458; www.visitcolumbiamall.com. Anchored by Dillard's, JCPenney, Sears, Barnes and Noble, and Target, the shopping mall houses more than 100 stores, including Abercrombie & Fitch, Lids, Aeropostale, Coldwater Creek, Merle Norman, Eddie Bauer, Footlocker, Talbots, Hollister, Gymboree, and Victoria's Secret.

The District. 11 S. 10th St.; (573) 442-6816; www.discoverthedistrict.com. The 43-block area has more than 100 retailers and unique specialty stores offering men's, women's, and children's apparel, gifts, jewelry, furniture, appliances, antiques, vintage clothing and accessories, bookstores, and wine and gourmet food shops. There are plenty of affordable parking garages nearby—rates are only about 50 cents an hour.

Maude Vintage. 818 E. Broadway; (573) 449-3320; www.maudevintage.com. Specializing in men's and women's clothing from the early 1980s and before, the shop also showcases dozens of designers who have created unique, specialized lines of "recombinated" items ranging from clothes and accessories to music and art. They also have more than 3,500 square feet of space devoted to costume rentals.

Poppy. 920 E. Broadway, #1; (573) 442-3223; www.poppyarts.com. The shop features a unique selection of contemporary crafts and folk art from around the country, including handcrafted jewelry, pet-themed gifts and decor, furniture and accessories by STICKS Furniture, wooden dollhouses and children's toys, seasonal decor, and original artworks in ceramic and metal. They also stock a stylish mix of purses, hats, gloves, scarves, and other accessories. Open daily.

where to eat

Addison's. 709 Cherry St.; (573) 256-1995; www.addisonssophias.com/addisons. Addison's is a casual, trendy restaurant with an eclectic menu of appetizers, salads, pasta dishes, and "S.M.M.s"—Sandwich Making Materials—like the Black Bean and Thai Peanut

Wrap (black beans, ginger rice, wonton curls, tomatoes, scallions, carrots, cheddar cheese, and romaine lettuce in a soft tomato tortilla with an Asian ginger-peanut dressing). Known for their Nachos Bianco (Italian pasta chips topped with Asiago cheese sauce, tomatoes, scallions, kalamata olives, banana peppers, mozzarella cheese, and chicken or chorizo sausage). Addison's also offers specialties like Ahi Tuna Amuse-Bouche (seasoned tomato tortilla crisps topped with lemon cream cheese, raw ahi tuna, pickled ginger, scallions, red pepper, sesame seeds, and cilantro and finished with a honey-soy reduction and wasabi) and their Jalapeño Smothered Pork Chop (grilled 12-ounce brown-sugar-brined pork chop topped with pepper jack cheese sauce, blistered jalapeños, tomatoes, and scallions). $$.

Blufftop Bistro. Les Bourgeois Vineyards, 14020 W. Hwy. BB; (800) 690-1830; http://missouriwine.com/blufftop-bistro.php. This wine garden and bistro offers spectacular views and a menu of house-smoked meats, locally grown produce, fresh seafood, and hearty pastas. Lunch options include the Maine Shrimp Roll (poached shrimp, tomatoes, lettuce, pickled onion, and Old Bay aioli on a toasted roll) and Pork Tacos (cinnamon-orange pork carnitas, grilled flour tortillas, ancho avocado cream, coriander tomato relish, and *queso fresco*), salads, and appetizers. For dinner try the pan-seared scallops, porcini-rubbed rib eye steak, or Mushroom Eggplant Napoleon (fried polenta, white wine tomato sauce, mozzarella, and basil oil). The bistro also offers a Sunday brunch with menu items like Cajun eggs Florentine, ricotta and orange pancakes, and Gorgonzola cheesecake with toasted bread, tomato sauce, and pesto. $$–$$$.

Flat Branch Pub & Brewing. 115 S. 5th St,; (573) 499-0400; www.flatbranch.com. The microbrewery features a dozen brews on tap that change daily, like Katy Trail Pale Ale, Green Chili Beer, Owens Preemie-um Porter, and Oil Change Oatmeal Stout. There's also a full bar with more than 35 scotches, 9 bourbons, and a variety of additional libations. In addition to such entrees as bangers and mash, shepherd's pie, meat loaf, and ribs, the pub is renowned for their Chokes 'n Cheese (creamy artichoke dip served hot in a bread boule with fresh carrots, broccoli, and celery on the side) appetizer and the half-pound Flat Branch Burger (topped with Chokes 'n Cheese dip and served on a toasted artisan bun). The menu also includes the Flat Branch Veggie Burger (house-made burger of oats, dirty rice, tofu, red pepper, pecans, and portobello mushrooms) and an array of brick-oven pizzas, salads, and sandwiches. Open daily. $–$$.

The Heidelberg. 410 S. 9th St.; (573) 449-6927; www.theheidelberg.com. A popular place to tailgate and brunch prior to Mizzou football games, the Heidelberg is a Columbia tradition. It offers a menu of adult beverages and inexpensive pub grub appetizers, burgers, pizzas, sandwiches, and salads. There's also a Sunday brunch buffet featuring everything from made-to-order omelets and biscuits and gravy to chili, chicken wings, and cobbler. $$.

Lakota Coffee Company. 24 S. 9th St.; (573) 874-2852; www.lakotacoffee.com. Lakota features fresh-roasted specialty coffees, coffee drinks, loose-leaf tea, smoothies, frappes, and a lunch menu of cold sandwiches and hot paninis like the Turkey Bacon Heaven (maple honey turkey, bacon, Gouda cheese, lettuce, tomato, and mayonnaise) and the half-pounder known as the Beast (maple honey turkey, Black Forest ham, provolone cheese, lots of bacon, lettuce, tomato, and a drizzling of honey mustard on Hawaiian pineapple bread). $.

Main Squeeze Natural Foods Cafe & Juice Bar. 28 S. 9th St.; (573) 817-5616; www .main-squeeze.com. Main Squeeze is healthy eating at its best, with a menu of all-natural foods and using organic ingredients when available. Try the Catalpa Tree Burrito (brown rice, refried beans, Monterey jack cheese, tomato, and red onion in a sprouted wheat tortilla, topped with spicy enchilada sauce, sour cream, sunflower seeds, and sprouts), Don't Be Gruel (brown rice, seasoned beans, tofu, Monterey jack cheese, homemade salsa, green goddess, and red onion), or a fresh glass of Elvis Parsley juice (carrot, celery, spinach, parsley, and beets). An extensive breakfast menu is available on Sat and Sun. The super-fresh, all-vegetarian menu has a number of vegan options available as well. Get it to go in some of their earth-friendly packaging. Open daily. $.

Shakespeare's Pizza. 225 S. 9th St.; (573) 449-2454; www.shakespeares.com. Shakespeare's is a Mizzou student tradition and was named "Best College Hangout in the Nation" by *Good Morning America* in 2010. The pizza here isn't fancy, it's just really good. Choose wheat or white crust—they make the dough fresh from scratch several times a day—and pick the meats and vegetables you prefer. They only use fresh veggies, never frozen, and slice their own pepperoni so they can make the pieces thick enough to satisfy their own preferences. Specialty pies include one named for the heart-healthy mayor called the Darwin (onions, green peppers, artichoke hearts, turkey, and tomatoes) and the Masterpiece, which includes copious amounts of every topping they have. Their cheese-free pizzas are vegan-friendly because there are no animal products in the crust or the sauce. $–$$.

Sophia's. 3915 S. Providence Rd.; (573) 874-8009; www.addisonssophias.com/sophias. Offering Southern European–influenced cuisine, the same folks who own Addison's run Sophia's. This restaurant offers a more genteel yet still casual dining experience for lunch, dinner, and Sunday brunch. Choose from tapas, salads, and pasta dishes along with entrees such as the Godiva Ahi Tuna (seared sushi-grade ahi tuna topped with a Godiva white chocolate liqueur sauce) and Brandy Cream Filet (grilled 8-ounce beef filet topped with brandy cream sauce over white cheddar mashers). Menu options are the same for lunch and dinner, with smaller portions served at lunch, and there's a very nice, reasonably priced wine list. $$.

Sparky's Homemade Ice Cream. 21 S. 9th St.; (573) 443-7400. Sparky's is known for it funny and offbeat flavors of ice cream, including such favorites as lavender honey, maple bacon, carrot cake, green tea, jalapeño chocolate, Thai black rice, and red wine ice cream made with wine from a local winery and dark chocolate chunks. They'll mix almost anything with ice cream—they made a special cicada flavor in 2011—and serve up concoctions like Red Bull and ice cream, a Guinness beer float, and other adults-only "booze shakes" such as White Russians and Grasshoppers. Ice-cream crepes with Nutella and whipped cream are the newest addition to the menu. Sparky's also has vegan-friendly sorbets in flavors like mango lime, strawberry lemonade, champagne peach, and banana caramel. $.

where to stay

The Gathering Place B&B. 606 S. College Ave.; (573) 440 1301; www.gatheringplace bedandbreakfast.com. Located across the street from the University of Missouri campus, the Gathering Place offers 5 guest suites, all with private bathrooms. The inn is operated by the College of Agriculture, Food and Natural Resources and serves as an educational capstone experience for a select group of students studying hotel and restaurant management. King, single, and double rooms are available, including the Textiles Room, which can accommodate up to 4 people with its 2 queen-size beds, and the spacious Chemistry Room, which has a king-size bed and lots of room to relax. Amenities include free Wi-Fi, a beautiful backyard courtyard, off-street parking, individually controlled room temperature, in-room cable TV, a gourmet breakfast, and a guest pass to the university's rec center if you want to work out. $$.

day trip 05

west

>>> **a capital affair:**
jefferson city, mo

jefferson city, mo

Perched on the northern edge of the Ozark Plateau near the geographic center of Missouri, Jefferson City was specifically created to serve as the state capital by the Missouri state legislature in 1821. The city was originally laid out by Daniel Morgan Boone, son of the famed frontiersman, and was named for US president Thomas Jefferson. Today "Jeff City" remains a hotbed of state politics and offers an all-American way of life for its 43,000 residents and the state lawmakers who call it home.

getting there

From St. Louis, follow I-44 West for about 43 miles, then take exit 247 to merge onto US 50 West toward Union/Jefferson City. Continue on US 50 West for a little more than 81 miles, then make a right onto Jefferson Street and take the second left onto W. Miller Street. Continue onto Washington Street and turn right.

where to go

Jefferson City Convention & Visitors Bureau. 100 E. High St.; (573) 632-2820; www .visitjeffersoncity.com. Stop by for a visitor's guide or some advice about where to go and what to see. You can book a tour of the old Missouri State Penitentiary here too. The CVB

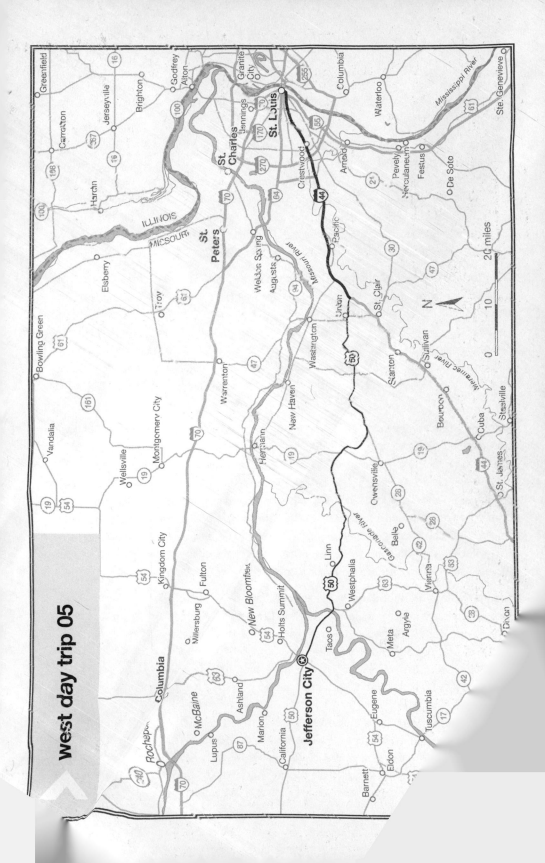

west day trip 05

is open Mon through Fri from 8 a.m. to 5 p.m. and Sat from 10 a.m. to 2 p.m. (Sat hours Apr through Oct only).

Jefferson Landing State Historic Site. 101 Jefferson St.; (573) 751-2854. The Jefferson Landing State Historic Site, which is a rare Missouri River landing, includes buildings dating back to the mid-1800s. The Lohman Building houses a transportation exhibit and features a 20-minute film called *Welcome to the Missouri State Capital* that offers the history of Jefferson City. The Union Hotel building—home to the city's Amtrak train station—also houses rotating exhibits about Missouri's history, art, and culture in the Elizabeth Rozier Gallery. Both offer free admission. Open Mar 1 through Labor Day. Closed Mon.

Missouri Governor's Mansion. 100 Madison St.; (573) 751-4141; http://mansion.mo .gov. Built in 1871, the 3-story Missouri Governor's Mansion is one of the oldest governor's homes in the US and has housed 35 of the state's governors. Designed by noted St. Louis architect George Ingham Barnett, the home is an example of Second Empire architecture and is listed on the National Register of Historic Places. Volunteer docents provide the free historical tours, which last approximately 20 to 30 minutes. Tours are available Tues, Wed, and Thurs from Mar through May, and Tues and Thurs only during the other months of the year.

Missouri State Museum. 201 W. Capitol Ave.; (573) 751-2854; www.mostateparks.com/ park/missouri-state-museum. The Missouri State Museum features a collection of 50,000 artifacts and objects representative of the state's cultural and natural history. It includes 2 main exhibit halls—the History Hall and the Resources Hall—as well as the Missouri Veterans Gallery and the Foundations Gallery, which features changing exhibits about state government and the state capitol. Museum staff members provide free guided tours of the capitol, Jefferson Landing State Historic Site, and the Governor's Mansion. Guided tours are available year-round, or you can pick up a self-guided tour map from the Capitol Tour Reservation Desk and strike out on your own.

Missouri State Penitentiary. 115 Lafayette St.; (866) 998-6998; www.visitmo.com/ missouri-state-penitentiary-tours.aspx. Built and opened for use in 1836, the Missouri State Penitentiary (MSP) would become known as the "bloodiest 47 acres in America." Before closing in 2004, MSP was the oldest continually operating penitentiary west of Mississippi River. Today's visitors aren't searched for contraband—they just have to wear hard hat while on the tours, which are led by former corrections offers or guards stationed inside the prison walls. The penitentiary is very rundown, which is why a hard hat is needed for the tours that showcase MSP's history with a walk through the control center, yard, industry area, exercise yard, and cellblocks in housing Unit A, built in 1868 to get a look at the dungeon cells where inmates often went mad, the gas chamber where 40 male and female inmates were executed, and cells of such famous inmates as light-heavyweight champion Sonny Liston and James Earl Ray, the man who killed

Dr. Martin Luther King Jr. Ray escaped from the prison in 1967 and assassinated Dr. King in 1968. Because of the nature of the tours, children under 10 years old are not permitted. All attendees must sign a waiver of liability, and children under 18 must have a parent or guardian's signature on their waiver. Due to the age of the facility, the tours are not wheelchair accessible.

Missouri Supreme Court Building. 207 W. High St.; (573) 751-4144; www.courts.mo .gov. The 3-story redbrick Supreme Court Building opened in 1907 and features French Renaissance architecture. Today it houses the offices of the Supreme Court clerk and the clerk's staff, 2 courtrooms, the office of the state attorney general, and the 2-story-high Supreme Court Library. The library contains more than 110,000 volumes, including state and federal court decisions, Missouri Approved Jury Instructions, state and federal statutes, legal periodicals, and treatises. In addition to free half-hour tours of the historic building, visitors are welcome to observe oral arguments, which are usually held between Sept and May each year. Tours available Mon through Fri only.

where to shop

Capital Mall. 3600 Country Club Dr.; (573) 893-5437; www.capitalmall.com. The enclosed shopping mall is anchored by 3 major retailers—JCPenney, Dillard's, and Sears—and populated with specialty stores such as Hibbett Sporting Goods, Payless Shoe Source, American Eagle Outfitters, Bath & Body Works, Buckle, and Radio Shack.

Downtown Book & Toy. 125 E. High St.; (573) 635-1185. A local, family-owned, full-service bookstore that's been around since 1984, they also stock an assortment of educational toys, games, and puzzles for all ages as well as magazines. The shop offers free gift wrapping and out-of-print book searches, in addition to discounts on new releases and *New York Times* bestsellers.

where to eat

Cafe via Roma. 105 W. High St.; (573) 636-8771; www.cafeviaroma.com. Casual cafe serving hot panini sandwiches, wraps, pasta dishes, and salads like the Volcano (house salad mix, hot Italian spiced chicken breast, pico de gallo, guacamole, sour cream, tortilla chips, and ranch dressing) and the Farmer's Salad (spring mix, hot roasted potatoes, crumbled bacon, hard-boiled egg, Roma tomato, croutons, and homemade house vinaigrette). Grab a fresh-baked scone, muffin, or cinnamon roll for breakfast, along with homemade quiche and breakfast paninis and wraps. Get your caffeine boost with a cappuccino, espresso, or other assorted coffee drinks. $.

Domenico's Italian Restaurant & Lounge. 3702 W. Truman Blvd.; (573) 893-5454; www .domenicosjeffcity.com. Choose from a menu of steak, seafood, chicken, veal, and past options served in a casual atmosphere. Dinner specialties include Beef Mudega (charbroi

14-ounce strip steak lightly breaded and topped with provel cheese, fresh mushrooms, and a white wine, lemon, and butter sauce), Horseradish Encrusted Salmon (oven-broiled filet topped with Japanese bread crumbs, Parmesan cheese, and horseradish, served over a dill cream sauce), and pasta dishes like the Hallie Special (linguine topped with a variety of vegetables and a red wine tomato sauce) and Carriage House Pasta (fettuccine tossed with artichoke hearts, black olives, and sautéed chicken breast, finished with cream and seasoned with oregano, basil, and fresh garlic). For dessert try the tiramisu (sweetened mascarpone cheese over espresso-soaked lady fingers dusted with cocoa) or a grown-up ice-cream drink like the Golden Cadillac (Galliano and white Crème de Cacao) or Pink Squirrel (Crème de Noya and white Crème de Cacao). $$.

Paddy Malone's Irish Pub. 700 W. Main St.; (573) 761-5900; www.paddymalonespub .com. Paddy Malone's is Jefferson City's oldest continually operating tavern, and it offers an authentic Irish pub atmosphere, casual dining, and a menu that has an assortment of freshly made appetizers, sandwiches, and burgers. Carnivores will love the Boo Boo Burger (half-pound burger, crispy bacon strips, and melted Guinness cheese sauce, served on grilled wheat berry toast) and the Yogi Burger (half-pound burger, breaded and deep-fried, topped with Thousand Island dressing and all the "fixin's" on Texas toast). Traditional grub includes bangers and mash, fish-and-chips, and nightly dinner specials such as locally raised and butchered steaks and chops. A dozen draughts are on tap, including Guinness, Smithwick's, Harp, Kilkenny Cream Ale, and Magner's Cider, alongside various microbrews and domestics. There's an extensive wine list and a full bar that offers 20-plus Irish and Scotch whiskies. Traditional Irish music sessions are held each month. Closed Sun year-round and on Sun and Mon during the summer. $$.

Prison Brews. 305 Ash St.; (573) 635-0678; www.prisonbrews.com. Quench your thirst with a cold one at the old Landwehr Dairy building, circa 1895, choosing from a large selection of handcrafted ales brewed on-site. The food menu features wood-fired oven-baked pizzas, soups, salads, burgers, and bratwursts made with Prison Brews' beer. Speaking of beer, the brew menu features a litany of seasonal beers like Cellmate Pale Ale, Misdemeanor Maibock, Pretty Boy Floyd Peach Wheat, Holding Cell Hefeweizen, and Deathrow Oatmeal Stout. Dine inside the walls or get out on the large outdoor patio and play a few games of bocce, also known as Italian lawn bowling. $–$$.

where to stay

Huber's Ferry Bed & Breakfast. 27 CR 501; (573) 455-2979; www.hubersferrybedand breakfast.com. Perched majestically atop the bluffs overlooking the Osage and Maries Rivers, the Huber's Ferry B&B house was built in 1881 and is listed on the National Register of Historic Places. The main inn features the 2-room William & Mary Suite, complete with fireplace and a soaking tub as well as a full private bath, and 2 smaller guest rooms. All have private bathrooms. The Wilhelmshaven is a separate building that includes a loft and a sitting area with a fireplace, television and DVD player, CD player, microwave, refrigerator, and an antique dining table. There's also a master bathroom with a 2-person jetted tub and a double shower. You can have a full breakfast with home-baked bread, seasonal fruits, a hot entree, juice, aromatic coffee, and specialty teas delivered in the morning, or trek to the main house for breakfast in the formal dining room. $$.

northwest

day trip 01

northwest

welcome to charm central:
st. charles, mo; troy, mo

History and charm are never in short supply in this part of Missouri, as St. Charles and neighboring Troy both have rich heritages that merge well with a decidedly family-friendly nature. Many of St. Charles's 65,000 and Troy's 14,000 residents make the trip to and from St. Louis every workday, with only a 30- to 60-minute commute each way.

st. charles, mo

The oldest city on the Missouri River, St. Charles is where explorers Meriwether Lewis and William Clark departed from in 1804, seeking a route to the Pacific Ocean by order of President Thomas Jefferson. Today the city offers locals and visitors a small-town atmosphere with big-city amenities nearby. Located alongside the Missouri River, the city was founded in 1769 by French-Canadian fur trader Louis Blanchette and named *Les Petites Cotes,* or the Little Hills. During the great westward expansion, thousands of pioneers passed through St. Charles and replenished supplies one last time before departing into the new territory. The historic community served as the state's first capital in 1821. Today it is the location of the annual Lewis and Clark Rendezvous and the origin of the Boone's Lick Trail.

getting there

St. Charles is only about 30 minutes from downtown St. Louis. Take I-70 West to the 5th Street exit.

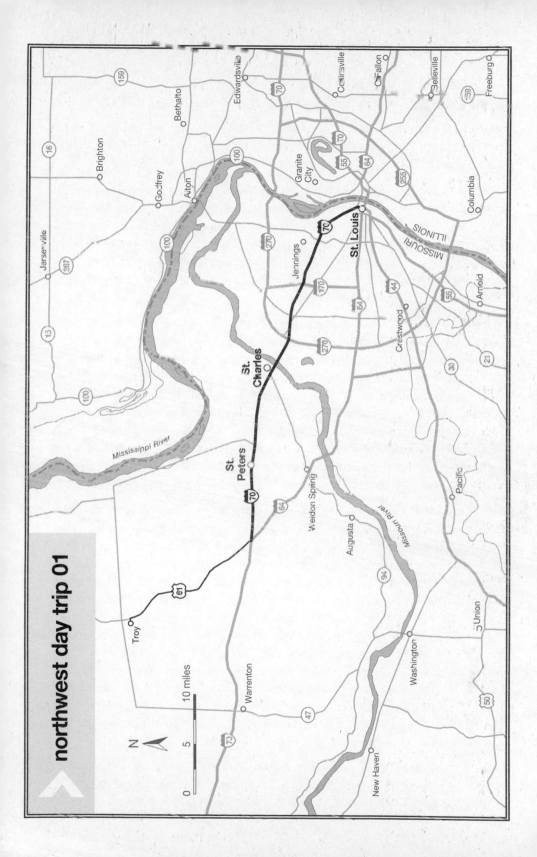

northwest day trip 01

where to go

Greater Saint Charles CVB. 230 S. Main St.; (800) 366-2427; www.historicstcharles .com. Stop by the St. Charles CVB's visitor information center and pick up some additional info about places to go, things to do, and stuff to eat in the area.

Ameristar Casino. St. Charles riverfront; (636) 949-7777; www.ameristarcasinos.com. If you're yearning for some modern-day gaming action, the 130,000-square-foot Ameristar Casino has more than 3,000 video poker and slot machines—including the Lord of the Rings slots—a variety of table games and live poker. The casino frequently hosts nationally known entertainers in the Bottleneck Blues Bar, and dining options include the Amerisports Bar & Grill, Bugatti's Steak & Pasta, Casino Bar Deli, Falcon Diner & The Bakery, King Cat Club, Landmark Buffet, and Pearl's Oyster Bar.

First Missouri State Capitol & State Historic Site. 200 S. Main St.; (636) 940-3322; www.mostateparks.com/park/first-missouri-state-capitol-state-historic-site. Located on St. Charles's Historic Main Street, the site was the first seat of the state's government. The building has been completely restored and furnished with period pieces from the 1820s, and interpretive programs explain what life was like in the early 1800s. In 1820 Governor Alexander McNair signed a bill making St. Charles the first capital of Missouri, and the new temporary capitol was located on the second floor of two adjoining Federal-style brick buildings. The space was divided and served as senate and house chambers, as well as an office for the governor and a small committee room. The site was used to run the state's government until 1826, when the new capitol in Jefferson City was completed.

Katy Trail State Park. (573) 449-7402; www.mostateparks.com/park/katy-trail-state-park. Feeling a little adventurous? The Katy Trail offers a unique opportunity for people of all ages and interests. Whether you are a bicyclist, hiker, nature lover, or history buff, the trail offers opportunities for recreation, a place to enjoy nature, and an avenue to discover the past. The trailhead located at Riverside and Boonslick Roads in St. Charles is at mile marker 39.5. Katy Trail State Park is built on the former corridor of the Missouri-Kansas-Texas Railroad, which is better known as "the Katy." When the railroad ceased operation of the route from St. Charles County to Sedalia, MO, in 1986, it was turned into an extraordinary long-distance hiking and bicycling trail that would eventually run almost 200 miles across the state. The section of trail between St. Charles and Boonville has been designated an official segment of the Lewis and Clark National Historic Trail, and the entire path is part of the American Discovery Trail. The trail also has been designated as a Millennium Legacy Trail. Bike rentals are available nearby at the Touring Cyclist (11816 St. Charles Rock Rd.; 314-739-4648; www.touringcyclist.com).

Lewis & Clark Boat House and Nature Center. Bishop's Landing, 1050 Riverside Dr.; (636) 947-3199; www.lewisandclarkcenter.org. This hands-on museum traces the journey of famed explorers Lewis and Clark as the Corps of Discovery navigated its way into the wilderness of the West. The center interprets the expedition through a collection of exhibits, literature, and educational programs. Museum exhibits focus on the role St. Charles played in the expedition, as well as the members of the expedition, the tools they used, the journals they kept, and the many Indian cultures they encountered. Detailed dioramas show the group's journey along the entire length of the Missouri River, the crossing of the Rocky Mountains, and the continued trek toward the Pacific Ocean. Located alongside the Missouri River, the center also offers exhibits that explain the river's ecosystem. For those looking to learn more about the explorers and their adventure, the Trading Post includes a good selection of books related to Lewis and Clark as well as general history and nature.

Each May the city hosts the Lewis & Clark Heritage Days, a reenactment of the encampment, complete with historically accurate costumed participants, black-powder rifle shoots, and frontier craft demonstrations. There are also 3 replicas of the boats used by the Corps of Discovery and additional exhibits about the expedition.

Mid-Rivers Golf Links. 4100 Mid Rivers Mall Dr.; (636) 939-3663; www.midriversgolf.com. Located about 2 miles from downtown St. Charles, the 18-hole course features 6,466 yards of golf from the longest tees for a par of 71. The Ned Story–designed course has a course rating of 70.9 and a slope rating of 125. The practice facilities include a 10,000-square-foot putting green, a 100-stall driving range, an irons-only area, and sand traps.

Shrine of St. Rose Philippine Duchesne. 619 N. 2nd St.; (636) 946-6127; www.ash 1818.org. The shrine attracts pilgrims from around the world who bring prayers and petitions to the fourth US saint. Its two entrances represent the shrine's Roman and St. Louis connections: The Roman connection is represented by the coat of arms of Pope Pius XII, who beatified Philippine, over the north entrance. The St. Louis connection is at the east entrance, which includes Cardinal Glennon's coat of arms and a mosaic of St. Louis, King of France. In addition to the actual shrine, visitors can tour the parlors of the early brick convent building, which Philippine called "the house where charity dwells," and see the small cell where she died at the age of 82. Items on display include primitive relics of the pioneer convent, books brought from France by Philippine and her fellow missionaries, and other articles representative of their religious and academic lives.

St. Charles County Family Arena. 2002 Arena Pkwy.; (636) 896-4200; www.familyarena .com. The 10,000-seat state-of-the-art performance center hosts trade shows; professional football, hockey, soccer, and basketball games; family events; and a variety of concerts. Recent shows have run the gamut from live performances by musicians Buddy Guy and Reba McIntire to circus performances and appearances by political pundits Sarah Palin and Glenn Beck.

Verizon Wireless Amphitheater. 14141 Riverport Dr.; (314) 298-9944; www.livenat` .com. Still called "Riverport" by the locals—the original, pre-sponsorship name of the f ity—the amphitheater is the largest outdoor venue in the metro area. From May to O

20,000-seat facility presents concerts by the country's hottest rock, country, pop, and R & B touring headliners. The only bad thing about the venue is the long postshow delay in getting out of the parking lot. However, if you plan ahead and pack a tailgate-style snack, you can hang out with fellow music fans after the show and have a real "locals" type of experience.

where to shop

Bass Pro Shops Sportsman's Warehouse. 1365 S. 5th St.; (636) 688-2500; www.bass pro.com. If you hunt, fish, or just enjoy the outdoors, welcome to mecca. There are 77,000 square feet of outdoor equipment, wildlife displays, and state-record replicas, as well as a 7,000-gallon aquarium and a shooting arcade. The store hosts a number of special events, including outdoor skill workshops, archery ranges, and weekend activities for the kids. Check out the Fish Feeding Show on Sat and Sun afternoons, as well as Family Saturdays with free crafts, demos, classes, and special guest appearances.

Centuries Past Antiques. 119 S. Main St.; (636) 946-1919. Located in the basement of a former US Post Office building, Centuries Past Antiques carries a wide variety of real antiques, vintage collectibles, and some generally unusual items. If you're looking for something really unique, check this shop first—they've had such items for sale as a Davy Crockett Halloween costume from the 1950s and antique Wade & Butcher straight razors, in addition to old cigarette advertising signs, antique cameras, historical memorabilia, coins and currency, vintage toys, jewelry and watches, furniture, music memorabilia, crystal, and china. Open daily.

Foundry Art Centre. 520 N. Main St.; (636) 255-0270; www.foundryartcentre.org. Residing inside a 1940s-era train car factory, the 36,800-square-foot building is now home to a collection of local artists' studios. The open glass fronts allow visitors to see the artists and interact with them as they create. Available artwork represents a variety of media, including oil painting, printmaking, wheel-thrown ceramics, sculpture, and watercolor. The Foundry's gift shop sells one-of-a-kind jewelry, candles, ceramics, books, puzzles, and home decor pieces.

Frenchtown. This historic St. Charles neighborhood offers more than 20 unique shops, including a variety of antiques stores. Frenchtown also boasts the US's largest selection of vintage architectural products, so if you're in the market for hardware, plumbing, molding, ceilings, intricate gingerbread, lighting accessories, weather vanes, or a cupola, this is the place for you.

Grandma's Cookies. 401 S. Main St.; (636) 947-0088. Freshly baked, delicious cookies and cupcakes served in what feels like your grandmother's kitchen. Chocolate chip cookies are the house specialty—served with milk! Closed Mon and Tues.

Historic Main Street. The 10-block-long, 200-year-old street was Missouri's first and largest historic district. Today a trolley travels along the street, which is home to more than 125 one-of-a-kind stores. Shop your way through collections of framed art, antiques, vintage and reproduction signs, Victorian accessories, lamps, collectibles, quilts—everything you can imagine is available here.

Main Street Books. 307 S. Main St.; (636) 949-0105; www.mainstreetbooks.net. This privately owned bookstore specializes in local history and guidebooks, children's titles, and books on the Civil War, Lewis and Clark, and western history. The friendly and knowledgeable staff provides great customer service. There's also a small selection of used books.

Moss Boutique. 424 S. Main St.; (636) 410-0625; www.nikmoss.com. Moss carries labels such as Silver Jeans, Mystree, Urban Behavior, and Costa Blanca and features custom designs, decorated jeans, and an international collection of unique accessories.

Reunion Revolution. New Town at St. Charles, 3257-1 Domain; (636) 724-3550; www.reunionrevolution.com. This quirky shop offers a variety of treasures from the 1950s through the 1980s as well as a host of militaria and historic uniforms from around the world. They also have items like war board games, military history books, and discharge papers. Music buffs will love the 45s, 78s, and LPs they stock, along with the vintage 45 and LP carrying cases, record company promotional items, concert posters, antique jukeboxes, and record players. The store also features more traditional antique items, including original oil and watercolor paintings, prints, furniture, and knickknacks.

where to eat

Lewis and Clark's American Restaurant & Public House. 217 S. Main St.; (636) 947-3334; www.lewisandclarksrestaurant.com. This popular eatery serves up burgers, pasta, and traditional American fare with a smattering of Mexican dishes in a 100-year-old, 3-story renovated building with a patio overlooking Main Street and the river. Try the blackened fish tacos, an Angus burger, or a specialty sandwich like the Eggplant Stack (lightly breaded deep-fried eggplant with spinach, cucumbers, tomatoes, Swiss cheese, and pesto ranch dressing) or the Jeff City (prime rib, cream cheese, tomato, lettuce, onion, and horseradish on marble rye). $–$$.

Little Hills Restaurant & Winery. 501 S. Main St.; (636) 946-9339; www.littlehillswinery .com. Lunch and dinner options range from salads, sandwiches, and wraps to salmon and steak. For a grown-up take on an old-school favorite, try Dave's Gourmet Grilled Cheese (American cheese, tomato, onions, peppers, and mushrooms served on sourdough bread with bacon "jam"). Dinner specialties include the Brie & Butternut Squash Ravioli (asparagus, red peppers, tomatoes, portobello mushrooms, and a delicate brie cheese crea sauce tossed with butternut squash ravioli) and Shrimp Davila (butter-fried shrimp ro in bread crumbs, baked, and topped with a white wine tomato and lemon-garlic sa

Breakfast is available on the weekends, and there's a good-size children's menu. Gluten-free options are also available, including gluten-free beers, along with a selection of wines from Little Hills Winery and others. $$.

Miss Aimee B's Tea Room. 837 First Capitol Dr.; (636) 946-4202; www.saucemagazine .com/missaimeeb. Enjoy indoor or outdoor dining for breakfast, lunch, or dessert in the Marten-Becker House, a historic home built in 1865. Try the Elegant Praline French Toast (thick French bread slices coated with pecans, oats, cinnamon, and brown sugar) for break-fast or the sandwich with the slightly confusing moniker, the Veggie BLT (bacon, lettuce, tomato, beets, cucumbers, onion, and baby Swiss on wheat with homemade dill spread) for lunch. And save room for the dessert called My Neighbor's Peach Bomb (a whole peach wrapped with piecrust, baked, and then drizzled generously with almond butter). $–$$.

Picasso's Coffee. 101 N. Main St.; (636) 925-2911; www.picassoscoffeehouse.com. A great place for weekday lunch, thanks to a menu of salads, grilled paninis, and sandwiches like the Old Man & the Sea (homemade tuna salad, spinach, and tomato on a croissant). In addition to the java, Picasso's serves up real fruit smoothies and fresh-baked goods. The coffeehouse attracts an eclectic crowd throughout the day, from college kids and stay-at-home moms to dreadlocked musicians and bikers fresh from the Katy Trail. Picasso's has a different art exhibit on display each month and live acoustic performances on Fri and Sat evenings. Nighttime beverage offerings expand to include a selection of wines, liqueurs, and craft and imported beers. $.

Riverside Sweets. 416 S. Main St.; (636) 724-4131. If you have a sweet tooth, you won't want to bypass this place. Numerous flavors of fresh homemade fudge, chocolates, tof-fees, and caramel apples are made on-site. Hand-dipped ice cream—26 flavors—along with shakes, malts, hot and cold drinks, peanut brittle, and a specialty called Oreo Cookie Bark are also offered. There may be a line but it moves quickly, so don't let that scare you off—and there's a downstairs seating area so you can sit and savor your treat. $.

Trailhead Brewing Co. 921 S. Riverside Dr.; (636) 946-2739; www.trailheadbrewing .com. In addition to a menu of gourmet pizzas, steaks, sandwiches, and salads, the popu-lar microbrewery offers a selection of handcrafted brews including Missouri Brown, Old Courthouse Stout, and Riverboat Raspberry. Trailhead's ale-battered fish-and-chips is a well-established house specialty, along with the barbecued smoked baby back ribs and center-cut pork loin medallions. There's something for the vegetarians too—try the Open Faced Porta Plank Stack (grilled portobello mushroom over deep-fried eggplant slices topped with red peppers and melted Swiss and Asiago cheese with a chipotle ranch dress-ing) or a Grist Mill Salad (mixed greens, tomatoes, feta cheese, walnuts, basil, and sweet ed onion with raspberry vinaigrette). $$.

where to stay

Ameristar Casino Resort Spa. One Ameristar Blvd.; (636) 949-7777; www.ameristar .com/St_Charles_Hotel.aspx. The $265 million luxury hotel and spa has almost 400 gener- ously sized suites with oversize baths, sunken living rooms, and floor-to-ceiling windows offering river or city views. The AAA Four-Diamond hotel recently added a 7,000-square- foot full-service spa that offers massage therapy, skin care, healing body rituals, nail therapy, and a hydro-circuit featuring steam, sauna, whirlpool, and Swiss shower. There's also an indoor-outdoor pool. $$–$$$.

Bittersweet Inn. 1101 N. 3rd St.; (636) 724-7778; www.bittersweetinn.com. Built in 1864, the inn is located in the Frenchtown district. The elegantly restored home features a veranda, garden, and spacious guest rooms and is outfitted with antique furnishings. There are 3 bedrooms with queen-size beds and private baths, along with 2 suites, including one with an adjoining room. All rooms feature sitting areas, air-conditioning, fluffy bathrobes, and ceiling fans. In addition to a gourmet breakfast, guests are treated to refreshments and homemade treats upon arrival. $$.

Boone's Colonial Inn. 322 S. Main St.; (888) 377-0003; www.boonescolonialinn.com. The inn is a 19th-century stone row house located in the heart of St. Charles's National Historic District. Guests can choose from 3 period suites with such luxuries as whirlpools and fire- places. Full gourmet breakfasts include special entrees like cheese-stuffed French toast with strawberry sauce or Eggs Olé, and private in-room breakfast service is also available. $$$.

troy, mo

To be clear, there are two Troys—one in Illinois and one in Missouri. Troy, MO, is a tiny town about 33 miles northwest of St. Charles that serves as a civilized outpost for visitors heading to and from Cuivre River State Park. Situated in the heart of Lincoln County, the town is mostly residential, with a few independent restaurants and shops sprinkled in. The community offers equal parts rural charm and suburban convenience, so you can find all of the necessary elements here for a trek into the wilderness or a quiet night on the town.

getting there

From St. Charles, take I-70 West about 16 miles to exit 210B, then merge onto US 61 North toward Hannibal and follow the famed Highway 61 about 14.5 miles to the Old Cap Au Gris Road exit. Turn left onto Old Cap Au Gris Road and continue onto Fair Street/Monroe Street for a little more than 0.5 mile. Turn right onto Main Street, then turn right onto E. Cherry Street/Old MO 47 North.

where to go

Cuivre River State Park. 678 Rte. 147; (636) 528-7247; www.mostateparks.com/camp grounds/cuivre-river-state-park. Cuivre (pronounced "quiver") River State Park is located in the Lincoln Hills region of Missouri and is chock-full of tall grass prairies; dense forests; rocky, sunny clearings; and an assortment of caves, sinkholes, springs, and rocky creeks. The visitor center features exhibits on the area's cultural and natural history, and park naturalists conduct nature hikes and evening campground programs. Workers from the Civilian Conservation Corps (CCC) and Works Progress Administration (WPA) built many of the park's roads, bridges, and other structures, several of which have been placed on the National Register of Historic Places. The park's scenic limestone bluffs offer great views of the Cuivre River and Big Sugar Creek, which is home to several species of fish that aren't usually found in northern Missouri. The 1,872-acre Lincoln Hills Natural Area is one of the largest natural areas in the Missouri state park system, and it includes the best remaining example of the unique landscape characteristic of the Lincoln Hills uplift.

There are a number of hiking trails throughout the park, and they meander through a mixture of prairies, savannas, woodlands, glades, sinkholes, bluffs, and streams. Backpack camping is allowed on the Lone Spring, Cuivre River–North Loop, and Big Sugar Creek Trails, and horses are allowed on the Cuivre River Trail, which can be accessed at the equestrian campground and day-use area. The park's camping options include basic, electric, and electric/water/sewer campsites; an equestrian campground; 3 group camps; and a special-use camping area. During the season, which runs from mid-April through October, available services include reservable campsites, a dump station, showers, water, laundry, and the ability to purchase firewood and ice. Located near the campground is Lake Lincoln, a 55-acre lake stocked with largemouth bass, sunfish, and channel catfish. There's also a swimming beach and a boat-launching area. The CCC-constructed camps are available for group rental and include cabins, a dining lodge, and recreation areas.

where to shop

Cherry Street Emporium. 180B Cherry St.; (636) 528-3599. Offering a little bit of everything, the Cherry Street Emporium sells an assortment of antiques, jewelry, linens, and one-of-a-kind crafts and artwork from local and regional artists.

My Three Ladies Wine Haus. 360 Main St.; (636) 528-4287. Located on downtown Troy's historic Main Street, the newly expanded shop stocks a large number of Missouri wines, snacks, wine-making equipment, and accessories. Closed Sun and Mon.

Three Monkeys Beadery. 235 E. Cherry St.; (636) 528-7786; www.threemonkeysbead .net. A friendly, locally owned bead shop and stained-glass studio that stocks an abundance of unique, quality items and American-made products. They offer 30-minute bracelet and earrings classes Mon through Fri and glass ornament classes every Sat morning. Call 24 hours in advance to register for a class.

where to eat

Cherry Street Grill & Pub. 892 Cherry St.; (636) 528-9999; www.cherrystreetgrill.com. Casual neighborhood restaurant serving a menu of appetizers, sandwiches, pasta dishes, St. Louis–style pizzas, and half-pound burgers like the Black & Blue Stuffed Burger (stuffed with blue cheese and seasoned with black pepper) and the Ole Ole Spicy Burger (topped with jalapeños, pepper jack cheese, and salsa). Entrees include a 12-ounce rib eye, a catfish platter, and a tilapia filet. $$.

Krumbly Burger. 70 Front St.; (636) 528-5646; www.troykrumblyburger.com. Serving the famed Midwestern loose-meat sandwich made with seasoned ground chuck on a steamed bun, Krumbly Burger is a Troy tradition that's been around for more than 20 years. The menu also includes chicken wraps, chili, taco salad bowls, sandwiches, burritos, tacos, and fried catfish and shrimp, as well as milk shakes, malts, ice-cream sundaes, and the Fried Delight (freshly fried tortilla shell filled with ice cream, drizzled with honey, and topped with cinnamon sugar). $.

day trip 02

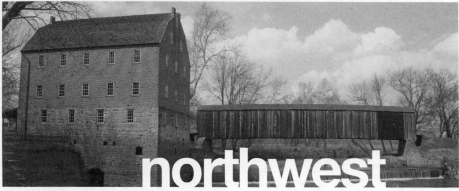

northwest

twain's town:
hannibal, mo

hannibal, mo

The town that shaped America's most beloved author welcomes visitors to Samuel Clemens's boyhood home, just 120 miles north of St. Louis. The Mark Twain Museum, Mark Twain Cave, guided trolley rides, and scenic riverboat cruises provide an authentic view of the town where young Sam Clemens created the adventures of Tom Sawyer, Huck Finn, and Becky Thatcher. The fabled Mississippi River town was founded in 1819 by Moses Bates and became known as "America's Hometown" thanks to the literary tales spun by its most famous native son. The tiny hamlet plays host to events straight out of the pages of Twain's books, such as fence-painting and frog-jumping contests. Today the town of 17,000 greets 21st-century visitors with a warm and friendly spirit in much the same way Twain described it in the late 1800s.

getting there

From downtown St. Louis, take I-64 West/US 40 West for about 39 miles to US 61 North. Follow US 61 for approximately 73 miles, then turn right onto Warren Barrett Drive and continue for 3.6 miles. Turn left onto S. Fifth Street, then take the third right onto Broadway Extended.

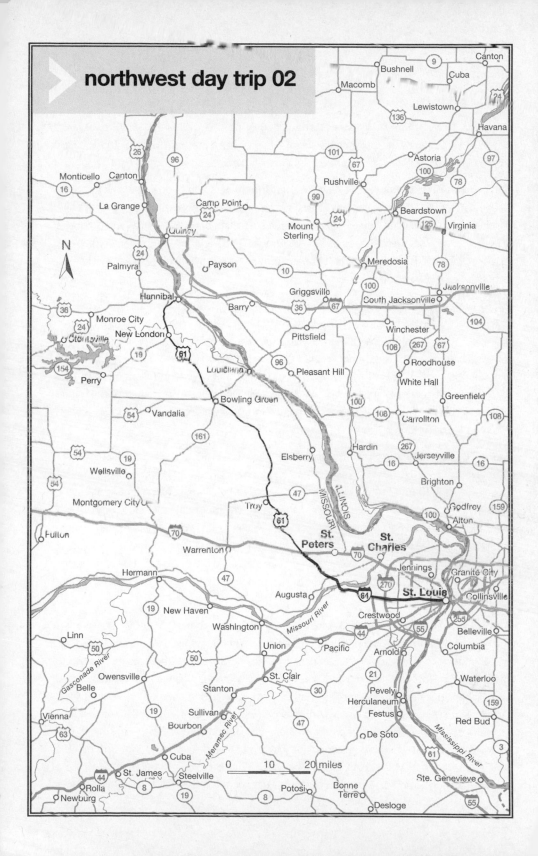

northwest day trip 02

where to go

Hannibal Convention & Visitors Bureau. 505 N. 3rd St.; (573) 221-2477; www.visit hannibal.com. Stop by the visitor center for info on special events and Twain-related activities taking place during your visit. You never know when a frog-jumping contest might pop up.

Cave Hollow West Winery. 300 Cave Hollow Rd., 1 mile south of downtown Hannibal on MO 79; (573) 221-1656; www.marktwaincave.com. Located on the grounds of the Mark Twain Cave Complex, the full-scale winery features a tasting bar and gift shop and produces such wines as Mark Twain Reserve and An Innocent Broad. Enjoy complimentary tastings indoors or sip some vino outside on the patio or the lawn. They offer live music and special events on select weekends.

Historic Hannibal Tours. 323 N. Main St.; (573) 494-2918. Located in what locals call the "Diorama Building" is a series of 16 3-D dioramas that illustrate the story of Tom Sawyer. There's one for each chapter of Mark Twain's famous work *The Adventures of Tom Sawyer*. The handcrafted scenes were created in the late 1960s by artist Art Sieving, and each diorama measures 40 by 40 by 30 feet. The storefront that houses the dioramas was built in 1840, and it served as the location of McDaniel's candy store. Today it houses Historic Hannibal Tours, a family-owned tour company that offers walking tours of Main Street and Haunted Hannibal Ghost Tours.

Mark Twain Birthplace State Historic Site. Mark Twain State Park, 37352 Shrine Rd., Stoutsville; (573) 565-3449; www.mostateparks.com/page/54981/general-information. Located about 40 miles southwest of Hannibal is the Mark Twain Birthplace State Historic Site. The museum and research library include the two-room cabin where Clemens was born along with several exhibits, including first editions of Twain's works, a handwritten manuscript of *The Adventures of Tom Sawyer,* and furnishings from Twain's Connecticut home. The site also has a public reading room for personal study and research. In the nearby village of Florida, there's a red granite monument that marks the cabin's original location.

Mark Twain Boyhood Home & Museum. 120 N. Main Street; (573) 221-9010; www .marktwainmuseum.org. The museum properties include 6 historically significant buildings and 2 interactive museums with collections that include a wealth of artifacts. In addition to Mark Twain's Boyhood Home, which has been designated a National Historic Landmark, visitors can tour the Huckleberry Finn House, J. M. Clemens Justice of the Peace Office, Grant's Drug Store, Museum Gallery, and Interpretive Center. The Museum Gallery, located in the historic Sonnenberg's Department Store building, features interactive exhibits that examine some of the author's major works, including *The Adventures of Tom Sawyer, The Adventures of Huckleberry Finn,* and *Roughing It.* The exhibits include a stagecoach, a steamboat replica, and 15 Norman Rockwell illustrations that were commissioned for special editions of Tom Sawyer and Huck Finn in the 1930s.

Mark Twain Cave Complex. 300 Cave Hollow Rd., 1 mile south of downtown Hannibal on MO 79; (573) 221-1656; www.marktwaincave.com. The complex offers 1-hour tours of the Mark Twain Cave—the one discovered in 1886 that showed up in Twain's books about Tom and Huck—and lantern tours of Cameron Cave, which was discovered in 1925. There's also a campground, visitor center, gift shop, and Sticks, Stones and Bones, where you can pan for semiprecious gemstones like amethyst, calcite, pyrite, and rose quartz.

Mark Twain Mississippi Riverboat. Center Street Landing; (573) 221-3222; www.mark twainriverboat.com. Take a ride on the Mighty Mississippi and see Hannibal the way Mark Twain and hundreds of riverboat captains have seen it. The 120-foot-long vessel takes landlubbers out for 1-hour sightseeing cruises that include commentary on river legends and history as well as background on sights like Jackson's Island and Lover's Leap. The 2-hour evening dinner cruises also feature live music.

Mark Twain State Park. 37352 Shrine Rd.; (573) 565-3440; www.mostateparks.com/ park/mark-twain-state-park. This 55,000-acre land and water project was established in the 1920s and named for famous author and Missouri native Samuel L. Clemens, also known as Mark Twain. Mark Twain State Park is located in the Salt River Hills, which got their name from the abundance of salt springs, or licks, in the area. The park is full of wildlife like white-tailed deer, turkeys, raccoons, squirrels, ospreys, northern harriers, bald eagles, and many species of waterfowl. There are plenty of camping options here, with both basic and electric sites available as well as modern showers and laundry facilities. The campground is located on Mark Twain Lake, where anglers can catch everything from bluegill, crappie, and catfish to largemouth bass, carp, walleye, and perch. There's also a public beach, a safe swimming area and changing house, 2 public boat ramps, and a fish-cleaning station located in the campground area. If sleeping under the stars isn't your idea of a good time, the park has climate-controlled camper cabins for rent. The Buzzard's Roost picnic area offers a shaded spot for picnickers, and the overlook provides a great view of Mark Twain Lake. There are 2 reservable shelter houses and a playground available as well. Hikers can set out on one of the park's 5 trails that range from 0.5 mile to 1.75 miles in length.

Norwoods Golf Club. 52651 Norwoods Pl.; (573) 248-1998; www.norwoodsgolfclub .com. The 18-hole course features 6,459 yards of golf from the longest tees for a par of 72. The course rating is 70.3, and it has a slope rating of 120 on bluegrass. Designed by Tracy Scott, the course offers 3 sets of tees and is a semi-challenging way to spend an afternoon. No tee times are necessary during the week. If you decide to head out to play a few holes, don't trust your GPS device. Call the clubhouse and let them tell you the best way to get there. Open year-round.

Sawyer's Creek Family Fun Park. 11011 MO 79 South; (573) 221-2200; www.sawyers creek.com. The park is an example of perpetual motion, with activities like miniature golf, bumper boats, water wars, an arcade, and Tom Sawyer's Wild Adventure, a laser-based activity through the graveyard with Tom and Huck. The Kiddie Zone, designed for wee ones from 6 months old through preschool, features a village called Hucksville where kids can work puzzles, crawl through tunnels, or "work" in a doctor's office, construction zone, or restaurant. Prices vary by activity.

where to shop

Alliance Art Gallery. 112 N. Main St.; (573) 221-2275; www.hannibalallianceartgallery.com. The gallery features an ever-changing collection of one-of-a-kind works for sale by at least a dozen local artists, including jewelry, paintings, photography, pottery, and sculptures. Closed Tues.

Ayers Pottery. 308 N. 3rd Street; (573) 221-6960; www.ayerspottery.com. Choose from reasonably priced handmade bowls, mugs, bakeware, dinnerware, plates, platters, and other items that are made on-site by the shop owner, veteran potter Steve Ayers. Designed to be functional as well as beautiful, all Ayers pottery items are microwaveable and safe for the oven and the dishwasher. Open daily.

Becky's Old Fashioned Ice Cream Parlor & Emporium. 318 N. Main St.; (573) 221-0822; www.beckythatcher.com. In addition to indulging in an ice-cream cone, sundae, milk shake, or malt, you can shop for a variety of traditional souvenirs and knickknacks emblazoned with Mark Twain's likeness, as well as Hannibal Christmas ornaments and coffee mugs. If you're looking for an educational keepsake, the shop features the Mark Twain for Teachers section that has books about regional history, the Mississippi River, and steamboats, along with classic children's books. They also stock Dover coloring books and paper dolls. Open year-round.

The Country Shop Collectibles & Gifts. 203 N. Main St.; (573) 221-2101; www.country shop203.com. Offering numerous lines of Ty plush and other collectible critters, including Cow Parade, Hot Diggitys, Painted Ponies, Thomas Dam Trolls, Faerie Glen, Garfield, Peanuts, Beasties, and Snow Buddies. The shop also stocks various afghans, lighthouses, wind chimes, bird feeders, and more.

The Gilded Age Antiques & Gifts. 215-217 N. Main St.; (314) 494-2918. The Gilded Age sells an assortment of treasures ranging from antique housewares, silver, and china to ornate frames and personal accessories from days gone by. The best thing about the shop is the range of prices—you can pick up an antique compact for $20 or drop six times that amount on a pair of woven leather baby shoes.

Mark Twain Book & Gift Shop. 213 Hill St.; (573) 221-2140. You can't leave Hannibal without picking up at least one book by its favorite son, so stop in and get a copy of *Life on the Mississippi* or a hardback version of *The Adventures of Tom Sawyer*. While you're there, check out some local artists' handiwork and browse the usual lineup of souvenirs.

Native American Trading Company & Gallery. 115 N. Main St.; (573) 248-3451. Located across from the Mark Twain Museum, the store sells Minnetonka moccasins, Nuwati Herbals products, and authentic headdresses and handcrafted items from the Navajo, Zuni, Hopi, Cherokee, Sioux, Mohawk, Ojibwa, and Acoma cultures. They also carry Mark Hopkins original bronze sculptures, sand paintings, Pendleton blankets, and Mill Creek sculptures. The gallery features artists like Bev Doolittle, Tim Cox, Herman Adams, Howard Terpning, J. D. Challenger, and Judy Larson. Open daily.

Pudd'N Heads. 115 Bird St.; (573) 248-1018. The shop features an assortment of items made by area artists and craftspeople such as handcrafted wood, cloth, florals, and jewelry. Known for their huge collection of sterling silver charms and bracelets, Pudd'N Heads also dabbles in antique glassware, custom-made furniture, and a variety of collectibles. Open year-round.

Starlight's Alpaca Products. 55105 Buffalo Ln., New London; (573) 267-3778; www .starlightalpacaranch.com. The Starlight Alpaca Ranch is home to more than 90 alpacas, and their on-site store offers a variety of items made from alpaca hair—or is it fur? Either way, you can pick up unique alpaca-made items, including sweaters, gloves and mittens, throws, and socks. They also sell ruanas that are made of fiber from Starlight's herd as well as an assortment of toy alpacas. Visitors are welcome to visit the ranch, but you have to call ahead and make an appointment. By the way, no alpacas were harmed in the writing of this entry.

Twain Town Souvenirs. 202 North St.; (573) 822-5780; www.twaintown.com. Traditional souvenir items are available here, including T-shirts, caps, mugs, key chains, sport bottles, magnets, plush toys, and Tom Sawyer–style straw hats. They also stock some books by Mark Twain, Hannibal's *Cooking in America's Hometown* cookbook, and Twain-related DVDs.

where to eat

Java Jive. 211 N. Main St.; (573) 221-1017. The "first coffee shop west of the Mississippi," thanks to its proximity to Old Man River, is situated at Ayers Pottery. They offer a variety of coffee and espresso drinks, teas, sodas, smoothies, desserts, and baked goods. Curl up on a sofa and take advantage of the free Wi-Fi during the day, or enjoy the occasional live music events at night. Open early morning to late night. $.

LaBinnah Bistro. 207 N. 5th St.; (573) 221-8207; www.gardenhousebedandbreakfast .com. The bistro offers an intimate dining experience inside a historic Victorian house that was built in 1870. To call the menu eclectic is a severe understatement, as choices include flavors from Africa, Louisiana, Turkey, the Mediterranean, and other places around the globe. Begin your global gastronomical adventure with some *dolmas yalandji* (traditional Turkish stuffed grape leaves with homemade yogurt dipping sauce) or the Trojan Salad (feta cheese, olives, tomato, cucumber, and carrots with greens, drizzled with homemade lemon dressing), and continue your taste buds' globe-trotting trek with an entree like Chicken Florentina (chicken breast with fresh spinach and mushrooms sautéed in a lemon and white wine sauce) or the African Peri-Peri (an exotic pork cutlet with exquisite pepper flavors and spices). Open for dinner only. $$.

Lula Belle's Restaurant. 111 Bird St.; (573) 221-6662; www.lulabelles.com. There is a limited lunch menu of sandwiches and salads, but the dinner choices expand to include pasta, seafood, and steak. Entrees range from Belle's stuffed boneless pork chop and Mississippi surf and turf (half a rack of ribs and a catfish filet) to herbed shrimp fettuccini and ahi tuna. Early-bird diners enjoy a specially priced menu with slightly smaller portions from 4 to 6 p.m. Call for reservations. $$–$$$.

Ole Planters Restaurant. 316 N. Main St.; (573) 221-4410. Located just a half block from the Mark Twain Museum, the Ole Planters Restaurant serves up home-style lunches and dinners, including daily specials and the "meat and three" plate lunch that features 3 vegetables and a choice of hickory-smoked pork and beef, pork tenderloins, or chicken-fried steak. Additional options include barbecue ribs, jumbo shrimp, prime rib, and homemade pies. There's also a full bar. Open daily for lunch but closed Tues and Sun nights. $–$$.

Rustic Oak Cabin Steakhouse. 22448 Hwy. J, Perry; (573) 565-2040; www.rusticoak steakhouse.com. Located about 26 miles outside of Hannibal in nearby Perry, the specialty here is—you guessed it—steak! Lunch and dinner options also include pasta, seafood, a good children's menu, and lots of desserts. Try a half pound of breaded green beans, some fried okra, or an order of the Inferno Breaded Hot Wings to start. The restaurant's char-grilled prime rib is the specialty of the house. If you've got room after dinner, check out the Chocolate Dipped Bundt Hot Lava Cake with vanilla ice cream. $$–$$$.

where to stay

Garth Woodside Mansion. 11069 New London Rd.; (573) 221-2789; www.garthmansion .com. Mark Twain slept here. Seriously. He was probably attracted to the historical Victorian estate because of its location among 39 acres of rolling meadows, woodlands, and flower gardens. You can even sleep in the same bedroom—the Samuel Clemens Room. There are 8 guest rooms available in the mansion itself, along with additional options in the estate's guest cottages and the Dowager House. In 2010 *AAA Traveler Magazine* chose the B&B as "Best of the Midwest." $$$.

Robards Mansion Bed & Breakfast. 215 N. 6th St.; (573) 248-1218. Constructed in 1871, the Robards mansion is an example of classic Italianate architecture, featuring massive woodwork and interior brick walls. Listed on the National Register of Historic Places, the B&B's guest rooms feature private baths, king- or queen-size beds, and in-room cable TV. Children are welcome; however, pets are not. $–$$.

Rockcliffe Mansion. 1000 Bird St.; (573) 221-4140; www.rockliffemansion.com. The 30-room mansion, circa 1900, was abandoned in 1924 by its owners, who walked away from the home and left 80 percent of its original contents. Today the historic home offers tours and overnight accommodations complete with turn-down service and chocolates, wine and cheese at check-in, and a gourmet 3-course breakfast. Four chamber rooms are available, or you can combine two rooms and create a suite. $$.

festivals & celebrations

january

Baby, it's cold outside, but that's just the way they like it in St. Charles, MO, for the **Fete De Glace Ice Carving Competition.** Held on North Main Street in late January, the festivities include professional ice carvers doing their thing with chain saws, power grinders, sanders, cold chisels, hand saws, and irons. Sip some hot chocolate or coffee and warm up at one of the fire pits along the perimeter so you can hang in for the whole show. (800) 366-2427; www.historicstcharles.com.

Throughout the month of January, bird watching takes on national importance in and around Alton, IL, as scores of majestic bald eagles flock to the area to nest and fish. On **Eagle Watch Weekend,** the Audubon Center at Riverlands in West Alton offers a prime eagle-viewing location, live eagle shows, and educational info at the designated Important Birding Area at the Riverlands Migratory Bird Sanctuary. Enjoy the view indoors or head out to the bird blind on the water's edge and watch as eagles swoop down and snatch fish from the (usually) unfrozen Mississippi River. (636) 899-0060; www.riverlands.audubon.org.

february

Catch a flick or 10 at Southern Illinois University's **Big Muddy Film Festival,** which is one of the longest-running student-organized film festivals in the country. The two-week-long festival, held in Carbondale, IL, is dedicated to supporting the work of emerging and accomplished filmmakers and video artists, and the list of visual options includes documentary, narrative, animation, and experimental entries from across the US and around the world. Additional activities include presentations by guest artists and a variety of panel discussions. (618) 453-7703; www.bigmuddyfilm.com.

Celebrate two great tastes that taste great together along the **Chocolate Wine Trail** in Hermann, MO. Held in mid-February, the weekend features pairings of luscious chocolates and wines at seven stops along the Hermann Wine Trail. Tickets sell out early, so if you have a ravenous sweet tooth or love someone who does, it's a good idea to plan ahead. (800) 932-8687; www.visithermann.com.

march

The students at Missouri University of Science and Technology in Rolla, MO, sure know how to throw a party. The century-old **Best Ever St. Pat's Celebration** includes everything from a raucous parade to knighting student representatives of university organizations as Missouri S&T pays homage to St. Patrick, the patron saint of engineers. The festival, which takes place the Saturday before St. Patrick's Day, includes live music, games, streets that are literally painted green, and a parade of student-made wooden shillelaghs. http://stpats .mst.edu/events.

On the fourth weekend of March each year, Hermann, MO, stakes its claim as the sausage capital of the state with the annual **Wurstfest,** celebrating the "Best of the Wurst." The citywide event includes a sausage making contest, German music and dancing, old-school sausage-making demonstrations, tastings and tours at local wineries, and a Wiener Dog Derby for four-legged competitors. (800) 932-8687; www.visithermann.com.

Columbia, MO's **True/False Film Fest** features the finest new nonfiction films while striving to debunk the notion that documentary films are stuffy and boring. The three-day festival offers films that push the boundaries of the genre and blur the line between documentary and narrative talking pictures. Films are screened in a variety of downtown venues, all located within walking distance of one another, ranging from the 1,200-seat historic Missouri Theatre to the 300-seat Blue Note nightclub to the tiny 85-seat Ragtag Cinema. (573) 442-6816; www.truefalse.org.

april

The people who attend the three-day **Cape Girardeau Storytelling Festival** each year are expecting to hear some tall tales, and the event is sure not to disappoint. Both local and national storytellers gather in Cape Girardeau, MO, in mid-April and spin stories that have been handed down through the generations – or maybe it just happened last week. All of the festival performances take place in Cape's historic downtown area along the mighty Mississippi River. (573) 335-1631.

If you thought your college's fraternity parties were a circus, you won't believe your eyes at the **Gamma Phi Circus Spring Show,** which takes place at Illinois State University's Redbird Arena in Normal, IL. Gamma Phi is the oldest collegiate circus in the country, and the troupe features tight-wire, silks, juggling, hand balancing, Russian swing, and German wheel acts. Plus some clowns. Real ones—not just guys like the joker you sat next to in psych class. The main difference between this event and a frat party is that this one offers family-friendly entertainment. (309) 438-2690; http://gammaphicircus.illinoisstate.edu.

may

When it comes to celebrating its connection to explorers Meriwether Lewis and William Clark, the city of St. Charles, MO, does it up right. In mid-May St. Chuck serves up **Lewis & Clark Heritage Days,** a weekend full of period music, weapon demonstrations, boat replicas, museum tours, crafts and foods from 1804, children's games, and more in Frontier Park. It all takes place in an authentic reenactment of the dynamic duo's camp that they set up in the area before heading northwestward on their exploration of the Louisiana Purchase. There's also a parade and a Sunday church service. www.lewisandclarkheritagedays.com.

Ste. Genevieve, MO's **Spring Garden Walk** offers visitors a chance to enjoy a kinder, gentler walk with Mother Nature through some of the town's historic private and public gardens. Held in mid-May, the annual stroll includes a guided walking tour, plein air painting, and sales of various plants and gardening items. Tours step off from the welcome center, which also stocks a supply of maps and event schedules. www.historicstegen.org.

june

What do you get when you assemble more than 1,000 air-cooled Volkswagens in Effingham, IL? Well, you get the **FunFest for Air-Cooled VW,** an annual event held in early June on the Mid-America Motorworks campus. In addition to the ultimate VW car show, the fest includes technical seminars, a fun-run road tour, Exhaust and Burnout Wars, family-friendly activities, live entertainment, a food fair, and a place to camp if you're so inclined. (217) 540-4200; www.funfestevents.com.

Downtown Arthur, IL, comes alive in early June with the annual **Arthur's Strawberry Jam,** a two-day festival featuring craft and food booths, kids' activities, a strawberry pie–eating contest, games, and live music. One of the highlights of the event is the Bluegrass Jam that's open to anyone with an acoustic instrument and a desire to sit in and pick and grin. There are plenty of sidewalk sales going on with the local merchants, as well as lots of ways to eat and drink your fill of strawberries. www.arthurfestivals.com.

Celebrate the spicy, multipurpose horseradish root at the **International Horseradish Festival** in Collinsville, IL. Held in early June, the kitschy event offers family-friendly fun, live music, food booths, a craft village, and such horseradish-specific activities as the Root Toss, Root Golf, Root Sacking Contests, a Bloody Mary–making contest, the Little Miss Horseradish Festival Pageant, a horseradish recipe contest, and the annual Horseradish Root Derby. (618) 344-2884; www.horseradishfestival.net.

july

America's Hometown, aka Hannibal, MO, celebrates its greatest fictional residents each July 4 with the **National Tom Sawyer Days** festival. The three days of events and activities are straight out of the pages of Mark Twain's books, and they include everything from the National Fence Painting Contest to a frog-jumping contest. There's also live entertainment, cave tours, and more. The event is sponsored by—who else?—the Hannibal Jaycees. (866) 263-4825; www.hannibaljaycees.org.

Get on board the **Great Egyptian Omnium Bike Race** and take a competitive ride through the unique terrain of the southern Illinois region. The area features hills and bluffs that make for a challenging course filled with natural beauty and plenty of elevation changes to keep things interesting. The race takes place over two days with three stages, and the criterium is held in downtown Marion, IL. (618) 997-3690; www.greategyptianomnium.com.

august

If it's August, it must be time to rodeo. Dust off those boots and make tracks for Sikeston, MO, and the annual **Sikeston Jaycee Bootheel Rodeo.** Festivities include top PRCA cowboys and cowgirls competing for more than $100,000 in prize money, along with concerts by national country music artists like Gretchen Wilson, Big & Rich, Blake Shelton, Trace Atkins, and Jason Aldean. (800) 455-2855; www.sikestonrodeo.com.

Don't let the summertime blues get ahold of you—shake them off with a trip to the annual **Old Capitol Blues & BBQ,** which sets up camp in downtown Springfield, IL. The two-day festival features a kids' zone; live entertainment; a barbecue competition with rib, pulled pork, brisket, and "anything goes" categories; and concerts by local bands and nationally known blues artists such as Jimmie Vaughan and Lou Ann Barton. (217) 544-1723; www .downtownspringfield.org.

september

Augusta, MO's **Augusta Harvest Festival** is really two festivals in one. It kicks off with a nighttime Concert and Picnic in the Vineyard, which includes a pumpkin wagon ride down a country lane to the site of the evening's festivities. The picnic portion of the event includes port sampling with the folks at Mount Pleasant Winery and gourmet picnic baskets full of delectable snacks to enjoy during the concert. The next day the celebration continues with A Taste of Historic Augusta, with harvest specials at shops, restaurants, and wineries, along with a premier dinner event showcasing area wineries. (636) 228-4005; w .augusta-chamber.org.

Enjoy live concerts by such national blues artists as Taj Mahal, Buddy Guy, Derek Trucks and Susan Tedeschi, Robert Cray, and Mavis Staples during the two-day **Roots N Blues N BBQ** festival in downtown Columbia, MO. Held in late September each year, the festival also hosts a half-marathon, a 10K race, and a barbecue cooking contest where more than 50 teams compete for top honors in everything from pork and brisket to ribs, chicken, and dessert. www.rootsnbluesnbbq.com.

Road warriors looking for an excuse to hit the highway should pack up the car and motor to Springfield, IL, for the **Annual International Route 66 Mother Road Festival.** Held in downtown Springfield, the free fest features more than 1,000 classic and just-plain-cool cars; live music from the '50s, '60s, and '70s; a nighttime car cruise; a poker race; and a tires burnout competition—so get your motor runnin'! (317) 236-6515; www.route66 fest.com.

october

Every October the Stephens College campus in Columbia, MO, transforms itself into a min-iature Hollywood East, because that's where the three-day **Citizen Jane Film Festival** is held. The festival, which takes place late in the month, features films made by women, and there are enough short and feature film screenings and panel discussions to make Kathryn Bigelow and Sofia Coppola jealous. There's also a special video art performance and instal-lation held in conjunction with the fest. www.citizenjanefilm.org.

Held in late October every year, the two-day **Apple Butter Festival** in historic Kimmswick, MO, includes live entertainment, hundreds of vendors, and a variety of crafts and food items available for sale. Watch the Kimmswick Historical Society as they make (and sell) their famous apple butter at the Apple Butter Pavilion on Market Street. (636) 464-7407.

november

'f you're looking to get in the good old-fashioned holiday spirit, check out the **Christmas aditions** festival in historic St. Charles, MO. Beginning the day after Thanksgiving and 'nuing through Christmas Eve, the downtown district celebrates the holidays with 'ld-school activities as chestnut roasting and caroling—plus there are authentically 'l Santas from around the world who wander the street. On Wednesday, Friday, 'y evenings, you can shop or dine by candlelight in S. Main Street shops and '00) 366-2427; www.stcharleschristmas.com.

Snows in Belleville, IL, goes all out with the Christmas decorations each 'ights Christmas Display includes more than 1.1 million lights as well 'olays, an interactive children's village, and an indoor laser show. Plus you can ride a real, live camel—outdoors, of course. The free lights display is open from mid-November through New Year's Day. www.wayoflights.org.

december

Take a trip overseas and back in time with a visit to the traditional German Christmas market at Stone Hill Winery in Hermann, MO. Held on the first weekend in December, the **Kristkindl Markt** features carolers and handmade crafts like wooden Santas, homemade soap, German glass Christmas ornaments, pottery, dried flower arrangements, and jewelry. Enjoy a hot cup of soup or some cider to really get into the spirit of things. (800) 909-9463; www.stonehillwinery.com.

Take a drive through the **Christmas Wonderland** spectacular light display at Rock Spring Park in Alton, IL. It features more than 2.5 million lights decorating trees and in a variety of unique displays. You can visit Old St. Nick and have your photo taken in the Santa Claus House. Take a carriage ride through the park or take advantage of the "walk-through night" when no cars are allowed. The display lights up the day after Thanksgiving and stays lit until the day after Christmas. (618) 465-6676; www.christmaswonderlandofalton.net.

index

Getaway ideas for the local traveler

Need a day away to relax, refresh, renew?
Just get in your car and go!

INSIDERS' GUIDE®

The acclaimed travel series that has sold more than 2 million copies!

Discover: Your Travel Destination.
Your Home. Your Home-to-Be.

Albuquerque

Anchorage &
  Southcentral
  Alaska

Atlanta

Austin

Baltimore

Baton Rouge

Boulder & Rocky Mountain
  National Park

Branson & the Ozark
  Mountains

California's Wine Country

Cape Cod & the Islands

Charleston

Charlotte

Chicago

Cincinnati

Civil War Sites in
  the Eastern Theater

Civil War Sites in the South

Colorado's Mountains

Dallas & Fort Worth

Denver

El Paso

Florida Keys & Key West

Gettysburg

Glacier National Park

Great Smoky Mountains

Greater Fort Lauderdale

Greater Tampa Bay Area

Hampton Roads

Houston

Hudson River Valley

Indianapolis

Jacksonville

Kansas City

Long Island

Louisville

Madison

Maine Coast

Memphis

Myrtle Beach &
  the Grand Strand

Nashville

New Orleans

New York City

North Carolina's
  Mountains

North Carolina's
  Outer Banks

North Carolina's
  Piedmont Triad

Oklahoma City

Orange County, CA

Oregon Coast

Palm Beach County

Palm Springs

Philadelphia &
  Pennsylvania Dutch
  Country

Phoenix

Portland, Maine

Portland, Oregon

Raleigh, Durham &
  Chapel Hill

Richmond, VA

Reno and Lake Tahoe

St. Louis

San Antonio

Santa Fe

Savannah & Hilton Head

Seattle

Shreveport

South Dakota's
  Black Hills Badlands

Southwest Florida

Tucson

Tulsa

Twin Cities

Washington, D.C.

Williamsburg & Virginia's
  Historic Triangle

Yellowstone
  & Grand Teton

Yosemite

**To order call 800-243-0495
or visit www.Insiders.com**